SOCIAL ASPECTS OF EDUCATION

SOCIAL ASPECTS OF EDUCATION

[Useful for B.Ed./M.Ed. Students and Other Competition Aspirants]

By
Muniruddin Qureshi

ANMOL PUBLICATIONS PVT. LTD.
NEW DELHI - 110 002 (INDIA)

ANMOL PUBLICATIONS PVT. LTD.
4374/4B, Ansari Road, Daryaganj
New Delhi - 110 002
Ph.: 23261597, 23278000
Visit us at: www.anmolpublications.com

Social Aspects of Education

First Published, 2005

ISBN 81-261-2183-1

PRINTED IN INDIA

Published by J.L. Kumar for Anmol Publications Pvt. Ltd., New Delhi - 110 002 and Printed at Mehra Offset Press, Delhi.

Contents

Preface

Education has a lasting impact on society. No Society can progress without education. Hence, its importance is not debatable. Apart from academic and scholarly effects, education also effects our society in social terms. It modifies and moulds various groups of populace into a civilized entity, known as society.

This book, basically a semi-textbook, presented with the intention of making it helpful for students, covers all social aspects of education. It discusses various trends, waves and streams of education in detail. And this very speciality makes it a valuable book on the subject.

This work is bound to be solidly beneficial for sociologists, planners, educationists and scholars as well.

The undersigned is confident of being acceptable in all circles.

Editor

1

Introduction

Society is a system or organization of mutual relations between human beings, implicit in certain communities and institutions. The school is a group and education an institution. Evidently, the school is an important part of society. Here we mean a specific society, not the general concept of society. And a specific society impliess a group of human beings living within the limits of a definite country and which is characterised by a specific culture. The school is related to this specific society. It is for this reason that different educationists have defined the objectives of education differently for different nations. In the past, in India the objective of education was salvation, while at about the same time in China education was intended for scholarship. As time passes, the aims of education in society change when its cultural patterns undergo change. For example, in modern China, the objective of education is to acquaint the educand with the ideology of Mao Tse Tung and to use him as a tool for implementing this ideology in practice.

Importance of School in Society

Explaining the intimate relationship between society and school, T. P. Nunn, the famous educationist writes, "A nation's schools, we might say, are an organ of its life, whose special function is to consolidate Its spiritual strength, to maintain its historic continuity, to secure its past achievement, to guarantee its future. Through its school a nation should become conscious of the abiding sources from which the best movements in its life have always drawn this inspiration, should come to share the dream of its nobler souls, should constantly submit itself to self criticism, should purge its ideals, should re-inform and redirect its impulses." This comment clearly indicates that the relationship between society and school is characterised by the following elements.

Keeping Moral Power. Schools keep the moral power of the society secure, and also maintain the social heritage of society. This social heritage is handed on by the schools to the following generation.

Preservation of Historical Continuity. Schools also protect the historical continuity of society. Schools perform the function of acquainting the new generation with the ancient myths and legends, and maintaining the patterns of behaviour in the form of traditions and customs.

Perservation of Social Heritage. Schools also help to keep alive the society's achievements in the past, and transfer it to the younger generation through the teaching of history and the social sciences.

Guardians of Future. Schools are the guardians of society's future, because educands are the future leaders of the nation. Schools shape the future of the country by achieving the complete development of these leaders. It is for this reason that the educator is often referred to as the architect of the nation.

Literary Function. Through the medium of the schools, the members of society are acquainted with those motives and inspirations which formed the basis of all the literary achievements of the past. This is achieved through the teaching of literature.

Instrument of Social Change. Schools also encourage considerable discussion and exchanges of opinion on the functioning, methods of working, customs and traditions existing in various parts of society. These elements are analysed and subjected to criticism in order to decide whether they should be retained or thrown out. In this way, schools are the source of social change.

Training of Leaders. Through the medium of the school, leaders in various spheres such as engineering, medicine, legal profession, teaching, literature, etc., are trained. In this sense the progress of society depends upon the progress of the schools.

It is evident from the foregoing of the intimate relationship between society and schools that development and progress of schools is essential for the progress of society. Before introducing any change in society on a large scale, it can be experimented within the school and its nature and consequences observed. It can then be introduced into society.

Impact of Society on School

It is evident from the intimate relationship that exists between society and school that both influence each other. The various points to be noted in the impact of society on school are the following:

Impact of Family. All the individuals, educators and educands, found in schools come from society, and hence it is only natural that their thinking should influence life in the school. It is generally accepted that the kind of family an educand comes from can be judged from his conduct in the school.

Impact of Social Change. Society is a dynamic and changeable structure. One can see effect of various social changes on schools.

Impact of Social Mores. Social conduct in society also has an influence upon the conduct of educand in schools. If social conduct deteriorates, there is no way of shielding the student from this deterioration and connsequently conduct in school will also reflect a fall in standard.

Impact of Social Needs. The curriculum of the schools is determined according to the needs of society, because parents always send their children to school in order to prepare them for society. They are given education so that they may become useful members of the society.

Impact of Social Institutions. The life of the school is profoundly influenced by all the major institutions of society, as family, religion, and economic institutions. From this standpoint one can compare the schools in Communist Russia with the schools of Democratic America.

Impact of Books. All the education that the educand imbibes in school through books and lectures, actually emanates from society, because books are little more than the accumulated experiences and ideas of the greatest figures in society.

Impact of School on Society

Society is influenced by the school in as great a measure as it itself influences schools. In this respect, the following points are to be considered as impact of school on society.

Leaders. Schools create the future leaders for all the spheres of society. It follows that the type of school will determine the calibre of leaders, and their calibre in turn will determine the nature of society that they will create.

Social Control. The school, like the family, is a social institution which socializes the individual and provides him some experience in social control. Therefore, the individual will learn to accept the kind of similar social control from society. For this reason, there is a great insistence in democratic countries that the atmosphere in school should also be democratic so that the educand can get used to democratic norms of social control.

Social Change. It has already been stated that the school plays an important part in social change because it subjects all the customs, traditions, mores, practices, etc., of society to continuous criticism. As a result of this criticism, some of these are maintained and others rejected. This determines the future of social change.

Useful Citizens. It is the function of school to provide useful citizens to society and make individuals independent and self-reliant.

Reform and Improvement. By exercising their right of criticism, the educands assess the weaknesses of society and thus prepare a blueprint for its future reformation and improvement.

Contribution of Society

Education amounts to a complete development of the child,

and an important aspect of this development is moral development. Society can play a positive role in the child's moral development in the school. In this connection, the following things should be noted:

Balanced Personality. If society itself is well organized, the child's personality will also be balanced and his moral development becomes possible.

Patterns of Moral Behaviour. The patterns of moral behaviour exhibited in the family and other social, the child to behave in the same in the same manner.

Assistance by Members. the child's moral development can take place more rapidly and positively if the educator is assisted by other members of society.

Responsibility of Society

The extent to which society can play an active part in making the school a powerful and affective medium of purveying education is evident from the impact it has on the school. It is clear that society has great responsibiliity in this direction. The following points should be noted in this connection:

Construction and Maintenance. Society should undertake to construct appropriate buildings for schools and also provide for their development and maintenance.

Guidance. It is the responsibility of society to see that educators get and guide the parents about possible future problems.

Bringing Society and Schoold Closer

The importance of close co-operation between school and society is evident from the foregoing discussion. The following are the means by which this can be done:

Cultural Function. School should frequently organize cultural functions of a kind which can make it possible various members of society to attend and participate in them.

Adult Literary Schemes. The relationship between society and the school can be give a more firm foundation by running social welfare schemes or adult literacy schemes in the school to educate the old and illiterate members of society.

Teacher-parent Associations. Co-operation can be further increased by forming associations consisting of teachers and parents.

Financial Assistance and Cooperation. School should win financial assistance and co-operation from various senior members of society for the organization, provision and development of the school.

School as Social Sub-system

Social Organisation. Sociology of education particularly studies the school as a social sub system. The social organization in the school consists of different roles and statuses for the educators and the educands. Among the teachers also there are different statuses and roles according to their seniority, qualifications, special skills and the position of the hierarchy of the school. The Headmaster in very school occupies a pivotal position, more responsibility, more administrative power and, therefore, the most important role. Similarly, among the educands also different students occupy different statuses and roles in the schools according to their seniority, special skills and allotted responsibilities, etc. For example, the chief prefect is overall incharge of the discipline among the students. Similarly, there are so many prefects which maintain discipline in the school. Every class has a monitor who maintains law and order in the classroom in the absence of the teacher and complains to the teacher about the defaulter student.

Social Roles. As a social system the school aims to prepare the students to occupy social roles. Youths utilize their capacities after leaving the school. In India most of the rural youths finish their studies after high school. Some of them do not go beyong the middle schools. Therefore, the functions of the middle schools and the high school in transmitting knowledge, skills and socialization are very important. As a social system the first function of the school is to transmit knowledge and skills to the younger generation. The technical schools transmit knowledge concerning so many trades. The agricultural institutions train the sons of cultivators about better means of the cultivation. All the schools impart knowledge of 3R's,i.e., reading, writing and arithmetic. This is necessary in order to help every male and female to skilfully manage the household affairs and also matters concerning every day life.

Transmission of Culture. Besides transmitting knowledge, the school as a social sub-system transmits culture to the younger generation. The customs and traditions, rules of etiquettes and manners are taught both by instruction and by example. The rules of the school discipline the educands and give them training in group activities. The mechanism of rewards and punishment makes this training a success. Most of the schools transmit the culture of their area in the younger generation. However, the urban public schools mostly tramsmit culture of the West which is not a healthy sign. This alienates the student from the culture all around him. Each school must train the educands in regional and national culture. However, efforts must be made to maintain human culture everywhere.

Perception and Identity Formation. The younger generation learns future roles by means of perception and identity formation both in the family and in the school. Extra-curricular activities in the school are important to develop individual differences and particular skills of the educands. Thus, some of them may develop social leadership qualities, other political leadership traits and so on.

Development of Individuality. An important function of education is the development of the individuality of the student. This is developed by the development of individual skills and the allotment of roles and statuses according to it. This should not be based upon favours and prejudices. As a social subsystem the school is the best place to teach equality, liberty and fraternity to the younger generation. It is the best preparation around for practice of democratic traits in the wider social situation.

Culture of the School. Each school has a particular culture. This be noticed in the comparison of the private and public schools, the rural and urban schools, the schools in the tribal areas, the boys and the girls schools, etc. culture is constituted of the norms, customs, traditions, rules of behaviour, attitudes, etc. All these arc reflected in the social life of the school. While in the outer society culture is transmitted without much change and refinement, in the school particular attention is given to transmit refined elements of culture. This is done through various means of socialization and the allotment of different statuses and roles to different students.

The school is an important place for achievement. Students arc accorded prizes, awards, statuses and roles according to their scholarly attainments and achievements in the sports and extra-curricular activities. It teaches hierarchy and functions according to it. The behaviour of the teachers among themselves and their behaviour towards the headmaster serve as examples to the students about behaviour among equals and the behaviour towards the seniors.

Socialization. The most important task of the social organization is socialization. This socialization requires acting according to allotted roles and statuses. The schools provide scope for the development of leadership qualities among these students particularly through the extra-curricular activities. Under the supervision of the teachers, they gradually learn to carry out responsible activities. The headmaster and the teachers should allow more and more freedom to the students and it makes. Them more responsible. They should follow the principle of least interference in the social relationships among the students. They should impart the knowledge of social customs and traditions and develop values of society among the students. Thus the school serves as an agency of cultural transmission. It weans the child from the family and makes him more independent. As the reliant, more individuated and a better adjusted person. The teachers should be competent, take interest in the activities of the students and provide maximum facilities. So much depends on their presenting proper examples because social learning very much depends upon role perception. The students should learn social commitment. This requires favourable examples from the teachers and the headmasters. Competence, responsibility, straight-forwardness, skill and dynamism are created among the students by the social organization of the school. As the educand learns commitment to his roles so he becomes a better member of society after leaving the institution.

Social Mobility. The school is an important centre for promoting social mobility. It presents an example of the fulfilment of social justice. It is a place where every social custom and tradition is analysed, evaluated and even questioned before acceptance is granted to it. Therefore, the school presents the forum for bringing about desirable social changes. If the new generation learns the defects of the pernicious customs and traditions, if fights for their change and replacement in the wider society. This is particularly true about the high school.

2

Impact of Socialization

The Definitions

Socialization is a social process, and it has been variously defined. Some of these definitions are the following:

V. V. Akolkar. "The process of adoption by the individual of the conventional patterns of behaviour is described as his socialization, because it occurs on account of his integration with others and his expression of the culture which operates through them."

E. A. Ross. "The development of we feeling in association and the growth in their capacity and will to act together."

E. S. Bogardus. Socialization is "the process whereby persons learn to behave dependably together on behalf of human welfare and in so doing experience social self-control, social responsibility and balanced personality."

Socialization then, is process by means of which the individual learns to behave according to the social traditions and conventions. The human child has a remarkable capacity to imitate others, and hence he develops according to the environment into which he is born. Man, being a social animal, tries to win the appreciation of the group in which he lives and hence he naturally tries to imitate the culture of that group. It is through socialization that he is transformed from the animal into the human, and it is socialization which gives him a balanced personality. The social aspect of the personality is no less important than the individual aspect. Socialization teaches him to retain control over himself in the interest of others. It evolves a we feeling or community feeling in him and thereby invests him with a sense of responsibility.

Process of Socialization

Individuals influence each other by imitation, suggestion and sympathy, besides which the process of socialization is furthered by many social institutions. Man is the product of many social processes such as praise and blame, cooperation and conflict, submission and ascendency, and these forces create the individual's personality. Education is the most potent agency of socialization available to society.

Socialization in the Family

The family plays a very significant part in the individual's socialization because the child spends his early formative years in the home. He learns much by observing the people around him, by imitating them, by indulging in activities which win their approval and avoiding those which bring their disapproval and immediate punishment. It is the family environment which can create good habits in him, because the child's moral code is conditioned by the system of reward and punishment It is the family. And, it is also in the family that criminal tendencies are first generated. In their *book New Light on Delinquency and its Treatment*, Healey and Bronner have pointed out that Juvenile delinquents are frequently found in those famines in which the fulfilment of social relationships has been hindered at one time or the other. Freud and other psychoanalysts have demonstrated that the child remains throughout life whatever he is made out to be in the family. In his *'Psychological Factors* in *Marital Happiness'*, Termann has theorised that only those individuals can enjoy marital bliss whose own parents had been happy and contented. In the preface to *Women of the Street'*, a depth study of the prostitutes of London, it has been commented that the problem of prostitution is, in reality, a problem of the relationship between the children and parents. Children become aberrant and spoilt when the family peace is vitiated, and it is in circumstances such as these that many thieves, robbers, murderers and prostitutes are first born.

The family plays a very significant, perhaps the most

significant role in the individual's development. Freud and other psychoanalysts believe that the impressions made upon the child's mind at home determine the child's personality as an adult, for in childhood, the child's mind is very flexible and susceptible to any influence. The parents' love for the child makes a deep impression on him. And, although it is true that excessive love and affection have detrimental effects, the complete absence of affection creates complexes in the child's mind, which later disbalance his personality. His personality is also influenced greatly by the behaviour of his brothers and sisters towards him. Alder, the famous psychologist, has stressed the fact that the order of the birth of children in the family distinctly and separately influences the personality of each child. The eldest child's mental make up differs from that of the last. Besides, all great thinkers and philosophers have admitted the importance of their mother's love as far as their personality development is concerned. In India, people often gauge the personality of a young marriageable girl by observing her mother. And, as far as marriages are concerned, more attention is paid to the prospective bridegroom's parentage than to his own personality, for the family makes a lot lot of difference. There is little possibility of a child having a balanced personality if the personalities of his parents are not balanced. Even the social and economic status of the family has a deep impact upon the child's personality.

The family's influence does not end with the individual's entrance into adolescence, for even then the influence continues. Complete absence of control often results in moral degeneration among the young people, while excessive control manifests itself in repressed personalities and narrow minds. Only reasonable restraint and freedom can help the individual to develop a balanced personality. After marriage, the individual's personality is also exposed to the influence of his partner's personality, his or her health, mental attitudes, family background, physical beauty, attainments, etc. The ability to beget children or not is another factor which plays a significant role in the individual's personality development. In fact, considerable literature has been devoted to the subject of family's influence upon the personality by sociologists, psychologists and anthropologists.

Socialization in the School

After the home, the child is exposed to the school which also influences him, for the school is nothing less than aminiature society to him. It socializes him, gives him an opportunity to manifest his qualities, instincts, drives and motives, and helps to develop his personality. For the child, the educator's personality and character provide a model which he strives to copy, thereby consciously or unconsciously moulding his personality. This is true only of those teachers who succeed in arousing in the child's mind an attachment and love for themselves. Every little action, every movement, speech, etc., impresses itself on the child's mind. On the other hand, he is often repelled by some teachers, and he wants to contradict them through every act. This repulsion may be conscious or unconscious, but it drives the child away from such a teacher. The child is attracted by the other teacher who wins his sympathy, and it is from this teacher that the child wants to win praise and appreciation. He fears the frown of his teacher, he imitates him persistently. Apart from the teacher the child is also influenced by his colleagues, and his status and role in his school groups plays a large part in determining the status and role he is to occupy in society in later life. During the process of education, the child's personality develops under the impact of the other personalities with whom he comes into contact. It the school the child is disciplined. He is aware that disobedience brings immediate growth and may even drive him to criminal activity. On the other hand, complete absence on control may either make him liberal, free and independent or impulsive and impish. Besides, the cultural programmes of the school also help to refine his attitudes.

In this manner, the human personality is profoundly influenced both by the home and the school. Of the two, the family influence lasts for a longer time and is more comprehensive.

It is evident from the foregoing account of social development during adolescence that at this stage the individual is in real need of guidance. Many factors such as the sex drive, choice of profession, adjustment within the family and the school, etc., present such problems to the young immature mind which it cannot easily solve, and it is here that the teachers' and parents' guidance is really desirable.

Process of Social Development

Education plays an important part in the child's social development at every stage, but this education is not the formal education the child derives from books and lectures. It includes the education that comes to the child from extracurricular activities, the atmosphere of the school, etc. Group camps always have a good effect on the individual's social development, for it helps to build his character and also develops many social qualities. He develops good habits, learns the elements of leadership and gets the opportunity to learn many kinds of skills. In the informal atmosphere of the camp, the members can meet more freely, and this in itself is education in social living In this manner, the teacher and the parent can cooperate with each other and create situations for the proper development of the child. The child aspires to the social values of his own group, on the one hand, he is equally anxious to win the love and esteem of his parents as well as of his teachers, although it can sometimes happen that out of loyalty to the group he may feel compelled to neglect his parents and teachers and their entreaties. For, he is particularly anxious to win esteem in the group. Sometimes, in the group he indulges in activities that are considered specially anti-social In the case of children who indulge in such activities, fundamentally a great responsibility lies in the environment within the home and family. In families where the parents have no hesitation in giving praise and affection to their children, it will be seen that the young individuals indulge in proper and desirable activity. On the other hand, neglect and consequently rebellious children are apt to indulge in detestable actions, and later on turn into Juvenile delinquents It is necessary that the teachers keep an eye on the development and active manifestation of such tendencies within the child groups within his domain. Groups provide opportunities for the development of the qualities of leadership, so that in their adult and more responsible years, the boys and girls can turn to leading the nation. It should be kept in mind that all children do not evince the same liking for the group. Some children tend to avoid groups and prefer to stay with one or two children of their choice. There may be occasions of conflict between these individualistic boys and the bigger groups. An, there is not essential rule the members of the group are intelligent while these boys and girls who tend to shun the group are slow-writted. It is perfectly possible for the opposite to be true. Secondly, there may be some personal reason which may actuate the individual to stay away from the group, but generally it is best to live in the group, as it benefits the individual's social development.

The child's social development is influenced in important manner, by the mutual interaction between child-hood groups, competition, conflict and co-operation.

Criteria of Social Development

According to Bridges, the following Table can help to reveal the extent to which a child's social development has taken place, if at all. Positive answers indicate development, while negative ones indicate the opposites

1. Played with another child.
2. Spoken to another child.
3. Occasionally made social contact by touching or pushing a child.
4. Imitated other children's actions.
5. Imitated children's words.
6. Imitated children's laughter.
7. Often spoke to other children.
8. Originated new play activity with other child.
9. Joined group of children in play.
10. Sought another child's approval.
11. Asked another child for help.
12. Always given up toys at fair request.
13. Usually waited turn.
14. Tried to defend own right to materials or place.
15. Pointed to others' errors.
16. Tried to help others.
17. Stopped work to aid another child.
18. Comforted another child.

Further indication of desirable adjustment can be measured in terms of the extent to which a child has not rather has:

19. Turned away to avoid another child's friendly advances.
20. Usually stayed out of group marching or games.
21. Claimed others' errors.
22. Interfered with others' work.
23. Destroyed others' work.
24. Created disorder in group or led others into mischief.
25. Frequently pulled or pushed others.
26. Frequently complained of other adults for own gain.
27. Harassed new child by scoffing or shunning.
28. Hit or pinched others for fun several times.
29. Bitten or spit at other for fun several times.
30. Teased in other ways, causing irritation or discomfort.

Family and Social Development

Human personality develops in a social environment. In the childhood the personality of an individual is very susceptible to change and variation. hc can bc turncd in practically any desired direction. The famous psychoanalyst S. Freud has contended that the personality of a man is formed in his childhood and the period after that marks only its development. In view of the fact that the experiences, habits, etc., acquired in childhood are so extremely important, the family situation also becomes important because the childhood of the individual is spent within the precincts of the home. The family situation can be regarded as comprehending three factors-(l) Relation of parents to child. (2) Order of the child's birth, and (3) Presence of brothers and sisters and other members in the family. The important role played may be clearly realized after these three aspects have been studied.

Relation between Child and his Parents. Having affected a psychological analysis of the importance of the parent child relationship the psychoanalysts have tried to show why the child is influenced to such a great extent by his parents and the relation in which he stands with them.

According to S. Freud the parents are particularly present before the child as ideals. They are more powerful and strong and can perform all activities efficiently. The child effects an identification with his rather unconsciously. He wants to become as his father. It is often seen that the young child dons the clothes of his father and imitates his manner of walking and talking. The child behaves precisely as do his mother and father. Besides identification, the second element in this is that of imitation. The child learns much by imitation. There are many activities that the child learns to perform merely by observing and imitating the older members of the family. For the child, the parents are as examples and it will be very difficult to prevent children from indulging in activity in which the parents themselves indulge particularly when they do so in front of the child. The difficulty arises because he feels that what the parents are doing should be done. In this both identification and imitation are included. The child also receives suggestions from his mother and father. The activities in which the mother and father indulge automatically suggest themselves to the child. In this way, the process of identification is not the only process that is activated in the relationships between the child and the parents but is supplemented by the process of imitation, suggestion and sympathy. According to Freud, the viewpoints of the male and female child towards their parents are not identical. Freud believes that the sex instinct is innately given in the individual and is present at birth. In this opinion, the child does not suck his mother's breast merely because he is hungry but also because it gives him pleasure. His mother is not exclusively the source of his nourishment but also the basis of his feelings of pleasure. Freud has further postulated the instinct for heterosexuality in children. Accordingly, the male child loves his mother more while the female child shows greater attachments to die male parent. The mother is the boys' beloved. Hence, naturally the father becomes his opponent and sometimes he sees that he is deprived of his mother's love only because of his father's presence. Often his mother loves him and goes this father when the latter comes. Consequently, the boy regards his lather as rival. On the one hand, he respects the father because he is the ideal, on the other, the child also hates him in his capacity of opponent.

Criminal Tendency and the Parent-Child Relationship. The misbehaviour of the parents or their neglect of the children are important factors due to which children often become juvenile delinquents. According to the report *Women of the Street,* an important research on the prostitutes of London, the problem of prostitution has its origin in the relationship between the child and the parents. Often when the child is deprived of parental love and is sternly punished frequently he is filled with the desire to revolt and disgust so much that he runs away from the home when he gets the opportunity to do so. Once away from the home he falls into criminal ways. If neglected by his parents the child feels helpless and alone as a result of which he develops many kinds of complexes. The child becomes a delinquent also when the parents try to conceal too much from him. For example, the children are very apt to ask their parents as to where they are often mislead. When they come to know of their true source from servants or from their friends they develop a sense of insecurity because they are deeply hurt when they come to know that their parents do many things that they would not have the children know. This sense of insecurity often lures children into sex crimes.

Need for Balance. In this way, both excessive neglect and excessive love and affection are not to be desired in the relationship between the child and parents. Both are the origin of difficulties. Concerning the personality and all kinds of problems take root in the mind of the child. Similarly, it is harmful both to place absolute control on the child as well as to leave him to his own mechanisms almost entirely. If the child is given too much freedom he does not develop any respect for authority and cannot be governed. If he is placed under excessive control, his personality is not allowed to develop and he is obsessed with a sense of inferiority and sometimes even turns to crime. The truth of the matter is that if the child is to be disciplined and educated a bitter pill must be swallowed. It is very difficult to bring up a child. In this connection it is necessary that there be much balance and understanding. Then there can be no one universal rule that can apply to all children. Some children are amenable to greater control while others respond to a lighter degree of authority. On the other hand all children are not similarly influenced by authority just as all children do not react in the same manner to parental love or neglect. All that has been said before is true in a general way but it is also open to exceptions.

Result of Discrimination. Sometimes parents discriminate between their children in behaving towards them. Their unlimited love and affection for One while only scolding and punishment for another. Sometimes it is the beautiful child that is loved while the ugly one is neglected and disregarded. Whatever the reasons at the root of this discriminatory behaviour it is bad because it arouses feelings of hatred for each other among the children. When the child observes that his brother or sister is being loved more than he is, he becomes anxious to revenge this injustice. Sometimes he is even seen possessed of aggressive tendencies. He also tries to harm the other children in one way or the other. He is seen to be disappointed, fearful, etc. But it is also possible that the child may try to win the admiration and love of others in society and at school by appearing to be better than others in order to make reparation for the deficiency in family love that has been accorded to it. Whatever the outcome, it is completely undesirable and psychologically unjustified to indulge in this kind of discrimination between the children.

Impact of the Character of Parents. The personality of the child is also appreciably influenced by the moral thoughts and conduct of the parents because usually the child looks upon his parents as ideals on which to mould his life. In order to inculcate morality in the children the parents should place an example before them in the form of their *mm* exemplary behaviour. There are very few children who can mould their behaviour according to social values and conceptions even when they have seen their parents indulge in theft, sexual immorality, falsehood, deception and other forms of misconduct. In Miss Eliott's study the parents in 67 percent broken homes and 44 percent unbroken homes were indulging in immoral behaviour. If the mother indulges in prostitution her daughters have no inhibition against it and they would have no difficulty in imitating her and proceeding towards immorality and corruption.

Impact of the Mutual Relation of Parents. The personality of the child is further open to another important influence viz., the mutual relation between husband and wife. If the husband misbehaves towards the wife then the child, particularly the male child, takes exception to it and this increases his hatred for the father. This can, under certain circumstances, lead to terrible consequences. Similarly, if the wife misbehaves with husband, the female child in particular is likely to dislike it and hence she hates her mother. Constant conflict and quarrelling between husband and wife leads to the creation of an atmosphere of insecurity in the home which is not at all conductive to the development of the child's personality. If the relations between husband and wife are good the children have a good and encouraging ideal in front of themselves which they can imitate to good effect. They then try to be good themselves. It is only natural for the child to develop some personality defects if the relation between his parents is not good.

Impact of the Broken Family. When the relation between the husband and wife deteriorate, the family is reduced to a broken family. This is because the relation between no two members retain their original charm and goodness. A broken family is one in which the family relations have been severed. Family does not means the living together of some individuals but rather the intimate and profound relations that exist between them. In the absence of this intimacy the family is disbanded/and in the broken family juvenile delinquents are reared and brought tip. In the broken family the children are not looked after or cared for. According to some specialists, the broken family tends to create the criminal tendency in the female children more than it does in the male child. In 1947 in Bombay there were 386 boys and 169 girls under the child care society. Of these two boys and two girls had their parents in jail serving sentence for some or the other crime while 2 boys and 5 girls were victims of harsh behaviour and 5 boys and 6 girls were victimized by immoral insecurity. In the broken family the relation between the husband-wife, parents-child and brother-sister do not remain healthy. Hence, it is natural for boys and girls to tread the path of mistakes, crime and degradation.

Impact of Siblings. The personality of the child is susceptible to the influence not only of the relationship between itself and its parents but also by the personality of his brothers and sisters. This influence seems to be more pronounced in the case of girls because they are not quite as exposed to external influences as the boys are. If the older children in the family indulge in criminal activity the younger are very likely to follow suit or at least to be profoundly influenced, if the sister is a criminal or indulges in immoral acts, the younger sister will also imitate her or at least she is, likely to do so. The individual is socialized in the family. If the child finds other children in the family who are not much older or younger than him then the child finds a good atmosphere in the family. If there is only one child in the family then 'he does not find a conducive social atmosphere for development and its development is to some extent adversely affected. But this deficiency can be compensated if the parents play with the children.

Impact of the Financial Status. The financial condition of the family also influences the development of the child's personality. If the financial condition is good and the parents can adequately satisfy the needs of the children then the children are generally not possessed with the sense of inferiority and want and they do not turn to crime. But if the financial condition of the family is extremely bad the personality of the child suffers. Merrill has written that if the income of the family is low the children also have to work and their education is thus left incomplete. The child's personality does not react very appreciably to the conditions of work. Many of the desires of the poor children are left unfulfilled in order to satisfy which they turn to criminal activity. Poverty induces feelings of dissatisfaction and inferiority. But this does not warrant the conclusion that the poverty of the family will inevitably have harmful effect upon the child's personality. Sometimes the children, both male and female, become delinquent even though, and sometimes because, the financial condition of the family is very good. On the other hand, the children of the poor learn the lesson of self-reliance from the very start.

From the foregoing description of the parent-child relationship and the effect of various family conditions on the personality of the child it is evident that they are very important. In fact, it is these elements that are responsible for the development of the main characteristics of the individual's personality.

Social Importance of the Family

Nuclear Situation in Society. Family is the first institution in the history of man. In the ancient age men lived in small families, which lacked any kind of organisation or permanence. But they served to fulfil simple biological needs. Generally, the family consisted of husband and wife and their offspring. The powerful men possessed many wives and thus they lived in big families with their wives and children. When man became oriented in agriculture many families formed a group and stayed permanently at some place for farming. When these people started partaking of each other's pain and happiness as neighbourly gestures, social relations increased and in this way family is that primary group which slowly evolved into nation.

Fundamental Social Unit. Family is fundamental unit of human society. Its foundation rest upon man's biological and psychological needs. In the modern age, many functions of the family have shifted to other institution but nevertheless, there are many biological and psychological needs which cannot satiate without a family. Havelock Ellis in his penetrative essays, has shown that the importance of mother's milk for the child cannot be obtained in any other manner. Psychologists have proved that the absence of family affection has a serious impact upon the child's development. Sexual passions can be satisfied even outside the family but it can never be the source of emotional fulfilment. That 'man is a social animal' implies that man cannot live without a family. Thus, family is a fundamental unit of society.

Unit of Division of Labour. In primitive societies the entire organization was based on family units. The division of labour in society is also based on the family. In the complex structure which is society today, the family has lost some of its importance, but even today the activities of most members are for the family or contiguous to it. It is seen that people work and labour for the comfort of their wives, children and other members of family than even for personal comforts. Thus, even now the family is the nucleus of a major part of man's activities.

Basis of Social Organisation. Proper social organization depends upon proper organization of families. If the families disintegrate in some society, then the society will never be safe. One major cause of social disorganization is family disorganization. Families develop the character of the members of society. Freud and other psychologists have proved that a child, when a man, exhibits the same character and mental tendencies which he acquires in the family. In the opinion of Alder, a man's role in the family determines his role in society.

Socialization of the Individual. In this way, a person is socialized in the family. Defining family, Merrill writes, "Family is an enduring association of parent and offspring whose primary functions are the socialization of the child and the satisfaction of the members." According to Dewey and Tufts the family is a social agency for the education and protection of the 'race. It is in the family that the child acquires such important qualities as sincerity, sympathy, self-submission and realizing responsibility, etc. It is the character developed in the family which helps the child in becoming an important and responsible member of society. Wright was quite correct in stating that in every family, the child gets an opportunity for free expression of thoughts and developing his entire personality. Psychologists have incontestably proved that the proper development of the child is impossible, without a good environment in the family. The tendencies and habits which he acquires in the family, he finds impossible to shed later on. According to Freud, the viewpoint of a child toward the senior in the family determines his attitude and viewpoint towards the elders in society. The child's education should be in the hands of the parents in family. The parents should participate in all the child's activities. A child learns much by imitating his superiors: It is the family which imparts practical education to the child concerning the customs in society, conduct, other important elements of culture, preservation of health, love, sympathy, co-operation, etc.

It is evident from the above account that family is the primary and fundamental unit. Confucious remarked quite correctly that if you want to improve society improve its families. Society will improve automatically when the families improve.

Conveyance of Traditions. The family moulds the character and personality of the individual. It is through the family that society imparts its culture to the individual, thus, the family is very important in the form of socializing agency. In the essay, the *Family Conveyance of Tradition,* Paul Schoreker wrote that a particular function of the family is to sanction children. Like marriage, institution of family is constituted by different elements of culture. It is due to this reason that it has religious, judicial, political, artistic and linguistic aspects. Whenever a new thought impresses itself on an age the family takes a new form in order that the upbringing and mental tendencies may be harmonious to that thought. Politics and law were dominant in Rome, so that family organization there was such as to ensure the upbringing of children in harmony with the culture. Today, the economic order is predominating. So the family has changed its form, it makes the mental tendencies concur with the new culture. In this way, the family makes individual harmonious with the culture of society.

In the family, the child acquires knowledge about the current customs, mores, traditions, etc.

Social Control. A social life is a web of relationship. In order to maintain these relations properly a system of rights and duties is organized which will avoid any conflict between the members of society and allow them to develop as complements to each other. In order to avoid any breach of this harmony between the individuals in society, the society applies numerous kinds of control on the individual. They are taught to obey the elders, have sympathy for the young and for others. A strict control over sex relationship is necessary for maintaining the social order, otherwise disintegration will spread over the complex social life of today. Relationships between men and women will lose their solidarity. Illegitimate children will be born with no one to look after them. Although the anthropologists Mead and Malinowski have discovered societies where control over sex relations is inordinately lax without disturbing the social order but such an order is completely contradictory to the thinking of today's cultured person. It is the family which does this work of controlling sex passions for society. In all cultures, the families exercise some degree of control over the unmarried members till they attain the matrimonial state. In the same way, the family acts as a preventive to individual in keeping him from "the habits and crimes like drinking, theft, etc. Not many parents could like their children to embark on careers of crime. Even the worst person tries to prevent his children from adopting bad habits.

3

Influence of Society

On the one hand, one finds numerous groups in contemporary Indian society, distinguished from each on the basis of language, religion, race, caste, tribe, geographical location, etc., while on the other, one also finds distinct economic classes. The processes of secularization, westernization, acculturation, industrialization and urbanization have led to remarkable changes everywhere. The impact of the West is evident enough, but it is accompanied by frantic attempts to rejuvenate ancient Indian values. The increasing complexity of economic problems has had the effect of economic classes leaving indelible marks on the personality of children. Increasing political awareness is another factor which is clearly evident. The most clear outcome of the interaction of all these tendencies is that the young generation has been presented with a fantastic variety of alternatives and differences of opinion, the extent of variety by its very nature rendering extremely difficult any determination of right and wrong. This disorganization of values is manifested through such undesirable activities as indiscipline, juvenile delinquency, pessimism, destructive and murderous tendencies, etc. In such a situation, the first duty of the educational organisation is to supplement the clear presentation of all possible alternatives before the younger generation with active encouragement in the choice of one alternative, so that there is some positive guidance.

Education and Society

Hence, education must not merely inculcate secularism, realism and liberality in the educand, but must also provide him with the ability to distinguish the right from the wrong. The young people are subject to a multiplicity of influences emanating from various sources, and for this reason it is essential that there should be some unity in all this diversity. The absence of such a unity will have disastrous consequences in the form of personality and social disorganisation. The first step in this direction is the creation of character, which will grant an adolescent the determination to be guided by his own opinion. It is essential that old and traditional values be explained to the younger generation in the interest of continuity with the older generation but this should not preclude consideration of new values which can lead to progress and development. Education can thus fulfil the needs of society only if it adopts a comprehensive and dynamic curriculum, a dynamic methodology of teaching and a dynamic philosophy of education.

Characteristics of Indian Society

In order to understand the social foundations of education, it would be interesting to glance at the characteristics of India society. The main features are the following:

Caste System. Caste can be defined as a hereditary intermarrying group which determines the individual's status in the social stratification by his occupation, etc. In defining caste it is necessary to highlight its characteristics features. Intermarriage is an essential feature, for its members cannot marry outside their group. There are similar though less rigid limitation and restrictions on the dietary habits of the members of a caste. The occupations of most of the castes are determined, and it is not possible to transfer from one caste to another. The brahmin has the highest place in the social stratification of castes.

It is evident from the foregoing account that caste is not identical with class, because in a class stratification is free, not rigid. Membership of the caste is determined by birth while the membership of the class is based on status, standard of living, and other objective factors. Members of the caste do not necessarily, have any caste consciousness but members of a class have a class consciousness. Class is much more flexible than caste, which is completely rigid. Compared to the class, caste groups have greater social distance between them, and it is not possible to transfer from one group to the next. Similarly, caste division is also much more rigid in that members of one caste cannot mix eat and drink with the members of another. In this manner the caste system presents a bigger obstacle to the progress of democracy. In the medieval period the caste played an important role in the organisation of Hindu society-it organised the Hindu society, it maintained social and political stability, helped in begetting good offspring, looked after social security, looked after the mental security of the members, functioned as a trade union, determined laws about education, provided technical training, maintained and transmitted hereditary knowledge of mechanical and technical processes, maintained the religious life, etc. The caste system continued to exist due to certain characteristics of Hindu society, such as religious influence, static society, rural social structure, geographic division, differences between tribes, absence of education, etc. But in the present day the caste structure is being weakened by many factors. Modern education, social reform movements, political movements, industrialization, means of communication and transport, increase in the value attached to money, emergence of new social classes, a modern system of laws, etc., are all helping in the decline of the traditional caste structure, but despite this one finds a steady increase in casteism also. Casteism is actually being encouraged by elections fought on the basis of caste, and it is being kept alive by petty politicians. In the modern context, the caste system is proving immeasurably harmful to society. The separation and division in society caused by untouchability is in fact due to casteism, which is causing social disorganisation in many other ways also. It is dividing the Indian society into a number of fragmented groups. Discrimination on caste grounds causes serious difficulties in the development of the individual, and this helps to maintain the inequalities of distribution of wealth and the means of production. Because the sculptors were believed to belong to the low castes, the art of sculptors has suffered a serious blow. Very often the protection of women is hindered in the name of protection of caste. Besides, the caste system is responsible for a number of other problems such as child's marriage, denial of widow remarriage, dowry, etc. Hence, the caste system is proving a very serious obstacle to social progress and the establishment of a democratic society. It is opposed to nationalism because it encourages casteism. In view of the situation, many sociologists have suggested many ways of eliminating caste system. But what is required even more than the elimination of the caste system is its refashioning or modification so that it may help in fostering the sentiment of nationality and also encourage the growth of democracy. The first step in this direction is to remove caste discrimination in the new generation through education. Co-education will also encourage intercaste marriages. Another way is to get rid of surnames which indicate the caste of a person. It is also necessary to keep strict control over caste meetings and caste associations. Ways must be found of stopping caste considerations from taking a part in political elections. In this way, the existing caste system is proving a hindrance to the development of democratic ideals through education, and in order to prevent its ill-effects from poisoning society, it is necessary that educational institutions should take the first step.

Social Classes. Classes in society are as common in India as they are in any part of the world. Class is a status group, and in any society the social status of one group always differs from that of another. In the words of Maclver, "A social class is any portion of community marked off from the rest by social status." The foundation of the class is the class consciousness. In every case, the member of one class is perfectly conscious of his own status in respect to and as differentiated from the status of some other group. For this reason, the child's developing mind and personality always bear the stamp of the social class in which he originated. Many schools cater to the children of one particular social class because members of other classes cannot bear the expenses of educating children in such schools. Class consciousness also tends to hinder the growth of democratic values, and for this reason the school should provide an atmosphere which may encourage the feeling of equality and underlay differences between children of different social classes. It is difficult to increase the feeling of brotherhood as long as class distinctions exist. But class consciousness cannot be eliminated without putting an end to economic disparity and other inequalities. For this social and economic reforms are essential.

Religious Groups. A significant characteristic feature of the Indian society is the plurality of religious groups and communities found here- Hindus, Muslims, Christians, Sikhs, Zorastrians to name only a small number. Even among Hindus there are a number of smaller communities such as the Sanatan dharma, the Arya samaj, etc. The Jians and the Buddhists also believe themselves to be separate communities, while the Shias and the Sunnis among the Muslims also claim to be distinct religious groups. Every one of such religious communities tries to strengthen the we feeling among its members and tries to help them progress in many ways. That they do something positive cannot be denied, but this stands in the way of developing any national sentiment. Certain religious groups are so fanatically opposed to certain other groups that communal tension between them is a regular feature, and it starts on the smallest excuse. Many political parties take advantages of this, and in order to secure their own advantage they keep on encouraging communalism. Apart from the damage to life and property during communal disturbances, considerable damage is done to the attitudes of the younger generation because the entire social atmosphere is vitiated. Without putting an end to this communalism, it is impossible to achieve the moral, spiritual and intellectual development of children. As long as it exists, it is also impossible to create any national unity or to create an atmosphere suitable to the development of democratic values and concepts.

Variety of Languages. Another feature of Indian society is the presence of more than a dozen languages and an almost impossible number of dialects. Although this variety is conducive to cultural prosperity, it also affords a useful opportunity to those who want to arouse linguistic sentimental attachments and create differences. As a result there have been very destructive riots and conflicts in many parts of the country, leading to loss of life and property, both public and private. If languages spreads rapidly, it only injures the mental development of the young people because they begin to hate other languages and refuse to learn them. Linguism also leads to hatred of the literature in the other tongue. Hence, this emotion also blunts moral and intellectual development.

Many Cultures. Although from the earliest times, it has been granted that India had a single culture, in fact this unity covered a remarkable diversity. India is such a big country that it should properly be called a subcontinent, and in different parts of this country, different cultures have been independently evolving. While all of them share certain common characteristics, they also differ from each other in many respects which influence the children brought up in them. There can be no denying that cultural variety adds to cultural pros erity but it can also encourage social disorganisation when the distinctions are used to create differences. In more recent years, political interests have inspired many people to demand separate slates on the basis of these cultural differences. In same cases these demands .have gone so far as to express a desire for secession from the centre.

Excessive Population. The population in India is growing at such a rapid pace lhat the excess of population has become a very complex and frightening problem. In such a situation it is becoming increasingly difficult to provide the necessities of life, proper education and a proper environment for everybody.

Poverty. As a result of the large population, the country is suffering from endemic poverty which serves to offset all the advantages of education.

Disorganisation of the Joint Family. The joint family system is rapidly breaking down in modern Indian society, and it is being replaced by centralized families, with the result that the individual is now subject to the influences of a different kind of family. Before making any national plan for social reformation, it is essential to keep in mind this change.

Disorganisation of Values. The present day society in India has lost all its faith in the traditional Indian values under the impact of westernization, secularization, urbanization and a host of similar influences. But the lost set of values has not been replaced by any more recent pattern, and consequently one finds complete disorganization of values. This is acting as a serious impediment to moral and spiritual development.

Marital Disorganisation. One finds a steady increase in the cases of disorganised marriages due to the system of dowry, increase in divorce rate, change in the functions of the family, marriage between incompatible people, etc. Marital disorganisation invariably has a bad effect on the development of children.

Materialism. Compared to the ancient Indian society, the contemporary social organisation is decidedly more materialistic. This is leading to individual and social disorganisation on the one hand, and to evil effects upon the social, moral, spiritual and intellectual development of the younger generation on the other.

Politicisation. After independence, political influences have penetrated every sphere of life the result that the sole motive governing every action is that of self interest and self-aggrandizement. Even in education, political interest can not be found at practically every level. This again is functioning as a very serious ;obstacle to all progress.

Social Disorganisation. Indian society is being rapidly fragmented into small units because of the influence of regionalism, linguism, casteism, untouchability, communalism, etc. As a consequence, one finds social disorganisation everywhere. This has a detrimental effect on the development of children.

Individual Disorgnisation. For the last few years, the tendency to indulge in various kinds of intoxicants is growing among the younger generation, more particularly among the students. The character level of students is falling rapidly under die influénce of alcohol, opium and other intoxicants and viewing of immoral films. Combined with this is the uncertainty about the future, which only tends to aggravate abnormalities, mental tension and personal disorganisation. All these are serious problems for the educational planners.

Economic Difficulties. Compared to the conditions existing in ancient and medieval India, there is far greater unemployment today. This has a direct impact upon the minds of educands. Besides, economic difficulties make it impossible to achieve the ideal of universal education.

Impact of Indian Society

Having seen the chief characteristics of Indian society, it is now possible to study the effect Indian society is likely to have on the child's development, and for this we will study its effect on each individual aspect of development.

Impact on Physical Development. Considerable attention has always been paid to bodily development in India from the very ancient times. Some kind of physical training has always been an inevitable part of school education, the tradition of yogic and other exercises starts from ancient times. In modern schools, efforts are made toward the physical development of the educand through such institutions as Scouting, Girl Guides, A. C. C., N. C. C., N.C.C.R., etc., in addition to which many schools also provide special training and guidance in some sports. Most of the contemporary Indian thinkers, among them Aurobindo and Vivekanand, had stressed the importance of physical education, but despite such physical education it is found that the health of the educands is generally below average. The poverty of the Indian nation is dearly reflected in their dull and weak faces, and it is only poverty which prevents the state from providing free nourishment to the educand. Education itself is so expensive that most families find it an almost intolerable burden. In addition to this, dietary habits also influence the health. As it is the food taken by Indians is lacking in many of the nourishing elements, besides which milk is very expensive and few people can afford to take it in the requisite quantity although it is essential. Again, one finds very few means of entertainment and recreation in India society. The result of this is that although the student can be compelled to stay from the matinee shows at cinema halls, he cannot be prevented from spending his leisure time in reading pornographic literature or in taking intoxicants. Cigarettes and other intoxicants are in common use in the lower and middle classes of Indian society. Children and adolescents imitate their seniors and also take to smoking, thus injuring their health. Another factor is the greater importance attached to smart, shiny and highly colourful clothes than to rich and nutritive food in many middle class families. Most of the young men and women living in cities are completely averse to physical effort of any kind. Their condition is made worse by a polluted atmosphere, absence of sanitation and hygienic living conditions, shortage of nutritious food, poverty irregular living habits, etc. Urban children are particularly subject to all these shortcomings, and thus their health is falling rapidly. The pity of it is that little if any effort is being made to check this landslide. There is little hope that one can foster for the coming generation when the future parents themselves suffer from so many shortcomings. In actual truth, although much importance is attached to physical education and training in theory, in actual practice, there is little physical education. Then, it is found that young men and women who complete the entire course of education, spending sixteen or seventeen years in schools and colleges, are far worse off in respect of health than those who study for a short time and then immediately adopt some career. As long as the educated class of the country suffers from such debility, there is little chance of any development or progress in the country.

Impact on Mental Development. Mental development is intimately related to physical development. Even when the child exists in embryo in the mother's womb, his health is influenced by the health of his mother, and if some nutritive elements are lacking in the nourishment conveyed to him, his mental development is retarded along with his physical development. After emerging from the womb, the child is influenced by the family. In India, little can be said in favour of the family if one considers the influence it exercises on the child's mental development. The child's mind is negatively influenced by the constant poverty, family disturbances and quarrels, quarrels between his parents, the large number of family members and other problems arising from this, frequent visitation of disease, etc. This is further complicated by the constant presence of such mental attitudes as casteism, communalism, etc. The feeling of communalism, is fostered in his mind from his earliest days and it is very soon supplemented by thoughts of untouchability. Not much later he is exposed to the realities of his family status as determined by its income, and the evil effects which emanate from this. Today the country provides the highest training and education in the spheres of agriculture, medicine, engineering, the arts, technology and almost any conceivable branch of learning, devised to develop the young and growing mind. But how many people can really derive any benefit from such institutes of higher learning ? Poverty effectively deprives even the most intelligent children of poor families of the highest education, for there is almost no arrangement of any financial assistance for them. Apart from this, the education provided in modern schools is also not free of defects, for it does nothing more than prepare the child for a profession or a job, and even that is often not available to the individual. In villages, many children do not attend even primary school. Most poor people are compelled to send even the youngest children out to some occupation so that they can augment the family income. In such conditions, it is futile to hope for the mental development of children. In recent years, radios, newspapers and other media of mass communication have just begun to penetrate to the villages, but as compared to the villages of Western countries, such means of mental development are still in short supply. In addition to this, such disorganising and disruptive tendencies as regionalism, linguism, etc., are only making minds more narrow and limited. What, then is the occasion for surprise if one finds little originality in most spheres ? Even after so many years of independent national life, we have not been able to give a national status to Hindi. In addition to conditions existing in the country are not conducive to the development of the literature of any language. English is still very influential and it carries with it a definite mental slavery. As a result of all these factors, mental development cannot be independent and unrestricted.

Impact on Emotional Development. Although many of the elements of Indian culture have succeeded in checking the growth of abnormalities of personality and mental disease, the present condition of society cannot be considered to be favourable to the emotional development of the coming generation. Increasing poverty, increasing population, family and marital disorganisation, uncertain future, rapidly increasing commodity prices, and other such factors influence the growing mind at a very early age and fill it with various kinds of fears and repressions. As a result of such sentiments as casteism, linguism, regionalism, communalism, etc., children begin early to hate many sections of society and also to fear them. How can brotherhood develop in such conditions ? The committee for national integration has given certain suggestions for evolving emotional unity and integration among the people, but all this amounts to letting off stem because all this activity is being countered by the encouragement to disruptive forces for political ends. Hatred and fear are being progressively encouraged, with the result that-conditions are deteriorating further. All these factors add up to create a very unhealthy atmosphere for the emotional development of the younger generation, and consequently one can see all the elements of individual disorganisation in the students of today-such elements as indiscipline, violence, disrespect, excessive sexual indulgence, crudity, use of intoxicants, gambling, etc.

Impact on Moral Development. Want of something and poverty are both mortal enemies of moral development, and both of these elements can be seen in most Indian families. The situation in towns is much worse than in rural areas because children see so many scenes of violence and crime, immorality and cruelty, that they cannot avoid them. Apart from any other influence, the cinema alone is responsible for a great degree of moral depravity and degradation, and it is next to impossible to shield young boys and girls from its influence. The film industry is more concerned with making huge profits than with the influence their films are likely to have on the moral fibre of the people. And hence, art is used as an excuse to cover up exhibitions of immorality, sexual indulgence and violence, all of which tend to undermine the moral character of adolescents. In villages, poverty effectively takes care of any moralistic leanings, and they, too, are called upon to face many odd circumstances. Because of their ignorance and lack of education, they are not even aware of their rights, besides which justice in Indian courts is neither inexpensive nor expeditious so that they may be encouraged to fight for their rights. Those who do struggle for their rights are soon destroyed and worn out, and those who do not succeed only in existing. The moral level of the villagers is lowered by lack of education, lack of sanitation and hygiene, insecurity, communalism, casteism and untouchability. One sometimes feels that the impersonal atmosphere of the towns is perhaps better and easier to contend with. In cities one finds certain areas designated as criminal areas, and children living here arc taught the fundamentals of crime in their very early years. In cities like Bombay a very large number of juveniles becoming involved in the illicit liquor, prostitution, gambling and other such markets which encourage juvenile delinquency on a large scale. The state can do little in such cases, and it is doing even less. The morals of the younger generation are further endangered by the disorganised set of moral and social values, caused by widespread differences of opinion about man-woman relations, sexual aberrations, earning of wealth, exploitation, the aim of life, the duties of the individual, relationships between members of the family, etc. It is difficult for the youth to decide what is wrong and what is right in any of these matters, and it is only natural that in the absence of any guiding principle they should feel obligated to follow on the smooth flow of instinctive needs and their satisfaction. This kind of disorganisation of personality and character throws a lot of responsibility upon the leaders in the social, educational, economic and political spheres. It can also be alleged that many leaders connive at this growth in moral degeneration because their interests are linked with this deterioration. The problem is so complex that moral and religious preaching in schools will do little to stem the root. What is required even more is to somehow do away with the set of circumstances which are responsible for lowering moral standards. Morality is not some thing to be taught, but a model to be presented by the conduct of elders, teachers and parents in the society. Moral education alone can never raise moral standards by itself. If a family is disorganised, the children cannot be saved by moralistic preaching. Characterless teachers cannot possibly achieve any moral improvement in the educand, and there can be no denying that the teaching profession is nowadays manned by individuals who have no moral values themselves and who do not hesitate even one minute to spread immorality among the educands. At the university level there is such great prevalence of nepotism, corruption, sexual indulgence and aberration, that if the truth be told, many parents would refuse to send their children for higher education to such institutions. Academic freedom is now merely a cloak for narrow mindedness. Even educational institutions are not free from the poison of casteism, communalism, linguism, regionalism, so much so that educational institutions are in fact playing a major role in spreading such disruptive sentiments among the younger generation. Briefly, there is a totality of circumstances which can only prevent any moral development in the child, and a detailed analysis of all of them would require a book of phenomenal size.

Impact on Social Development. The ideal of seeing oneself in all others has been part and parcel of Indian culture for ages, and as a consequence one finds that in India, particularly in the rural areas, there is a considerably high level of social exchange, organisation and adjustment. This is more true of the past than of the present, because in more recent years the detrimental effects of communalism, linguism, regionalism, etc., have been evident. They have cut into this social exchange and destroyed social feeling. Poverty and corruption have helped this disruptive process, and as a consequence one finds a very high incidence of disagreement, civil litigation, violence, theft, dacoity, prostitution, etc., in the villages, and sometimes even in the towns and cities. Social control has practically ceased to exist, and has been replaced by selfishness and individualism. Materialism has practically replaced interest in religion. One finds that educated or literate villagers have even less of the social consciousness than their uneducated counterparts because they are less amenable to social control. In the urbanized areas this lack of social consciousness seems to decrease in direct proportion, while in certain areas, such as the industrial and criminal infested areas, it has practically vanished. The disorganisation of the joint family has also been responsible for this deterioration in social feeling, a process which is being only encouraged by marital disagreements, maladjustment, etc. In schools and colleges one can see much the same kind of thing in the relationship between teacher and taught, and teacher and the school organisers. In the face of such disruptive factors, little can be done by organising a few isolated social programmes. Similarly, the efforts made by the committee for national integration are rapidly negated by the activities of political parties which are intent on spreading mutual hatred and jealousy among the various communities, social groups, classes, etc. On the one hand, people advocate the adoption of short programmes for encouraging social consciousness but on the other they themselves are responsible for growing gangsterism, groupism and other such anti-social activities within the school. All these are doing considerable harm to social development.

Impact on Aesthetic Development. The child's aesthetic development depends very much upon the beauty of the surroundings in which he is brought up, the beauty of the home, the school, the neighbourhood. In school his aesthetic development is helped along by some elementary training in the various arts, drawing and painting, singing, music, dramatics, etc. Many schools in the country provide specialized training in the arts. Efforts are also sometimes made to make the school buildings attractive and aesthetically appealing. But in actual fact the paucity of means makes such steps difficult and often colleges are not able to maintain beautiful buildings or lawns. In many cases one finds that the school or college present an appearance little better than some factory. Yet, it must be remembered that it is the home which plays a larger part in the aesthetic development of the child, and in this respect the home of a majority of children compares unfavourably with the school these children attend. Leaving aside the deliberate attempts at beautification, which require a definite economic standard, one finds that frequently children come from homes which do not even provide sufficient space for the large family to live cleanly and in normal privacy. In villages, one often finds the family and the domestic animals practically sharing a common shed, thus living in almost inconceivably unhygienic surroundings. How much aesthetic development can one expect from the child who spends much of his day playing naked in the dirty and dusty street outside his house: Towns are not much better than the villages in this respect, for many houses are not well lit, clean, located in densely populated areas, serviced by narrow, dark and appalling lanes. Little aesthetic progress can be expected from children living in such homes.

Impact of Spiritual Development. It has been the fond belief of many generations that Indian culture is basically spiritual, and that this inherent spirituality is steadily vanishing under the impact of such modern tendencies as westernization, urbanization, industrialization, that spiritual values are being rapidly replaced by more material and secular values. This process is also being hastened,by other cooperating factors such as endemic poverty, illiteracy, corruption, a numbering dirtiness, widespread communalism. Some educationists have advised the adoption of some kind of religious instruction in schools, and have been trying to convince the government that this would not constitute a violation of its professed secularism. Some political parties, the communist party among them, are violently averse to the adoption of any such moral or religious instruction and one finds that religious instruction has not been so far introduced in the curriculum of most schools. In cities and towns, much of the religious teaching is hiding only certain vested interests of a social or political nature. Another thing which must be considered is the influence of science and technology and the great frequency with which religious riots between sought to weaken man's faith in religion, but despite this the introduction of religious instruction in schools will have some beneficial effect on the child's spiritual development. Otherwise, there is little if anything to hope for, because the atmosphere and environment existing in the country would discourage any kind of interest in spiritual matters. Certain other educationists have advocated the propagation of ancient Indian cultural and moral values through courses in ancient history. In fact, the entire system of education can be successfully Indianized by teaching all subjects in the Indian context, and thus the ancient values can once again be made popular. Although many private institutions are engaged in useful work in the direction of spiritual development of the younger generation, the slate, too, must be convinced that the adoption of religious teaching in schools is not a reversal of its policy of secularism so that it can also play its part in introducing such education in institutions controlled or aided by it. Almost all educational philosophers of the country have supported this suggestion for moral instruction.

Impact on Cultural Development. In the good old days of ancient India education sought first of all to make the child cultured and civilized, but in the present day, educational institutions are concerned merely with acquainting the child with the various subjects put on the syllabus. The institutions care little whether the child acquires any culture in the process of education or not. Besides, the shortcomings that could be made up at home are not compensated because of the consistently widening generation gap and absence of social and family control. Society in general also provides a model only for such disruptive tendencies as classism, individualism, all of which promote selfishness, absolute liberty and disregard of laws. One finds little consideration and respect in the relations between teachers and students, parents and children, elder and young. Freedom and the rights of the individual are the call of the day, and they are only excuses for unbridled violence and indiscipline. Again, selfish politicians are encouraging instead of trying to arrest the process. Cultural development suffers another setback when the young see their elders raising their voice and hands against constituted authority in the form of the government. Even the social, educational, political and other circumstances obtaining in the country are net conducive to cultural development of any kind. Hence, one finds almost no cultural development in the present generation of children.

Suggestions for Reform

Having considered the impact of the Indian environment on the various aspects of the child's development, it is evident that considerable social reform will have to be undertaken, if the child's comprehensive development is to be ensured. This entire treatise was not to say that such conditions obtain in India alone, because such defective environment exists in many countries. Yet, instead of deriving consolation from this fact, it is better to try to improve things in our own country as best as we can, and according to our own lights. In trying to achieve the development of the child's character, care must be taken to see that it carries the impring of Indianization, for such characteristics development is natural. If proper social conditions and a healthy environment is to be created, in order to ilitate the child's development, it will be necessary for parents, teachers and administrators to cooperate. In fact, the process of education as a process of complete development is not different from the process of universal progress. If there is any drawback or shortcoming in any part of the country, it inevitably has an adverse effect on the development of the younger generation. Educational institutions are only a normal part of the social organisation, and hence they can achieve nothing by isolating themselves from the social pattern. Hence, if the educational policy is to be successful, it will have to be treated as part of the programme of general development.

Impact of Castes and Religious Groups

One finds many castes, religious groups and social classes in India. These form important elements in the child's social environment and they influence his development. This influence can be briefly described as under:

Influence of Castes. Under the Hindu social organisation, it is caste which determines the individual's status and position to the social hierarchy. One finds elements of the caste system even among the Muslims. In the caste, the professions and occupations of the lower castes are predetermined and fixed, and the child aims at adopting the occupation of his own caste. Since the child is almost compelled to adopt the same profession as his forefathers he is inevitably exposed to the rules of untouchability which operate between his caste and a superior caste. This creates very undesirable prejudices and gives rise to extreme narrow mindedness in the child. Although there are some ad vantages in adopting the hereditary occupation, it is undeniably unscientific in that it fails to consider the individual differences of the children and does not consider the actual suitability of the child to the particular occupation. The caste system has had the effect of splitting the society into many small segments, and this fragmentation obviously hinders the development of national unity. Besides, it is also responsible for the child's awareness of discrimination and distinction between individuals and the consequent feelings of superiority and inferiority. In this way, the presence of many different castes hinders the child's mental progress.

Impact of Religious Groups. In India one can see many religious groups such as Hindus, Muslims, Christians, Buddhists, etc., and some people have gone so far as to consider the Sikhs and Jains as distinct groups although, in fact, they are part of the Hindu community. Most of these religious groups have established and are maintaining many individual schools in which general religion is taught, along with their own respective religious teachings. Most of these schools try to inculcate a particular set of religious principles in the educand. In many ways the teaching of religious principles can be of benefit to the child and the community, but when teaching in one school contradicts or ridicules teaching in another school. It naturally gives rise to a consciousness of differences between one religious and another. The immediate consequence of this is communalism, which n instilled into the child's tender mind, and this prevents him from identifying himself with other members of the nation, and thus national unity suffers. The best course is to inculcate the general principles of religion, stressing the fact that all religion are one and the same for without this, religion can only lead to narrowminded thinking.

Impact of Social Classes. Social class is the most potent influence on the child. On the one hand, we find a steady breakdown of discrimination based on religion and caste, but on the other we find a growing consciousness of the class one comes from thus intensifying the feeling of difference. This awareness, that one belongs to the lower, middle or upper class, is communicated to the child also. Consequently, children coming from the lower classes start with the feeling of inferiority, of being poor, of deprivation of the good things of life. In reaction to this inferiority, many of them turn to criminal activity, because children from the upper classes find pleasure in displaying their superiority which has already created in them pride, vanity and a number of other ignominious emotions and sentiments. Comparatively, the child from the middle classes is less susceptible to either extreme of emotion for superiority on the one hand is reduced by consciousness of inferiority on the other, and this explains the reason way most middle class children show better performances in academic work than children from either of the two other classes. Some political ideologies ado reinforce this awareness of the difference of class. It may have some dubious advantages, but it cannot be denied that on the whole it has a detrimental effect on the child's development, and that it practically obviates the possibility of ever generating any humane sentiments in them.

It is neither possible nor desirable to eliminate religious groups, classes or castes from society in order to protect the child from the evil influences of these social institutions. It is more practical to try to create an environment, at home and in school, which would counter such influences, or at least not reinforce them. The educator can take upon himself the duty of explaining to the child that discrimination on the basis of any one of these is artificial, and that it is not a sound criterion for distinguishing between one human being and another. This will help to make the children more humane and liberal in their approach.

4

Influence of Community

Community is a group of human beings living in a clearly defined geographical area, having a specific name, possessing common customs, traditions and mores which bind one member of the group to another. Examples of such communities in India would be the Hindu community and the Muslim community. Although the chief features of a community are a geographical area, a specific name, the possession of common customs and traditions, and primarily a group of human beings, the most significant element in it is the feeling which acts as a cohesive force. It creates in members of the community a sense of identification with the group, the desire to make sacrifices and contributions, and the desire to depend upon the group. Thus, the feeling is successfully created and then strengthened by education. In recent years, this community feeling has broken the bonds of narrow nationalism and seems to be moving in the direction of an all comprehending internationalism, and in this, too, education has made significant contribution. On the other hand, the community itself is an important medium of education. Education is essential for converting the young men and women into useful members of society, but this education does not aim merely at a chance in their patterns of behaviour. What is required is a modification of the behaviour patterns not of a few individuals but of the entire community, because such a drastic change is required for the interaction between various communities living in society. According to one simple classification, communities are divided into the rural and the urban, and the impact of each respective community can be seen in the behaviour of its members.

Responsibility of Community towards Education

It is clear from the foregoing discussion that community has great responsibility towards education, for it itself is a medium of education. As Crow and Crow has commented, "A community cannot expect something for nothing, if it wishes its young people to serve their community well, it must provide whatever educational advantages are needed by the young people, individually and collectively, to prepare themselves for that service." Briefly, the community has the following responsibilities towards education:

Educational Control. In a democratic state, education should be controlled by the state because only then can they ensure that democratic ideals will be instilled into the young men and women receiving education. Hence, it is the leaders of society who give decisions regarding the curricula, general organization and administration, finances, methods of examination, etc., of the schools.

Control of Schools. The duty of the community does not end with providing finances and other means with which to establish schools. The community must also undertake the responsibility of selecting those individuals who can be relied upon to run the schools in a way in keeping with the ideals of the community. Besides, educators influence the life of the community very greatly, and hence the community must also ensure the contract, selection and appointment of educators.

Co-operation between Educators and Citizens. Modern educationists are of the opinion that the educator should establish contact not only with the parents of his wards but also with the leaders of society, so that educators, parents and leaders can get together and decide the curricula, the ideals of education, the manner of day-to-day administration of schools, etc.

Providing the Informal Means of Education. Outside the school, there are many agencies such as reading rooms, dramatic societies, museums, libraries, etc., which contribute in an important measure to the education of the child. Besides, the child's education cannot be really complete unless society also produces a mass of good literature and allows scope for the expression as looking after the maintenance of college lawns and gardens, maintaining discipline among the students, looking after the sports equipment and caring for the sports grounds, arranging cultural programmes and issuing invitations, etc. In addition, the student should also be guided on how he can face this responsibility effectively and successfully. Extra- curricular activities should generally be undertaken collectively. Different kinds of programmes help in evolving different kinds of qualities. For example, debates and discussions produce good orators. Art competitions bring out the natural artists. By maintaining a good tone in the college, good characters can be produced, because a good atmosphere in the college encourages self-confidence, self-respect and a strong determination.

Although individual or personnel education is being given in the modern age, there is no denying the value of community programmes in colleges as a way of evolving democratic values and also as a means of producing the leaders of the future. Hence, education in the modern democratic state should be both collective and individual.

Educational Impact of the Community

Community has a comprehensive educational impact. In this connection the following points are noteworthy:

Impact on Physical Development. In every country, there arc certain agencies of local self-government, for example, municipalities which are responsible for public hygiene and sanitation. Even at the international and national level some such committees are formed to safeguard the health of the citizens, because physical health is directly dependent upon public hygiene. In most big towns, citizens contribute liberally to the establishment of public hospitals which serve the poorer sections of society which are themselves incapable of paying for medical services. In addition, many societies also provide gymnasia and other facilities for physical exercise. In India gymnasia have been traditionally attached to various places of worship so that young people can bring to physical health the devotion often given to worship. Here young people were encouraged to attend such gymnasia and to take care of physical health under the guidance of physical culture experts and religious leaders. There apparently seems to be a decline of interest in this direction over the last few years, but nevertheless even now one finds such gymnasia attached to temples, etc. Every educated community takes care of the physical well being of its young by making provisions for nutritious food, occasions for rest, plenty of physical exercise, etc.

Impact on Mental Development. The community can play an important role in the mental development of its citizens by providing musical competitions, cultural functions, dramatic performances, seminars, etc. Besides, every enlightened community also builds libraries and reading rooms and encourages people to use them because mental development is hastened in the process of acquiring knowledge. All such means of mental development are now considered necessary adjuncts of any civilized community.

Impact on Cultural Development. Every community has its own distinctive customs, modes, mores, modes of behaviour, traditions, ideals, etc., which are transferred to the younger generation through the process of socialization. This socialization process has so profound an influence upon the individual citizens that one can find distinctive patterns of behaviour evolving in them which serve to distinguish them from members of any other community having a different set of ideals and traditions etc. In order to maintain the vital force of society, it becomes necessary to make some changes in these adjuncts of culture from time to time. Here, too, the leaders of the community have to assert themselves. It is for them to reflect on the existing state of affairs, to analyse and see the defect, to suggest ways and means of changing the cultural complex in order to effect improvements. Besides, the culture of a community also undergoes natural change and transformation by becoming the best medium of cultural development.

Political Impact. "The political ideology of a community is reflected in the extent to which educational opportunities are offered to all its members and in the responsibility assumed by its political leaders for the educational progress of the community." One can conceive the political impact of the community on citizens by comparing the political thinking of the citizens of democratic America and communist Russia. In a communist country the community aims at spreading communist ideology among the people while in a democratic state the community is inclined to develop democratic ideals among the people, and all its efforts are directed towards such development

Economic Impact. Different kinds of industries, jobs and professions develop only in a community, not in the solitude of an individual The child examines his own ideas and the conduct of various individuals involved in different professions and occupations. Frequently, one finds that adolescents develop some interest in one or the other profession. On the other hand, some professions can be learnt with the help of neighbours, family members, the community, etc. In certain cases the profession of an individual is determined by the community, for it is the community which decides the profession to be adopted by the child when he reaches adulthood. In India, for example, in the past, the profession of an individual was determined by his caste. Although now nobody pays attention to the claims of the caste system in this connection, there is no denying that the choice of profession is often limited by the type of people one comes into contact with, the local institutions and committees, which condition one's thinking. It is from them that one learns how to earn one's livelihood. It is therefore evident that the community influences the life of the individual to a very great extent.

Moral and Character Development. Community has an impact not only on the physical and mental development of the individual, but also on his moral and character development. Every society has its own code of ethic which differs in some degree from that of other societies, and this difference is reflected in the behaviour of its citizens. In order to see this effect of the community on the moral development of the individual, one can compare members of a civilized community with those of a tribal society and see the difference between their moral ideas and characters. Whatever the difference between the moral levels of two communities, there is no community which incompletely devoid of any moral values and standards. Even the most backward society has some primitive moral code and it tries to instil these moral ideas into the younger generation. It is the community which provides the environment for the character development of the child. If this environment is favourable it will create good character while on the contrary one will find defective character formation if the environment itself is defective. Hence, in this respect the duties of the community are self evident.

Impact on Social Development. Community is responsible for developing the community sentiment among its citizens, and this community sentiment creates in them a feeling and sense of responsibility towards the community which brings with it awareness of certain duties. Most of the intelligent people in a community try to create responsible citizens out of their children. It is the society which socializes the individual. In Indian society the individual's socialization is achieved through a variety of religious functions deliberately intended to create social consciousness in the child participating in the function. This awareness of the society around one is manifested in each individual's desire to win the praise of the members of the community and an equally strong desire to avoid winning their criticism and disrespect. He is afraid of being ostracized. But it must be remembered·that development of social consciousness does not imply a blind following of the traditional rules and customs of society. Many people do reflect upon the nature and value of all these customs, and if they Find them defective they raise their voices against such customs and vigourously arouse people to get rid of them. This is the beginning of social reform movements, and if members of the community cooperate with the revolutionaries, social reform takes place. But all this takes place within the society, because, the process of development and improvement of society occur within the society, not outside it. Hence the community plays an important part in the individual's social development.

Educational Impact. All the various influences that can be seen emanating from the community have an educational impact, inasmuch as they help the process of education. Apart from this, the community also has some impact upon formal education. The different classes of the community contribute to establish educational institutions. In India, one finds various institutions financed and run by Hindus and Muslims, and among Hindus by brahmins, jats, sikhs and other religious groups. Generally, such institutions aim at educating children belonging to their own communities. In addition such communities also try to provide the informal means of education such as reading rooms, libraries, dramatic societies, etc.

Educational Importance of the Community

Community makes important contribution to both formal and informal forms of education. The child develops first within the limited sphere of his own family and then steps out into the larger surroundings of the community which unconsciously influence his language, thinking, modes of living, habits, ideas, etc. In fact, every aspect of his development is consciously or unconsciously influenced by the community. In the words of Francis J.Brown, "Changing the behaviour of individuals is not enough, education must seek to modify community patterns of behaviour through close and constant interaction with the total culture of the community." From the very beginning, the child's behaviour, habits, his dress, etc., are all determined by the community. It is the community which determines his attitudes towards various religions, tribes, classes, individuals and objects, and in this way community aids the family in socializing the child but it differs from the family in that it continues to influence the child even after the family has stopped doing so. The community's approved patterns of behaviour are enforced on the individual through school discipline, while the moral and ethical code of the community is reflected in the personalities of the teachers which also influence the individual.

In India, from very ancient times, community has played a very significant role in the education of men and women. And even in present day education, one can see the impact of the community in every sphere. A democratic government was established in the country after it won independence, and this government presented democratic ideals to the country. The government also put forward the suggestion of universal and free education. It also undertook the task of establishing educational institutions to provide education at every level. Some of this burden was take over by some communities. Libraries, reading rooms, museums, art galleries, dramatic clubs, etc., have been established in all the larger towns. The community is playing a steadily increasing role in education in the country.

Development of Community Sentiments

Although modern psychology refuses to believe in the existence of collective or group mind, distinct from the mind of the individual, it does utilise the rules of human behaviour in a group situation to interpret the behaviour of school children in the environment of the school. The school is a psychological group, and communal sentiment can be generated in it by discipline, cooperation and other behaviour among the students. The conditions required for generating a collective or group mind enumerated by Mcdougall can be of great use in creating such a group mind in school. These conditions are the following:

Permanence of the Group. As far as possible, physical permanence of the group in the school be maintained. Certain changes do occur with the incoming new students and those leaving the institution, and with the construction of new buildings and other additions. But more frequently the same student spends five or six, or even more years in the same institution. This feeling of permanence can be enhanced by retaining the same teachers and not changing them too frequently, by maintaining the same rules, etc. If this is done, the students get the impression that this community feeling or sentiment can be developed in them by making them feel a part of a small community.

Members to Analyse the Norms of the Group. Every student is a member of the community of the school, but he can evolve a community feeling towards it when he conceives it as a community and understands his own place and duties in it. Aware of the rules educators should help the student by acquainting the student with the nature of the school, explaining to him the *modus operandi* which prevails and by reminding him of his own duties towards the institution. If this is done, every student will be able to do his bit in achieving the ideals of the school.

Contact with Other Groups. It is also essential that the student should identify himself with his own institution, by distinguishing between his school and any other group. He can develop a community feeling only if he has occasion to meet other groups. This can be done by providing an opportunity to hold healthy competition in the field of games and sports, dramatic activity, cultural activity, etc., between one institution and another. But the entire proceeding must be organized in an atmosphere of cordiality and friendly competition, for otherwise it will defeat its purpose by destroying the community feeling. Members participating in such competitions see themselves not only as individuals but also as active representatives of their own institution, and they try to win honour for their group. This helps to develop strong ties with the institution.

Developing a Community Tradition. Although students come and go from the institution, it is possible to maintain the community feeling by developing a specific and highly distinct community tradition by maintaining contact with the old students of the school. Old Students Association helps to conserving this community tradition by holding meetings in the old school and achieving contact with the present generation of students. Every college has some traditions of its own, such as a high degree of discipline or a remarkable academic record. These traditions can be maintained by providing opportunities for contact between the older generation of students and the present generation, and also by verbal recapitulation to which the teacher can frequently resort. This encourages the present student community to maintain that tradition, and thus the communal life of the school can continue indefinitely.

Dividing the Functions of Members. In every group, the responsibility for different functions is given to different individuals. Without this division of labour, it is not possible to achieve efficiency in the work of the group. The same principle can also be applied in school, the lawns, the play grounds, organisation of cultural programmes, etc. He regards all such work as his private domain, feels possessive about it and thus develops a community sentiment.

In addition to the above factors which can be helpful in creating a community mind in the school, certain other factors can also be used. For example, frequent meetings of the entire school community creates a sense of unity and singleness. A healthy atmosphere can also be created inviting the parents of the students to participate in or at least to witness some school performances. Teachers of literature, music and art can help to create healthy emotions and sentiments in the college. Early morning community gathering for prayers or a community parade later in the day can also be fairly useful. Consciousness of living as a community can also be further intensified by the collective performance of many functions such as annual prize distribution, celebration of national festivals,, elections to various committees, etc. In this, it is the tone of the college which has an important influence. A good tone can be generated only through discipline, cooperation, obedience of rules, a high moral level and good mutual relations. For this the teachers themselves must present the correct models and ideals, and they should also work towards closer contact with the educand. Teachers are the leaders of the students and therefore they must present the correct model in all those activities which the student is likely to imitate and which may help in his development.

Development of Leadership

Leadership occupies an important place in the sphere of education because it is the school which creates the future leaders of the nation. Although all individuals do not possess the same qualities of leadership, the atmosphere of the school helps to develop these qualities. Quite a few teachers become the leaders in school, but they are also supplemented by some student leaders from among the students themselves. And, generally, these student leaders are more influential than the teachers as leaders. This tends to make communication between the two on many aspects of development rather difficult. And in truth, most students of the present day are not willing to regard their teacher as leader. Hence, the teacher can remedy the situation by enlisting the help of the student leader to create the desired atmosphere in the school. In order to develop the qualities of leadership among the students, they should be entrusted with various jobs of responsibility.

5

Blessings of Democracy

Abraham Lincoln defined democracy as a government of the people, by the people and for the people. Despite the frequent attempts at defining democracy, this is probably the most accurate description. In a democracy one finds a government of the people which is made up of the elected representatives of the people, elected on the basis of adult suffrage. The ideals of democracy are liberty, equality and fraternity. Democracy aims to establish political, economic and social equality, and gives every individual the constitutional right to express his own opinion, to associate with any group, to indulge in any legitimate action. The final objective of democracy is not merely successful government but the creation of an ideal society in which people have the greatest chance of evolving brotherhood. Democracy seeks to create an environment which is conducive to the highest and most beneficial development of the human personality. The principles of democracy were described in the following words as part of America's Declaration of Independence in 1776: "We hold these to be self evident that all men are created equal, that they are endowed by their creator with certain inalienable rights, that among these are life, liberty, and the pursuit of happiness, that to secure these rights, governments are instituted, deriving their just powers from the consent of the governed." It was implied that men were born equal in respect of their rights and that they would. remain so. The objective of political society is to defend man's natural and unobtrusive rights; the right to freedom, property, security and opposition to injustice. The element of absolute authority basically inheres in the nation. No organization, no individual, can bring into play a power which is not clearly pertaining to him.

The word democracy is derived from the Greek words *demos* and *kratein,* of which the former means the people and the latter means administration or government. This is borne out by earlier descriptions of the conditions sought to be created by democracy.

Basic Ideals of Democracy

According to Sir Cripps, "By democracy we mean a system of government in which every adult citizen is equally free to express his views and desires, upon all subjects in whatever way he wishes and influences the majority of his fellow citizens to decide according to those view and to implement those desires." As far as a definition of a democratic state is concerned, the above definition is quite appropriate. But, as Dr. S.Radhakrishnan pointed out in his University report, democracy is not merely a political system but a way of life which affords equality to every one, irrespective of the differences of race, religion, creed and economic status.

This equality implies equal freedom and equal rights. In fact, democracy is a very comprehensive concept which can be interpreted in three ways -political, social and economic. The creation of democracy depends upon the extent to which the ideals of freedom, equality and brotherhood can be concretized in all three spheres. Before going on to a detailed discussion of democracy in these three spheres, it is necessary to clarify these three fundamental ideals.

Liberty. Liberty is a prerequisite of the success of democracy. John Stuart Mill attached the greatest importance to the liberty of the individual. But liberty does not imply complete wilfulness, for, freedom is not absolute but subject to control imposed by the individual's own conscience. Liberty implies the freedom given to the individual to develop his own abilities as he thinks best, without being conditioned or restricted by any external factor. But the freedom of a large number of people is possible only when no single individual has unlimited power and no individual misuses the rights given to him.

Equality. If democracy is to be successful it is necessary for every individual to be socially, politically and economically equal. Generally speaking, no privileges or special rights should be given to any class of people in a democracy. But equality also does not imply a deliberate neglect of individual differences between one person and another. Stated more accurately, equality actually means an equality of purpose, because equality cannot be used as the basis for ignoring differences between individuals. Lord Haldane was quite correct when he said that one cannot make all people equal because nature is far too powerful. While one woman is born beautiful, another is ugly, and this creates great differences. One man is born with remarkable intelligence, while another is remarkable for the lack of it. Thus the concept of equality should be abandoned, for it has governed the minds of people long enough, with little good effect. In democracy it is perfectly practical to give certain privileges to a backward class of people in order to give them an opportunity to raise themselves to the levels of others, but all such efforts should be exceptions, not the rule. In this way, offices in the administration or government should be open to all those who have the abilities and qualities required for such jobs. Every adult should have the right to vote. Every individual should have the opportunity to get employment which will bring him a wage sufficient to allow him to live well Unemployment, famine and such conditions can prove fatal to democracy.

Fraternity. It is important to achieve the ideal of brotherhood in a democracy because this is the only way of removing the psychological obstacles to democracy. The real difficulty lies not in the establishment of a democratic government but as a means or agency. Brotherhood is the chief characteristic of a democratic society, and cooperation the basis on which members of such a society work together. If a democratic society is to be created it is essential that every effort be made to increase brotherhood and cooperation. G. D. H. Cole is correct when he says, "A democrat is someone who has a physical glow of sympathy and love for any one, who comes to him honestly, looking for sympathy and help; a man is not a democrat, however justly he may try to behave to his fellow men, unless he feels like that." Hence, the establishment of a democratic society requires a complete change in the ideas, personalities and patterns of behaviour of the people. And for this all these people must develop totally. It is difficult even to conceive of democracy in the absence of a liberal mind, sympathy, love, consciousness of social responsibility, a high character and a developed personality.

Aspects of Democracy

The following are the important aspects or areas of democracy:

Political Democracy. As has already been pointed out earlier, the three ideals of democracy have to be translated into reality in the political, economic and social spheres. It is, therefore, important to understand these three aspects. In its political aspect, democracy can be defined in the words of Lord Bryce, "Democracy is the form of government in which ruling power of a state is legally vested, not in any particular individual or class but in the members of the community as a whole." In a democracy, legally every individual is equal, because law and justice are the same for every one. Although a democratic government is the representative of the majority it takes care to protect every right of the minorities residing within its territories. Every individual has complete right to think as he chooses and to express his opinion. Citizens are not discriminated against on the basis of sex, race, religion or any other ground which distinguishes them from others.

Social Democracy. In its social as pect, democracy lies in emphasis upon equality and brotherhood between all individuals. In the words of Dewey, "Such a society must have a type of education which gives individuals a personal interest in social relationship and control, and habits of mind which secure social change without introducing disorder." The social feeling of a democratic society is best expressed in Kant's famous moral formula, "So act as to treat humanity whether in thine own person or in that of any other, always as an end and never as a means." From this principle Kant derives the practical suggestion, "Try always to perfect thyself and try to conduce to the happiness of others, by bringing about favourable circumstances, as you cannot make others perfect." The democratic individual, therefore, functions as one member of a special government of ends. And this system of ends is the state of democratic ideals. As Kant puts it, "Act as a member of kingdom of ends." Implicit in this is the notion that one should treat oneself and every other individual as something having inherent value, one should act as the member of a state in which every person treats the good of another as no less valuable than his own good. In such a state or country, 911 die others should also behave so that everyone is not a means but an end. Every one should endeavour to promote the good of another while trying to achieve his own ends.

Economic Democracy. The economic aspect of democracy comprehends the rights of individuals to economic independence and equality. In democratic societies all individuals have the right to earn wealth without interfering in or obstructing the rights of other people. This liberty to earn wealth is limited or restricted by the right to equality because, despite the freedom to earn and accumulate wealth, no individual in a democracy has the right to control the means of production in such a way that his possession may obstruct the economic freedom of other people or his wealth may create a chasm between his position and that of others. In order to maintain the right to equality, all democratic societies enact legislation in order to protect the rights of the working class or backward classes. Democracy is opposed to capitalism and it does not approve excessive economic differences between individuals. Because it believes in brotherhood, democracy is opposed to any kind of economic exploitation.

Need of Education in Democracy

Aldous Huxley has remarked, "If your aim is liberty and democracy, then you must teach people the arts of being free and of governing themselves." Democracy can never be successful, in the event of lack of education. In a democracy the government is composed of the elected representatives of the people and if the people are uneducated they can never elect the right leaders and consequently can never create the right kind of government. In fact, it is impossible even to hope for democracy in the absence of education. It is difficult to expect a citizen to behave responsibly if he is not even aware of his rights and duties. Bertrand Russell has commented, "Democracy in its modern form would be quite impossible in a nation where many men cannot read." The truth of the matter is that education is a prerequisite of democracy. Only after proper education should the citizen be invested with his democratic rights. As Fichte, the German philosopher has commented, "Only the nation which has first solved in actual practice the problem of educating perfect men will then solve the problem of the perfect state." Although Fichte made this comment in the context of autocratic states, it cannot be doubted that the perfection of even a democratic state can be judged only by the extent to which it contains educated people. As Hetherington puts it, "Democratic government, at least, demands an educated people." Throwing light on the objectives of education in the 1949 meeting of the Universities Commission, Dr. Radhakrishnan stressed the fact that the democratic state recognises the importance of the individual, and it is the process of development of this individual which is called education. Hence, education is absolutely necessary for establishing a democratic society. Dewey has pointed out that democracy is inconceivable without education,' because education can generate and instil the qualities which democracy demands as a prerequisite. Philosophers of the ancient Greek city state were aware of the significance of education. Both Plato and Aristotle laid stress on the importance of education for the success of democracy. Ernest Barker comments, "To Plato education was the most important function of the state and the department of education the most important state department which was particularly advocated for producing the philosopher kings to improve the men's minds for becoming virtuous beings." Plato, in his famous text, *The Republic,* stressed not only the importance of education for democracy but even formulated a plan for the education of men and women which made all kinds of development -physical, mental, moral and aesthetic-possible. Aristotle was of the opinion that the aim of the state is to make possible the achievement of the highest moral level and this can be reached through education alone. Thus, education is the most important function of die state. From one point of view, the state itself is a school in which the individual learns citizenship. These truths were known not only to the Ancient Greeks but also to Indian thinkers of ancient times. India has been the home of democratic ideals and principles from ancient times. Hermitages and places of worship were used as schools in which the sages tried to produce ideal citizens who could become useful members of society. But the modem age needs democratic education far more than was needed in ancient Greece or ancient India because modem democracies are so vast and their problems so complex that the eduction of citizens is even more imperative today.

Importance of Education in Democracy

The importance of education for a democratic state is fairly evident from the foregoing account. The following points can be stressed in this connection:

Knowledge of Rights and Duties. If democracy is to a success, it is essential that every citizen should be aware of his rights and duties because only then can be take active productive part in the affairs of the state. This knowledge of rights and duties can be obtained only through education. Education socializes the individual so that he develops consciousness of duty.

Development of Humane Qualities. If the ideal of brotherhood is to be achieved by a democratic state, it is necessary for it to develop humane qualities in its members. Kant's moral concepts, quoted earlier, throw important light on this. Only through education such qualities as a high moral character, sociability, benevolence, patience, pity, sympathy aad brotherhood, etc., can be developed in the individual.

Faith in Democratic Ideals. In order to make democracy a success, it is essential that its citizens must have faith in the democratic ideals. And this can be brought about only when they are adequately educated

life is not the satisfaction of gross physical desires. The ideals of freedom, liberty, brotherhood, are more valuable and necessary. No one but the educated individual can understand the circumstances and needs of another person before passing judgement on him. Only such a person can accept the ideal of equality after recognizing human values as being the end to be achieved.

Fulfilment Political Duties. In a democracy the government is elected by the people, and hence the responsibility for electing a good government devolves upon them. And, if the people are unable to understand their political rights or to fulfil their political responsibilities, it is foolish to hope for a democratic government. This ability to recognise where one's duty lies can come only through education. Educated people can properly assess the qualities and shortcomings of the various individuals who are fighting the elections, and of die various political parties and their plans and policies which they profess. In India, in the absence of education the ignorant people are persuaded to vote the wrong person, with the result that the government of the country has failed time and again. Corruption is rampant. The Mudaliar Report points oat that if democracy is anything more than voting blindly, then every individual must accept the task of independently thinking about all social, political and economic problems before deciding upon the party he wishes to support But this is possible only when the entire electorate is educated to think independently.

Protection and Transmission of Culture. In any state, ideals can be achieved only when change is accompanied by a parallel continuity, and this continuity with the past is maintained only through culture, the social heritage, which is passed on to the new generation through the medium of education. Hence, education is also required for transmuting culture to future generations and for protecting it.

Preventing Exploitation. The ideals of democracy are opposed to exploitation of every kind, but if political, social and economic exploitation is to be eliminated from society, it is essential to have universal and compulsory education. It its absence, the rich and powerful people will never give up their advantage and habit, while the poor will never become sufficiently conscious of their rights or their ability to organize together and counter this exploitation. Educated people in a country are aware of their rights and they have the intelligence and training to fight exploitation or violation of their rights. Hence, education is the only real foundation on which democracy can be based.

Education for Democracy in India

India is not merely a modern democratic state but a country which is traditionally inclined towards democracy. A democratic constitution was adopted after independence. In 1938 Jawahar Lal Nehru had said, "The Indian Constitution seeks to establish a popular government in the country on the basis of democratic principles outlined earlier. For this every citizen must participate in the administration, through his right to vote and to be elected. Every individual is guaranteed and given equal status and opportunity, because no one is discriminated against on the basis of religion, race, caste, community, sex, or on any other grounds. The government is responsible to the people and its elected representatives."

Provisions in Indian Constitution

In order to achieve this objective of democracy, education is as necessary in India as anywhere else, a truth which the Indian people have been quick to realise. In the words of F. W. Thames, "Education is no exotic in India. There has been no country where the love of learning had so early an origin or has exercised so lasting and powerful an influence. From the simple poet of the Vedic age to the Bengali philosopher of the present day there has been an uninterrupted succession of teachers and scholars." Not only did the Indian constitution accept the ideals of democracy, it considered education the prime responsibility of the state. In Article 45 of the Constitution it has been stated that every state must arrange for the provision of free and compulsory education to all children up to the age of 14, within ten-years of the date of inception of the Constitution. After the achievement of independence, a new phase began in the history of education. Articles 29 and 30 of the constitution give fundamental rights to every individual in connection with education and cultural development. According to article 20, every Indian national living in any part of India will have the right to maintain his own specific language, script and his culture. No person can be refused right of admission to any educational institution, established by the state, by reason of religion, race, caste language or any other similar consideration. According to article 30, every minority community will have the right to establish and maintain educational institutions of its own choice, irrespective of whether the minority is a linguistic or religious one. The state will also not refuse aid to any such institution created by a religious or linguistic minority. Articles 45 and 46 determine the policy for education as part and parcel of the directive principles. According to article 45, the state will make every effort to provide free and compulsory education, within ten years, to every child below the age of 14. According to article 46, the state will pay special attention to the educational and economic interests of all backward classes, especially the scheduled castes and scheduled tribes. It also entrusts the state with the duty of protecting such tribes from social injustice and exploitation of every kind. The Indian Constitution laid the foundation for a federal government in which the functions of the state government have some duties with respect to education. It has been realised that there must be coordination between the central and state authority on education for a balanced development of the country. The modern Indian state is a welfare state whose objective is the complete development of its people. This welfare can be achieved only through education. Little surprise therefore if all the leaders of the nation stress the importance of education as a first step to improving the future of the nation.

Views of Secondary Education Commission

The democratic ideals which the existing educational policy is trying to achieve have been outlined most precisely in the Secondary Education Commission's explanation of the objectives of education:

Development of Democratic Citizenship. The success of democracy depends largely upon the people's awareness of their rights and duties and the extent to which people fulfill their responsibilities. Education aims at developing this ability in the people, because education teaches the man to think and distinguish between right and wrong. He can understand social, economic and political issues, and reflect on the possibility of solving such problems. He can decide upon the political party or the leadership which should be entrusted with the task of forming a government and undertaking administration. He does this after thinking on the problems facing the country and considering the ability of each group or leader to face such problems. He can express his ideas and suggestions through lectures, essays, articles, etc. He can organize new movements or constitute various kinds of committees to solve the problems facing the country. It is the duty of the state to insist upon a syllabus which can be expected to generate such democratic awareness among the children being educated.

Training in Skilful Living. Democracy can be said to have succeeded only if can trans late the democratic ideals to its society. And, for this, socialization of the individual through education is essential. It is desirable, to develop such social qualities as collective feeling, cooperation, discipline, tolerance, sympathy, brotherhood, etc. in the individual. Education must also aim to create faith in social justice and the willingness to rebel against injustice. Education helps people in adjusting to each other, and the educated individual is generally tolerant and liberal. Although he may differ from other people in their opinions, he has the ability to adjust to such people because he can understand their attitudes. Hence, education is the only means of removing the obstacles in the path of democracy, and also of achieving some adjustment between people who differ from each other in respect of language, race, caste, religion, sex, etc.

Development of Personality. The success of a democratic society also depends upon whether mature men and women form the majority or minority in its population. Democracy can succeed only if most of its members have developed mature personalities, because a mature person has gone through physical, mental, social, ethical and spiritual development. Hence, education should aim at the development of all aspects of the educands' personality through various kinds of training. Keeping this in view, most schools and colleges now provide many kinds of extra curricular training, which supplements all that is taught as part of curriculum.

Developing Vocational Skill. The Secondary Education Commission has pointed out that another aim of education it to develop some vocational skill in the educand. No nation can progress in the absence of economic progress. The first duty of the state is to provide a system and means of education which imparts some vocational and professional skills to the educands so that they can earn their livelihood at the same time as they contribute to the nation's economic growth. The country urgently needs skilled craftsmen, engineers, doctors, teachers and administrators. For this, specialized colleges are required. Every child should be given the right to choose a profession of his own liking, and he should be given the opportunity to acquire the highest training and education in this profession.

Developing Leadership. The success of a democracy depends upon the capabilities of the leadership. The democratic government is a decentralized government, and for that reason it requires skilled leadership at many different levels of administration. The democratic government is run by the elected representatives of the people, who should be possessed of special qualities. Expert leadership is required for development and progress in every sphere-political, social, economic, artistic, scientific and cultural. Education should aim at evolving such leadership, because without doing this education cannot make any real contribution to democracy, for, then it is leaving unfulfilled one of its important responsibilities. The element of leadership can be encouraged through many kinds of curricular and extra curricular activities in schools and colleges.

Apart from these objectives of education laid down specifically by the Secondary Education Commission, it is desirable to reflect upon some other objectives, which have significance in view of the fact that India is a democracy. In fact, the aims of education vary a little bit with the level of education - the primary, secondary and university education- a fact which has been recognised by the different education commissions established from time to time. The aim of education, at the primary level, is to develop the child's mind by presenting the fundamental elements in the various areas of knowledge, and also to give him an opportunity to develop all his abilities -physical, mental, moral, motor, creative imagination, etc. At this stage attention should be paid to physical development no less than mental development, but attention must also be paid to the burden such an education places on the child. The education imparted should not become a burden.

At the secondary level, attention should be focused on discovering the interests and abilities of every adolescent, and then developing such abilities. Education should be concerned not merely with the general welfare of society but also with the self realization and personal development of each individual.

Recommendations of Indian Universities Commission

The Indian Universities Commission has laid down the following objectives of university education in the country:

1. Providing leadership in politics, administration, professions, industry and commerce;
2. Training intellectual leaders of culture and creating inventors;
3. Causing spiritual development in the educand;
4. Protecting the culture and civilization of the country and instilling the youth with the ideals of this culture; and

5. Discovering the inherent qualities of individuals and developing them through training.

Steps to Establish Democracy in India

Development of Emotional Integration. For the success of democracy, education must have an additional objective of promoting integration among the citizens of this country which has an unlimited variety of races, tribes, languages, religions, communities, etc. Without- this the ideal of brotherhood cannot be realized besides, such a situation also encourages the growth of disorganizing and disruptive forces which hinder the country's growth.

Promotion of Internationalism. Addressing the Indians leaving the country and going abroad, Pt. Jawahar Lal Nehru said that Indians did not have to go to far away lands in search of a present, a search which was absolutely essential because living apart from others in the modern world implied backwardness. The old world has changed, the old bonds have been destroyed and life is becoming steadily more international. Nehru told the Indians that they would have to play their part in this increasing internationalism, and if they were to make success of it, was necessary for them to live in close contact with the world. They must go to all parts of the world, travel to the remotest corners, meet other people and learn to live with them. It is, therefore, necessary that Indian education, particularly at the university level, should seek to create a feeling for internationalism. UNESCO, the international organization, has laid stress on education for international adjustment. Speaking to the American Committee for teacher's training colleges in Chicago in 1956, Walter H. C. Lewis, the former director general of UNESCO said, "In education for international understanding we should try to promote a comprehension of the way of life, the values and the aspirations of the world." For the development of internationalism it is essential that members of every nation must rise above the considerations of nationalism and culture and learn to appreciate the cultures, values and life patterns of other people. Liberality of mind is very desirable. Actually the democratic ideal which exists within the bounds of one nation is not different from the democratic ideal comprehending the entire world. Both are based on tolerance and liberality, and both stress the importance of liberty, equality and fraternity.

Prerequistes for Democratic Education. In India it has been recognized everywhere that education must have the foregoing objectives for the success of democracy, although one is aware of the absence of any concrete step in this direction, up to the present. In order to achieve a higher level of democratization in the educational pattern, it is essential to pay attention to the following things:

Elimination of Discrimination. Efforts must be done to put an end to the discrimination practised in educational institutions established by religion. The selection of educands, the appointment of teachers, the fashioning of the syllabi are all apparently influenced by caste and communal considerations. All such things must be prevented. The state should penalize all such institutions by refusing them grants and other financial aid to compel them to give up such undemocratic practices.

Elimination of Regionalism: Regional considerations and affiliations are also seen influencing the selection of candidates and appointment of teachers in many parts of the country. Such practices cannot be prevented without the intervention of the central authority.

Hindi as National Congress. Arrangement should be made for the teaching of Hindi, the all India language, and English, the international language, in addition to the languages being taught in each region and state. Some people oppose the teaching of English while others are averse to learning Hindi. But it must be realized that Hindi is essential for developing nationalism while without English we cannot participate in any movement for internationalism. Both of them are important for achieving the democratic ideal, and it is to be regretted that the centre gives little evidence of dear thinking on the issue.

Information of Syllabi. The syllabi at all levels of education - primary, secondary and university levels - need to be reformed in order to lay greater emphasis upon democratic tendencies through the proper teaching of history and geography. Democratic tendencies should be actively encouraged.

Better Working Conditions. In most Indian schools and colleges, the working conditions and pay scales of teachers are far from satisfactory. Few universities provide sufficient facilities for research and higher studies. Appointments of teachers are made more on the basis of personal considerations than on the actual merits of each individual. So long as such conditions are allowed to exist, there is little hope for democracy. Hence, it is desirable that the government should study the situation, punish the culprits and provide more facilities for teachers and research enthusiasts.

Travel Facilities. In order to achieve the objectives of nationalism and internationalism, students and teachers should be given facilities for domestic and foreign travel, because such facilities are practically nonexistent at present.

Acquaintence with Culture. *At* each level of education, the educand should be acquainted-with ancient Indian culture and knowledge. Little has been done in this direction so far.

Improvements in Syllabi. If democratic ideals are to be achieved, the syllabi at every level need to be drastically changed. The following things should be considered in this connection:

Wide based Syllabi. In order to achieve the democratic ideals discussed earlier, and also to achieve the comprehensive development of child's personality, it is desirable that the syllabi at the primary, secondary and university levels should be wide based. The educational pattern in India has been evolved after keeping this point in view but it is regretted that the shortage of means has made implementation difficult.

Variety and Flexibility. At the various levels of education, the curriculum should be flexible and varied, not rule-bound and rigid. This is desirable, because only then can the curriculum accommodate the brilliant as well as the average educand. At the secondary and university levels this is all the more essential because the syllabus must provide each educand with a reasonable choice for selecting subjects that he would like to study. It must also be flexible in order to permit some minor adjustments according to the level of educands studying it.

Based on Local Requirements. India is a large country with a remarkable variety of races and tribes, languages and dress, etc. The syllabi should take into account local requirements. It would be better to give primary education to the children residing in different parts of the country in their respective mother tongues. At the secondary level and later at the university the educand should be given an opportunity to learn both Hindi and English. Ignorance of English will handicap them and leave them ignorant of a very big chunk of knowledge.

Creation of Social Consciousness. The curriculum should invariably provide certain programmes which can be expected to create social consciousness and a desire for responsible community life. But this sentiment for community life should be in keeping with the sentiments of nationalism and internationalism.

Earning One's Livelihood. The syllabus must include the teaching of subjects which the student can study and later on turn to account for earning his livelihood. In deciding the syllabi for the teaching of professional subjects, it is essential to keep in mind the situations the education will be required to face in practical life and also the extent to which the present syllabus is helping to prepare him for those situations.

Improvements in School Administration. Another aspect of educational reform is introducing the following changes in the pattern of school administration in the country. The pity of it is that little if any work has been done in this direction.

More Rights to Teachers. Educators should have say in determining the policy of the school, in preparing the syllabus and in other matters pertaining to the school. The educator must experience a sense of being free from shackles so that he may be able to work enthusiastically.

Greater Freedom to Educators. Educators should be given greater freedom in framing the syllabus, in selecting the methods of teaching, studying, research, etc. Without freedom little creative and original work can be expected. Only when the educators are given freedom to act and to think for themselves they can be expected to make new discoveries in science, literature and art, etc.

Democratic Environment in Schools. Cooperation and brotherhood should form the basis of relations between teacher and taught, between the educator and the administrators or organisers of the school, between the vice-chancellor and the teachers of the university, etc. The principle of equality should not be sacrificed in the name of discipline, for the latter is perfectly possible even when everyone is treated as equal. Defects should be removed and faults rectified democratically and liberally, not in an authoritarian manner.

Improvements in the Conditions of the Educator. The educator is also an important element in the teaching pattern, like the educand. The working conditions of teachers can hardly be said to be-satisfactory in this country. Arrangements should he made for training them adequately, and their selection should be made on merit, not on personal considerations and whims of the powers that be. They should be encouraged to study further and go in for research work. Their scales of pay should be made equal to the scales of pay of people who are as well qualified as they are. Payment should be made on the basis of equal pay for equal work. Their work should be free from officious interruptions from the administrative staff. Seminars and institutes be organized from time to time in order to improve their efficiency by informing them of the latest discoveries in then-respective spheres.

Improvement in Methods of Teaching. In a democracy, even the teaching methods adopted inside the school should be essentially democratic In this connection, the following suggestions can be given:

Encouragement to Cooperation. All work should be done with the cooperation of the principal and the head of department, between the head and the educator, between the educator and the educand, and between one educand and another. This helps to evolve the sense of cooperation and sense of community so essential for democracy.

Stress on Activity. According to John Dewey, one of .the most famous exponents of democratic education, the child should be taught by actually doing some action. By taking an active part in the process of teaching, the educand learns self control, self discipline and self inspiration, all of which are essential for the success of democracy.

Independence. Liberty is the fundamental principle of democracy, and hence the democratic method of teaching also has no place for any external pressures. It permits the educand to ask any questions coming to his mind, to express his own opinion and to make any criticism which suggests itself to him. Democratic education aims at training the individual to think for himself. Great stress is placed on the child's independence in all modem teaching techniques, such as Montessori method. Project method, Dalton method. Heuristic method, etc. In all such democratic techniques the teacher serves only as the guide whose task is to encourage, guide and direct the child who learns for himself and moves in the path of knowledge.

Based on all-round Development. Teaching methods in a democratic society should be so designed as to promote and encourage development of every aspect of the child's personality. Care should be taken to see that no aspect is repressed, so that all-around comprehensive development becomes possible. The democratic citizen would be handicapped by a lop sided development of personality because it would render him unfit for performance of duties in one sphere or the other. In proportion to the greater rights given to a citizen in democracy, his duties and responsibilities also tend to be greater than those of an individual in some other society. Hence, education must be so designed as to create such abilities in the child as self dependence, self realiance, dedication to duty, ability to dutiful responsibilities, etc.

Establishment of Discipline. Discipline has special value in the democratic pattern of education because the educands passing through the phase of education have themselves to grow up and take part in administration.

They have to consider the success of democracy. In other patterns of government too much discipline and training in discipline are not quite so necessary. The greatest discipline is self discipline, it is self control, it involves changes in one's own tendencies and desires, according to the demands of the community and the society. It is absolutely essential for the members of a democratic society to be disciplined. And this is possible only when school and university students are taught the lesson of discipline. In schools the educator should be impartial in his behaviour towards all the educands. Most of the work of the school should be performed by the educands, under the guidance and supervision of the educators. Self governing units such as students unions, students committees, and students parliaments should be created so that the educands may be trained in democratic activities and life. He should be able to take active and intelligent part in such activities. The educand's activities should be hindered or obstructed by his own organizations and institutions, not by the official administered. Social control will thus teach them to be disciplined. The teacher himself must prove himself to be model of discipline. Even the state should avoid unnecessary interference in the working of educational institutions. Finally, it can be said that only the voluntary cooperation of the educators, guardians and administrators can help to create a truly democratic environment in which the educand can learn to-be disciplined.

6

Sociological Foundation of Education

In reaction to Rousseau's individualism, there emerged in the nineteenth century a sociological tendency in education. One major cause of this was the emergence of sociology among the other social sciences. The sociological tendency brought many suggestions for reform in various spheres of education, the methods of teaching, etc. The sociological tendency is the attempt to apply sociological principles to the process of teaching.

Evolution of Sociological Tendency

The sociological tendency in education emerged as a result of following causes:

The Development of Sociology. The science of sociology had its beginnings in the writings of August Comte, a seventeenth century writer. Many other scholars also expressed their opinion on the subject, and thus the literature on the subject began to grow rapidly. Later on, sociological literature on education led to the emergence of a distinct branch which came to be known as educational sociology. It aimed at applying sociological concepts and understanding to the problems of education, and this encouraged the development of the sociological tendency in education.

Influence of the French Revolution. 'The French Revolution brought to the front 'the ideals of liberty, equality and fraternity, which were later accepted as the objectives of education for social welfare. Because of the principle of equality, education for everyone became compulsory.

Influence of the Industrial Revolution. The industrial and professional revolution drew the attention of the people to the labour class, and it was found that education was necessary for it. Social consciousness also emerged in various classes, and this led to a reduction in the impulse for individualism. This also encouraged the sociological tendency.

Social Objective of Education. From the earliest times, individualist ideas have always been accompanied by social or collective ideals in every part of the world, and these latter ideals and their proponents have stressed the importance of social objectives. Even in the field'of education some social thinkers have laid more stress on the, social aims of eduction than on the individual aims.

Impact of Democracy. In modern democratic societies, the social and political education of the masses came to be regarded as compulsory, because it is the people who elect the representatives to form the government. and hence, it became the aim of education to turn every individual into a useful citizen of a democratic state.

Sociological and Psychological Tendency

It is believed that there is intimate relationship, between the sociological and the psychological tendencies in modern education. Such educationists asPestalozzi, Herbart and Froebel, who encourage the use of psychology in education, also admit the influence of sociological factors in the child's development. Pestalozzi wanted the education of the child to "be such that it could lead to the welfare of the family and the nation and society, along with the child's own welfare. According to Herbart, the aim of education is the moral development of the individual, so that he can develop the ability to bring about social welfare. Thus, both Herbart and Pestalozzi, wanted to educate the child to be such that it could lead to the welfare of the family and the nation and society along with the child's own welfare. According to Herbart, the aim of education is the moral development of the individual, so that he can develop the ability to bring about social welfare. Thus, both Herbart and Pestalozzi, wanted to educate the child for social welfare. Even the thinking of Froebel reflects some sociological inclination, for he conceives of the school as a miniature society. In kindergarten education he has placed special emphasis upon the aspect of education. Thus, the proponents of the psychological foundation in education believe the social aim to be important, while, at the same time, those in favour of the social objectives of education do not in any way, detract from the importance of psychological elements in education. Obviously, then, both the foundation complement each other. In educating the child, it is therefore, important to pay attention to both his psychological and his social condition, for neither is less important than the other. The child enters the world possessed of the psychological elements, but these psychological elements develop in the social environment. Hence both must be studied in the child's education.

The scientific tendency in education places a lot of emphasis upon the importance of science. Spencer was one of the proponents of science, and he has said that science should be made the basis of education. Education, according to him, aimed at preparing the individual for the complete life. He believed that knowledge of the various physical and social sciences must supplement knowledge of literature, art and music. Sociology and Psychology are important social sciences. Hence, the scientific, sociological and Psychological tendencies are intimately related to each other. All three of them aim at the complete development of the individual in order to make him a useful member of society. These tendencies differ only in respect of the emphasis they place on their respective spheres. All three of them to fashion education in such a manner that it should culminate in the happiness of the individual and the welfare of society. Both the sociological and the scientific tendencies, have stressed the social objectives of education both have opposed the traditional methods of discipline, and both have demanded radical changes in the curriculum. Both are opposed to social distinctions and both want the child to study the natural and physical sciences. But despite these similarities, the two differ from each other in the following respect:

1. While scientists believe science to be supreme, the sociologists believe society to be the most important.

2. The scientist may also be an individualist but the sociologist is invariably in favour of collectivism.

Despite these two minor differences, both aim at social welfare. Because individual and society are two aspects of a single fact, and are therefore supplements to each other, the scientific and the sociological tendencies of education are also complementary.

Characteristics of Sociological Tendency

Stress on Professional or Vocational Education. The sociological tendency lays stress on enabling, the child to earn his livelihood through professional education.

Opposition to Individualism. The sociological tendency was born out of reaction to individualism. It stresses the importance of collective society, as against the individual.

Social Progress as the Aim of Education. Social welfare is the aim ascribed to education by the sociological tendency. Children should be trained only for this through a system of free compulsory education. This should make them members of society.

Faith in Democracy. The sociological tendency also evinces faith in democracy. In a democracy, education is based on the cooperation between the state and society, and besides, the success of democracy depends upon the education of its members.

Clarification of Social Problems. The sociological tendency clarifies social problems and suggests ways and means of solving them through education. Many social reforms can be brought about, by education, and it can create an entirely new generation which may be free of the defects inherent in the older generation.

Raising the Standard of Social Life. The sociological aim of education is to raise the standard of social life by achieving the child's comprehensive development. Education must train the individual to fulfil his social responsibilities. If it fails to do this, education cannot be said to have any utility.

Importance to Social Sciences. The presence of the sociological tendency in education has led to greater importance being attached to the social sciences, so that the child can understand social phenomena and problems, and thus be enabled to make some positive contribution to social welfare.

Importance to Social Life in the School. Social life within the college has been recognized as important because of the sociological tendency. It is now suggested that authorities should encourage the formation of committees which train child for later social life.

Education as an Agency of Social Progress. According to sociologists, education is the best means of social control, social change and thus, finally, of social progress can be easily brought about through education. Social control becomes a measure of self control through education because education socializes the individual.

Impact of Sociological Tendency

It is evident from the foregoing account of the sociological tendency in education that it has had widespread influence upon the meaning, objectives.

Functions of education upon the curriculum, the methods of teaching, the school organisation, etc. These influences can be briefly enumerated as follows:

Meaning of Education. According to educational sociologists, education is a social process which socializes the child and causes certain changes in his behaviour. In this way, even in defining education, the sociologists have stressed its social aspects.

Objective of Education. According to them, the objective or aim of education is to evolve those social qualities and a social feeling in the child which will enable him to understand his responsibility to society and nation, and to become the ideal citizen of his country, and train him to fulfil his duties. Such aims of education as education for citizenship and education for social life are influenced by the sociological tendency.

Functions of Education. Elucidating the functions of education, the educational sociologists have stressed the social functions of education. In his *Brief Course in the History of Education* Munro lays down the following four functions of education.

Spread of Knowledge. The first function of education is to provide various kinds of knowledge to the child. This develops the child's mind, and without this no other development is possible.

Social Control. The child undergoes a process of socialization in educational institutions and is thus subjected to social control. But social control through education eventually becomes self control for the child so that he has no difficulty in accepting it. Hence, in every society schools instil the elements of social control into the younger generation through the process of education.

Protection of the Social Heritage. Education is one important medium of transferring social heritage and culture from one generation to the next, because it is through education that the new generation is acquainted with the culture and civilization of society. And it is through education that the new generation is taught to adopt this culture. The new generation makes its own contribution to this social heritage, intensifies it and, in its turn, passes it on to its successor.

Social Development. Social development is also one of the important aims of education because, without this individual development is not possible. The school is itself a miniature form of society, for in the school the educators try to create an ideal social environment in order to inculcate the best possible picture of society in the minds of the educands. After leaving the school, the educand retains this picture of the ideal society in his mind and tries to recreate it in reality. Through education the individual develops the qualities required for the ideal citizen of society, and when most of the members of society have these qualities, it is only natural that society will develop.

Organisation of Curriculum. Educational sociologists have provided a number of valuable suggestions about reorganizing the curriculum of education. They suggest that the curriculum should be based mainly on sodal ideals and values, and the curriculum should provide for the introduction of social subjects and collective activities. The curriculum should be revised from time to time, according to the needs of the society, because it should always educate the individual to be the servant of society and to fulfil his responsibilities towards the family. Hence, sufficient importance must be attached to professional and scientific subjects in the curriculum, which should be flexible and variable so that it can be made to accommodate all social changes and social necessities.

Methods of Teaching. The sociological tendency also laid stress on the induction of social elements in the methods of teaching so that education can evolve essential social qualities in children. Some examples of this are the Dalton method, the project method, etc. Educational sociology gives suggestions for, changes in teaching methods from the viewpoint of social dynamics.

Administrative Techniques. Before the impact of the sociological tendency, efforts at administration and discipline were individualistic but the sociological influence laid stress on the social or collective methods. Collective methods stress the fact that administration and discipline should be collective, not individual. It is desirable to create such an atmosphere in the college that social discipline should naturally emerge in the educand so that he may not indulge in activities harmful to the individual or society at large. In this way, community feeling was made the basis of discipline. It is seen in many circumstances that, much better discipline can be established, through the influence of social control and public opinion than is possible through individual methods.

Child Education Movement. As a result of the sociological tendency, there began a movement for the education of infants. Many infant schools were established in America and in many European counties. Most of them aimed at providing education organisation, between the school on one side and the community and the home on the other, between education and the means of transport and communications, between education and the democratic or totalitarian states. It makes a study of such varied problems as the status and function of teachers, the organisation-of- educands, relationship between religion and education, sex education, the organisation of educational institutions, freedom of thought in higher education, etc. Educational sociology, like the other branches of sociology, is not merely a theoretical, but a practical science, and by virtue of its practicality, it gives suggestions concerning the reform of education.

Definition of Educational Sociology

The following definitions of educational sociology will make it easier to comprehend the nature, scope and importance of the subject:

Brown. "Educational sociology is the study of the interaction of the individual and his cultural environment." It is evident from this definition that it studies the effect of the cultural environment on the individual, and also the ways and means by which this cultural environment can be changed.

Carter. "Educational sociology is the study of those phases of sociology that are of significance for educative processes, especially the study of those that point to valuable programme of learning and control of learning processes." Putting it simply, this discipline is sociology in the field of education. It caries out experiment to make the application of sociological principles more active and effective.

Ottoway. "Educational sociology starts with the assumption that education is an activity which goes on in the society and the society in its turn determines the nature of education." Modern educationists agree that the process of education is made possible by the family, school, community and other parts of society. The educational system of a society will bear resemblance to the nature of society itself, although this does not imply that society cannot be changed through education. In fact, both society and education influence each other, and educational sociology makes a study of this interaction.

Value of Educational Sociology

The importance of educational sociology is hinted at in the foregoing account. Actually, the importance of sociology in general is identical to the importance of educational sociology in the field of education. The sociologist undertakes to define and to educate various social institutions and tries to collect data pertaining to them. He examines the various elements of culture and propounds principles to explain their dynamic nature. He gives suggestions about how a society can be transformed into or put on the path to democracy. His suggestions are very useful for bringing about social changes. He studies the various aspects of social life and determines the nature of each aspect and of social relations. The sociologist is of particular importance in a country like India, where there is immense scope for social reformation. Applying this knowledge of sociology to the field of education, one discovers the importance of educational sociology in that it can help in the calculated and programmed reformation of education. Only the sociologist can clarify the various elements, the importance of general principles underlying the social aspect of education. He will be able to define and assess the importance of the social elements which influence the process of learning. Making a detailed analysis of the individual nature of contemporary Indian society, the sociologist can advise the kind of teaching methodology which should be adopted here. In addition to this, his advice will also be helpful in removing obstacles which will inevitably bar the way of any educational reform. With the aid of the sociologist it will be possible to solve the problem of mass illiteracy which exists in the country today. The following points may be emphasized to underline the importance and place of sociology of education:

Stress on Professional or Vocational Education. The sociological tendency lays stress on enabling the child to earn his livelihood through professional education.

Opposition to Individualism. The sociological tendency was born out of reaction to individualism. It stresses the importance of society, as against the individual.

Social Progress as the Aim of Education. Social welfare is the aim ascribed to education by the sociological tendency. Children should be trained only for this through a system of free and compulsory education. This should make them responsible members of society.

Faith in Democracy. The sociological tendency also evinces faith in democracy. In a democracy, education is based on the cooperation between the state and society, and besides, the success of democracy depends upon the education of its members.

Clarification of Social Problems. The sociological tendency clarifies social problems and suggests ways and means of solving them through education. Many social reforms can be brought about by education, and it can create an entirely new generation which may be free of the defects inherent in the older generation.

Raising the Standard of Social Life. The sociological aim of education is to raise the standard of social life by achieving the child's comprehensive development. Education must train the individual to fulfil his social responsibilities. If it fails to do this, education cannot be said to have any utility.

Importance to Social Sciences. The presence of the sociological tendency in education has led to greater importance being attached to the social sciences, so that the child can understand social phenomena and prqblems, and thus be enabled to make some positive contribution to social welfare.

Importance to Social Life in the School. Social life within the school has been recognized as important because of the sociological tendency. It is now suggested that authorities should encourage the formation of committees which train the child for late social life.

Education as an Agency of Social Progress. According to sociologists, education is the best means of social control, social change and thus, finally, of social progress. All social-changes that may become necessary for social progress can be easily brought about through education. Social control becomes a measure of self control through education because education socializes the individual.

Scope of Educational Sociology

Educational sociology, as the name indicates, is the sociological study of educational·institutions and processes. It maybe defined as the study of education from the sociological stand point. It is the study of the inter relationship of education and the social system. It centers upon the study of social institutions and their role in education. It includes the inter-relationships of education with Kinship, social stratification, attitude of knowledge, international relationships besides the organizational pattern of educational institutions, the teacher-pupil relationships, the teacher-teacher relationships and finally student-student relationships.

The scope of sociology of education, as is clear by its definition given above, includes almost all the elements of general sociology with particular reference to education. Thus it includes the study of relationship of education to the other aspects of social system particularly kinship, social ratification, political organization, knowledge and attitudes to knowledge.

Education and Kinship. Both education and kingship are important institutions of socialisation in the society. Every society introduces gradual socialisation of a child through complex processes which, give the child individual identity and the ability to acquire social status and fulfil roles according to it. In the kinship system the most important role towards socialisation is performed by parental family. The school transfers knowledge from one generation to another and develops intellectual ability. Both kinship and educational institutions develop the value system in a society.

Family is an enduring association of parents and children. Its primary functions are the satisfaction of the members and the socialization of the child. It is a social agency for the education and protection of the race. It is in the family that the child acquires such important qualities as sincerity, sympathy, self submission and consciousness of responsibility, etc. It is the character developed in the family which helps the child in becoming an important and responsible member of society. In every family, the child gets an opportunity for free expression of thoughts and development of his entire personality. Psychologists have incontestably proved that the proper development of the child is impossible without a good environment in the family. The tendencies and habits which he acquires in the family, he finds impossible to shed later on. According to Freud, the viewpoint of a child towards the elders in the family determines his attitude and viewpoint towards the elders in society. The child's first school is his home and family. The child's education should be in the hands of the parents in family. The parents should participate in all the child's activities. A child learns much by imitating his superiors. It is the family which imparts, practical education to the child concerning the customs in society, conduct, other important elements of culture, preservation of health, love, sympathy, co-operation, etc. According to M. S.Gore and I.P.Desai, "The points of contract between the educational and the kinship systems are thus many and varied. The extent to which they work at cross purposes in any given society is a point of examination and study for the sociologist of education. He is further interested in determining the conditions under which the two systems are likely to support or conflict with each other."

The School as a Social System. After the home, the child is exposed to the school which also influences him, for the school is nothing less than a miniature society to him. It socializes him, gives him an opportunity to manifest his qualities, instincts, drives and motives and helps to develop his personality. For the child, the educator's personality and character provide a model which he strives to copy, thereby consciously or unconsciously moulding his personality. This is true only of those teachers who succeed in arousing in the child's mind an attachment and love for themselves. Every little action, every movement, speech, etc., impresses itself on the child's mind. On the other hand, he is often repelled by some teachers, and he wants to contradict them through every act. This repulsion may be conscious or unconscious, but it drives the child away from such a teacher. The child is attracted by the other teacher who wins his sympathy, and it is from this teacher that the/child wants to win praise and appreciation. He fears the frown of his teacher, he imitates him persistently. Apart from the teacher the child is also influenced by his colleagues, and his status and role in his school group plays a large part in determining the status and role he is to occupy in society in later life. During the process of education, the child's personality develops under the impact of the other personalities with whom he comes into contact. In the school the child is disciplined. He is aware that disobedience brings immediate punishment, but too strict a system of discipline restricts the child's mental growth and may even drive him to criminal activity. On the other hand, complete absence of control may either make him liberal, free and independent or impulsive and impish. Besides, the cultural programmes of the school also help to refine his attitudes.

In this manner, the human personality is profoundly influenced both by the home and the school. Of the two, the family influence lasts for a longer time and is more comprehensive.

Education and Social Stratification. Social stratification whether open or close, is very much concerned with education. Social mobility is very much influenced by castes, religious groups and classes. All these influence the mental progress of the child through education. Thus social stratification governs the type of education which a particular individual will be able to secure. This is clear from the influence of castes, religious groups and classes upon education in India.

Influence of Castes. Under the Hindu social organization, it is caste which determines the individual's status and position in the social hierarchy. One finds elements of the caste system even among the Muslims. In the caste, the professions and occupations of the lower castes are predetermined and fixed, and the child aims at adopting the occupation of his own caste. Since the child is almost compelled to adopt the same profession as his forefathers, he is inevitably exposed to the rules of untouchability which operate between his caste and a superior caste. This creates very undesirable prejudices and gives rise to narrow mindedness in the child. Although there are some advantages in adopting the hereditary occupation, it is undeniably unscientific, in that it fails to consider the individual differences of the children and, does not consider the actual suitability of the child to that particular occupation. The caste system has had the effect of splitting the society into many small segments, and this fragmentation obviously hinders the development of national unity. Besides, it is also responsible for the child's awareness of discrimination and distinction between individuals and the consequent feelings of superiority and inferiority. In this way, the presence of many different castes hinders the child's mental progress.

Impact of Religious Groups. In India one can see many religious groups such as Hindus, Muslims, Christians, Buddhists, Sikhs and Jains, etc. Most of these religious groups have established and are maintaining many religious Schools in which general religion is taught, along with their own respective religious teachings. Most of these schools try to inculcate a particular set of religious principles in the educand. In many ways the teaching of religious principles can be of benefit to the child and the community, but when teaching in the school contradicts or ridicules teaching in another school, it naturally gives rise to a consciousness of differences between one religion and another. The immediate consequence of this is communalism which is instilled into the child's tender mind, and this prevents him from identifying himself with other members of the nation, and thus - national unity suffers. The best course is to inculcate the general principle of religion, stressing the fact that all religions are one and the same, for without this, religion can only lead to narrow minded thinking.

Impact of Classes. Social class has the most potent influence on the child. On the one hand, we find a steady breakdown of discrimination based on religion and caste, but on the other we find a growing consciousness of the class one comes from, thus intensifying the feeling of difference. This awareness, that one belongs to the lower, middle or upper class is communicated to the child also. Consequently, children coming from the lower classes start with the feeling of inferiority of being poor, of deprivation of the good things of life. In reaction to this inferiority many of them turn to criminal activity, because children from the upper classes find pleasure in displaying their superiority which has already created in them pride and vanity and a number of other ignominious emotions and sentiments. Comparatively, the child from the middle classes is less susceptible to either extremes. The emotion of superiorty on the one hand is reduced by consciousness of inferiority on the other, and this explains the reason why most middle class children show better performances in academic work, than children from either of the two other classes. Some political ideologies also reinforce this awareness of the difference of class. It may have some dubious advantages, but it cannot be denied that on the whole it has a detrimental effect on the child's development, and that it practically obviates the possibility of ever generating any humane sentiments in them.

Education and the Political System. In modern societies, one finds that education is provided in government controlled institutions as well as privately managed institutions. Many educational institutions are also controlled and managed by religious institutions. And even among the government or state controlled institutions, one finds that some are administered by the central authority and others by state or local self governing bodies. Another aspect of the state control of education is to determine the spheres which the state should take under its own wings and the areas which can be safely left to the control of the people. In the present day, ever government, be it totalitarian or democratic, must contribute to education. There is no doubt that in a democracy the government is elected by the people, but it cannot be denied that the people themselves cannot evolve an educational pattern which may look after the educational needs of every individual. At the same time, it is also realised that democracy cannot be successful in the absence of universal education. Hence, modern democratic states play a large part in educational planning and organization.

Having accepted that the state must exercise control over the educational system, it becomes necessary to determine the exient to which this control should be exercised. Historically viewed, education has been carried on in every state through a variety of means and agencies. On the one hand, one finds colleges and schools run by individuals for profit while on the other one comes across institutions created by religious groups or philanthropists who have collected funds from private individuals for this purpose. In addition, one finds state aided institutions in every country. Even J. S. Mill, who objects to state control of education, has admitted that state should establish some ideal educational institutions which may serve as models and which may inspire the people to create similar institutions. Mill objects to the state control of education on the ground that the state tries to educate the people along lines which support its own ideology and thus it controls the ideas of the people. This belief is not completely without logic and supporting evidence, because communist states do try to control the thinking of the younger generations by intellectually feeding them on communist literature. It amounts to slow brainwashing. Much the same tendency has been seen in the past in totalitarian states which also try to control the thinking of the people by making educational institutions the centers of state's propaganda. This is unfair and improper. In fact, state control in education should be exercised with the sole purpose of preventing encroachment upon the political and social independence and freedom of the people, because this is essential for a proper development of personality. In the second place, the state has at its disposal unlimited means and resources which enable it to arrange for education on a large scale, something which is beyond the reach of private individuals and groups of individuals. Briefly speaking, it is desirable that state control of education should be guided by the principle of the least possible infringement of the liberties of the people. The welfare state provides for education. on precisely this principle. With the establishment of democratic government, the sphere of education is widening rapidly with the result that the responsibilities of the state are increasing. The state imposes taxes on the people in order to finance education and then compels people to send their children to schools and colleges. It also supervises educational arrangements in institutions not controlled by it to ensure uniform standards, and also to provide financial aid to them.

Education and Democracy. Aldous Huxley has remarked, "If your aim is liberty and democracy, then you must teach people the arts of being free and of governing themselves." Democracy can never be successful without education. Wherever democracy has been unsuccessful, it has been because of the lack of education. In a democracy the government is composed of the elected representatives of the people and if the people are uneducated they can never elect the right leaders and consequently can never create the right kind of government. It fact, it is impossible even to hope for democracy in the absence of education. It is difficult to expect a citizen to behave responsibly if he is not even aware of his rights and duties. Bertrand Russell has commented, "Democracy in its modern form would be quite impossible in a nation where many men cannot read." The truth of the matter is that education is a prerequisite of democracy. Only after proper education should the citizen be invested with his democratic rights. As Fichte, the German philosopher has commented, "Only the nation which has first solved in actual practice the problem of educating perfect men will then solve the problem of the perfect state." Although Fichte made this comment in the context of autocratic states, it cannot be doubted that the perfection of even a democratic state can be judged only by the extent lo which it contains educated people. As Hetherington puts it, "Democratic government, at least, demands an educated people," Throwing light on the objectives of education in the 1949 meeting of the Universities Commission, Dr. S. Radhakrashnan stressed the fact that the democratic state recognises the importance of the individual, and it is the process of development of this individual which is called education. Hence, education is absolutely necessary for establishing a democratic society. Dewey has pointed out that democracy is inconceivable without education, because education alone can generate and instil the qualities which democracy demands as a prerequisite. Philosophers of the ancient Greek city state were aware of the significance of education. Both Plato and Aristotle laid stress on the importance of education for the success of democracy. Ernesk Barker comments, "To Plato education was the most important function of the state and the department of education the most important state department which was particularly advocated for producing the philosopher kind to improve the men's minds for becoming circuitous being." Plato, in his famous text, *The Republic*, stressed not only the importance of education for democracy but even formulated a plan for the, education of men and women which made all kinds of development physical, mental, moral and aesthetic-possible. Aristotle was of the opinion that the aim of the state is to make possible the achievement of the highest moral level and this can be reached through education alone. Thus, education is the most important function of the state. From one point of view, the state itself is a school in which the individual learns citizenship. Aristotle suggested that the aim of education was to produce good citizens. These truths were known not only to the Ancient Greeks but also to Indian thinkers of ancient times. Hermitages and places of worship, were used :is schools in which the sages tried to create ideal citizens who could become useful members of society. But the modern age needs democratic education far more than was needed in ancient Greece or ancient India because modern democracies are so vast and their problems so complex that the education of citizens' is even more imperative today.

Education and the Attitude to Knowledge. The sociologist is interested in the social attitudes towards the sources, the limits and the validity of knowledge. With the change in these social attitudes one finds a considerable interest in the interaction among educators and the educand in educational institutions. In the ancient times knowledge was limited and attained through some limited means. It was acquired by few and individually circulated on the basis of *Guru-Shishya* relationship. Therefore, the attitude towards knowledge was of awe and reverence. The teacher was feared and respected, his word was the law. People refused admission to a student purely on personal grounds. The student, on the other hand, considered knowledge to be a treasure deposited with few persons who must be obeyed in order to learn. He had high respect for knowledge since most of the knowledgeable persons belonged to high caste or high social status. Thus the teacher-taught relationship in ancient India or Greece was very much governed by attitude to knowledge.

This attitude to knowledge has considerably changed in the modern times. The growth of knowledge in all directions, the substitution of new and sometimes absolutely opposite theories for the older ones, have led to the growing relation that no knowledge is final. Knowledge is unlimited and can be achieved by innumerable means. The one single factor that has come out to be the most certain concerning knowledge in our own time is the realisation that no knowledge is final and the only means of knowledge. In every field of knowledge today multisided, holistic, integral and total approach is considered to be wiser. All statements are taken as tentative. All theories are merely probable. Again, the fast growth of knowledge is making the old attitudes irrelevant. For example, in the early wake of science scientific knowledge was considered to be most certain and the scientific attitude used to challenge religious and spiritual experiences. With the growth of so many theories in different branches of knowledge scholars used to adhere to this or that ism. But today scholars work in specific areas rather than under banner of ism. Most of the scholars today are realising that the knowledge attained by non-scientific, intuitive, psychic or spiritual methods is no less or more valid than scientific knowledge. The world of knowledge is drifting towards a pluralistic, catholic, agnostic, mystic, holistic and integral approach. Therefore, the student's approach towards knowledge is altered. He is an agnostic if not a cynic. This agnosticism or cynicism has flown to him from the teacher himself. The data of knowledge is much more complex to be finally explained by a single formula or even by a conglomeration of formulae. The sociologist is interested in knowing how this change in the attitude to knowledge influences teacher-taught relationship, inter-teacher relation, teacher's role in society, teacher-administrator relationship, in brief all interaction within the educational system.

Interaction within Educational System. The most important area in the scope of sociology of education is however, social interaction within the educational system. The educational system involves three social constituents-teachers, students, administrators and in a small measure the society or the community at large. All these constituents constantly change within themselves and in their interaction. The educational sociologist analysis the factors of this change, observes the direction of change and finds out cause-affect relationship. A deeper analysis of the social interactions within the educational system will give a better insight in the scope of sociology of education.

Teacher-Administrator Relationship. At the fringe of the social organization in the educational institutions is the teacher-administrator relationship. The administrator is the employer or the agent of the employer. He is the leader, the supervisor and the guide of the teacher. With the authority vested in him, he gives rewards and punishments for successes and failures. Therefore, the personality and the way of teaching is very much influenced by teacher administrator relationship. The nature of the administrator changes according to the types of management. In government institutions the government officer is the administrator. In aided institutions the management constituted by a president, a secretary, a nominee of the government and influential members elected by the donors constituting the general body of management. The executive body works for a limited term and is elected by the general body. It is answerable to the government, the general management body and the public at large. In practice the secretary wields most of the power. If his behaviour is autocratic it has no adverse effect upon the morable of the teachers. If he acts democratically it has a healthier influence upon the teachers.

Teacher-teacher Relationship. In every educational institution today there are more than one teachers. Therefore, the educational sociologist is interested in knowing teacher-teacher relationship. This relationship maybe fraternal or marred by rivalry. While the fraternity results in cooperation, team spirit and goodwill, rivalry leads to mud slinging, favouritism and factionism. Even in small institutions or university or college departments two or more camps may be found among teachers giving vent to jealousy and rivalry against each other. The groups are based upon castes, religion, region, language, nationality, seniority, qualification or cadre. These groups maybe seen from primary to university level involving dissensions among students seeking favour from this or that camp.

Student-Student Interaction. The interaction among students is governed by age, classes, sex, study habits, extra curricular activities and so many other factors. The most intimate interaction is provided by the classroom situation. Interaction everywhere may be cohesive or divisive. It may increase cooperation or conflict. The most important dimension for improving interaction is provided by extra-curricular activities, the debating societies, the dramatic clubs, literary associations, teams for sports and games and batches of excursions. All these provide scope for more intimate relationships resulting in deeper interactions. Sometimes teachers by favour or disfavour, create groups among students and increase jealousies and rivalries. The educational sociologist analysis the conditions of student-student interaction, the cohesive, divisive sources, the consequences, the factors, of social change and social control etc.

Teacher-Taught Relationship. The most important field of interaction within an educational system is the teacher-taught relationship. Formerly, the teacher himself laid down the rules of admission, syllabi, teaching schedule, teaching methods and practically every detail of education. Today, the rules and syllabi are framed by experts or the government bodies while teaching schedule is prescribed by the principal or the time table incharge. Therefore, the teacher is confined only to teaching of his subject according to time table. He is appointed on his job on a particular salary scale and under certain conditions. Teaching today is a profession with all its advantages and limitations. The following are the factors governing teacher-taught relationship:

Age. The distinction of age creates respects on the part of the younger and leadership on the part of the elder. In teacher-taught relationship the distinction of age is in inverse correlation with the level of education. Thus it is maximum at the primary level and minimum at the university level. The bigger age gap allows for the development of teacher-taught relationship based upon respect, fear and reverence. The smaller age gap makes for more intimacy, love, affection and more interaction between the teacher and taught.

Teacher's Status. In some societies the hereditary status of the teacher is high. He is an all knowing and infallible person. He may punish or reward according to his own judgement. In modern democratic societies, however, the authority of the teacher is eroded along with the authority of the administrator. Therefore, there are more interaction in the present day institutions in comparison to the institutions of ancient past.

Status and Attitude of Knowledge. If these are marked by a certain finality the teacher wields more authority over the students. If these are tentative and probable, as it is today, the authority of the teacher is proportionately eroded.

Mode of Acquiring Knowledge Formerly, teacher's words were unquestionable. He commanded total loyalty. Today, however the mode of acquiring knowledge is multiple, tentative and creative.

Therefore, teacher-taught relationship has become more informal, less based upon fear and more intimate.

Image of the Teacher in Society. Formerly, the image of the teacher was almost the highest in the society. Therefore, even the princes used to touch feet of their teachers. If a scholar came to a court even the king left his seat. Today, with the contractural system of education, the teacher is a professional person if not a poor member of the society. With the erosion of the image of the teacher in society, the interaction between the teacher and taught has considerably changed.

Self image of the Teacher and the Student. The self image to today's teacher is professional person delivering goods, making out his living and at the most pursuing knowledge. He is one among equals, never superior and occasionally even inferior. The self image of the student, on the other hand, is no more of a submissive disciple obeying his teacher but an individual making the best of education to further his own aim in life.

Role of the Teacher. The teacher -taught relationship change according to change in the teacher's role in education. Formerly, he was independent and sovereign. Today he is subordinate and dependent upon the management, the government, the wider community and even the student. This role again changes on various levels of education such as primary, secondary and university. It also changes according to the type of management of the educational institutions, the private, the religious or the government management. This role again is governed by personal traits, seniority, qualifications, cadre, economic condition and innumerable other factors. The educational sociologist analysis the change of role and the consequent changes in the teacher-taught relationships.

Mode of Standardisation. As most of the educational institutions today receive financial aid, the government lays down uniform modes of standardisation about the syllabi, the teaching methods and the evaluation techniques at various levels of education. Some times there is an examining body governing all the students in a state such as U. P. Board of Secondary Education. Each university arranges for examinations and evaluation of all the students of all the colleges affiliated to it. This mode of standardisation has eliminated the value of personal qualities and scholarship of the teachers. The teachers and the students now concentrate upon text books and even notes; books with the sole aim of preparing for the examination and achieving better success. In the end it may be noted that the scope and type of interaction between the educators and the educand is today becoming more and more complex and changing fast. This requires an occasional review by the sociologists of education.

Area of Influence

As sociology began to grow, it also began to branch out into many directions, creating many branches such as rural sociology, urban sociology, and more recently the sociological approach to educational phenomena. Despite its being a new branch, many American institutions of higher education have arranged for a special study of educational sociology. Not much research work has been done on this branch of learning, but all sociologists agree that there are great possibilities for sociological studies in the field of education. Many sociologists have come to feel that schools can perform the function of important laboratories for sociological studies. According to Merton and Hugo, "If the process of socialization in medicine is to be understood, it is necessary to make a sociological analysis of culture and relationships in medical colleges." Schools have been treated as laboratories by Parsons, Staffer and Klukhohn in their studies of levels of ambition and social dynamics. According to Neil Gross,, the afield of educational sociology comprehends the following four kinds of research:

1. Social structure and functions of the school;

2. Classroom as a form of social profession; and

3. Education as career or profession.

Research on these and allied subjects and problems will inevitably yield important information. Educational sociology makes a study of relationships between eduction and the social organization, between the school on one side and the community and the home on the other, between education and the means of transport and communications, between education and the democratic or totalitarian states. It makes a study of such varied problems as the status and function of teachers, the organization of educands, relationship between religion and education, sex education, the organisation of educational institutions, freedom of thought in higher education, etc. Educational sociology, like the other branches of sociology, is not merely a theoretical, but a practical science, and by virtue of its practicality, it gives suggestions concerning the reform of education.

7

Social Control and Education

Meaning of Social Control

Social control is the control of society over the individual. Some of man's tendencies are beneficial to society while others are detrimental to his interests. There can be no question of controlling the beneficial tendencies. Thus, social control is exercised by society over the undesirable or harmful tendencies of man. But is social control merely negative? Is controlling some tendencies its sole function? No, social control creates those conditions in which man can be socialised and be prevented from performing anti-social activities. Some control comprehends all those processes, methods, mores, patterns, etc., which render assistance in this work. In this way, the term social control is fairly comprehensive. This is not governmental control. Governmental control is based upon law and is enforced upon the individual externally. Social control is self control. In keeps on changing in accordance with the changes in society.

Definition of Social Control

The various definitions of social control, as provided by the sociologists, are not identical. Some main definitions are the following:

Brearly. "Social control is a collective term for those processes and agencies, planned and unplanned, by which individuals are taught, persuaded or compelled to conform to the usages and values of the group to which they belong." It is clear from this definition that social control includes those laws by which an individual behaves in concurrence with the mores of group.

Gillin and Gillin. "Social control is that system of measures suggestion, persuasion, restraint and coercion by whatever means, including physical force, by which a society brings into conformity to the approved pattern of behaviour a subgroup or by which a group moulds into conformity its members."

Maclver and Page. "By social control is meant the way in which the entire social order coheres and maintains itself, how it operates, as a changing equilibrium.

Gurvitch and Moore. "Social control can be defined as the sum total or rather the whole of cultural patterns, social symbols, collective spiritual meanings, values, ideas and ideals, as well as acts or processes, directly connected with them, whereby, inclusive of society, every particular group and every participating individual member overcome tensions and conflicts within themselves through temporary equilibria and take steps for new creative efforts."

This definition of social control is adequately "comprehensive. It has taken into account both the negative and creative aspects of social control and has indicated the means and processes of social control.

Types of Social Control

Karl Mannheim has accepted the following two types of social control:

Direct Social Control. This is the control exercised upon the individual by the reactions of the people living in proximity-Such control is found ixisting in the family, neighbourhood, play group, and other primary groups. An individual is deeply influenced by the opinion and views of his parents, colleagues, neighbours and those who work with him. His behaviour is determined or controlled by their criticism, derogation, praise, suggestion or persuasion, etc. This is direct control.

Indirect Social Control. This is the control exercised upon the individual by factors which are separated from him. Control of the individual by secondary groups is of this type. Its prominent means are traditions, institutions, customs, rationalised behaviour, changes in situations and social mechanism, etc. The means of social control are invisible and subtle. In the existing complex society, the influence of the opinion, law, custom, etc., is controlled in this way. It is not that there are no individuals behind this control but these individuals are not seen by the persons affected.

Agencies of Social Control

It would have become evident from the foregoing description of the various types of social control, that there are many direct and indirect, formal and informal means of social control. Among the important means of social control Ross has enumerated family, educational system, belief and religion, social suggestion, social ideal, ritual and festival, art, leadership, law and administration besides physical force. Giddings has accepted the importance of belief, social direction or guidance, religion, ideals, social festivals, art, leadership, intellectual factors, education and propaganda, law and administration and force, as means of social control.

Role of Education in Social Control

According to Ruskin, "Education consists in making people polite what they ought to be." The ideals and patterns in these are promoted through education. Here the word "education" is used in a comprehensive sense. It is only in this meaning of the word that the sociologist studies or contemplates it. Education teaches man to live according to Nature. Education gives him ability to succeed in this struggle for existence. Education is an art of adaptation. For man, adaptation is more social than natural. Hence, education adapts man to society. In this way, education is an important means of social control.

Education is in the family, school, playground, club, office, in fact, everywhere-At every place the individual is taught something and socialized. In the family, in school, on playground, he learns to follow the opinion and advice of others and learns to comply with the traditions and mores. Theoretical education, viz., reading and writing .serves to form the intellectual base for all this and with practical education he learns to put this into practice. The organization or system of society is disrupted and thrown into confusion when the educational system contradicts or when the activity of education does not function correctly, and social control fails to function. Hence, education is a necessary condition for the proper exercise of social control. In the absence of an appropriate and organized education social control remains merely an arbitrary pressure which cannot continue for long.

Without proper education the harmony of the individual and society is not merely difficult but well nigh impossible. Education makes social control normal. It makes social control self control and the individual does not experience its burden.

8

Socialistic Pattern

Definition of Adult Education

Mukherjee. "Adult education may be defined very broadly so as to include all instruction, formal or informal, to adults."

K. G. Saiyeden. "Adult education includes political and civil as well as moral education." What was called adult education before winning Independence is today called social education. But the aims of social education are more comprehensive than those of adult education. Its main aim is to bring a socialistic pattern of society through education.

What is Social Education ?

Abul Kalam Azad. The erstwhile education minister Maulana Abul Kalam Azad explained the meaning of adult education while inaguguratíng the UNESCO seminar on village adult education in 1949. He said that social education implied education for making a man complete. It will make him literate so that he has access to the knowledge of the world. It will tell him how he should adapt to his environment and how he should take maximum advantage of his physical circumstances. It will teach him handicrafts and more efficient method of production so that he may achieve economic prosperity. It will teach him the fundamentals of personal and social hygiene so that this domestic life maybe happy and prosperous. And finally, this education will train him in citizenship so that he may be able to cooperate with his government in making the country strong and in establishing peace in the world, for which some knowledge is essential. In the beginning, social education or adult education was interpreted only in the sense of granting literacy to the unread adult, but now it has come to comprehend every kind of education for the adult.

"Social education is the stimulation in each citizen of a greater awareness of the advantages of the pattern of society as conceived in the constitution and a persistent desire for progress towards a pattern socially, economically and culturally."

Purpose of Social Education

In the past, adult education limited itself to creating some limited literacy in the adult so that he could read and write letters, read religious texts and comprehend accounts. But social education today is far more comprehensive. In this connection, the following aims of social education have been stated in a booklet *Social Education in India* published by the government of India. The following are the aims set down there :

(a) Individual Objectives. Social education, from the individual standpoint, aims at the achievement of the following objectives:

1. Mental development of adults.
2. Development of their professional ability.
3. Their physical development.
4. Development of their social skills.
5. Their cultural development.
6. Their self-development.

(b) Social objectives. Social education has the following social objectives:

1. Development of social unity.
2. Protection and development of national resources.
3. Organization of co-operative communities and institutions.
4. Inclusion of the social ideal.

Main Aims

It is evident from the foregoing list of the purpose of social education that its aim is very comprehensive. In India after independence, a committee was appointed under the chairmanship of Mr. Mohan Lal Saxena to advise the government on the expansion of adult education in the country. This committee re-christened adult education and called it social education, and determined the following aims for it:

1. To awaken the citizens towards their rights and duties, and to encourage the sense of social service among them.
2. Creating love for democracy among the citizens and training them in democratic government.
3. Acquainting the citizens with the problems confronting the country and the world.
4. Creating a sense of respect and admiration for Indian culture through the teaching of history, geography and culture.
5. Providing the citizens with an opportunity for cultural mixing and getting pleasure through organization of songs and dramatic activities.
6. Acquainting the citizens with specific moral values through community discussions and teaching.
7. Providing necessary knowledge of language and arithmetic and encouraging the spread of knowledge.
8. Educating the citizens to use their leisure for economic production and prosperity through teaching handicraft and others skills.
9. Continuing the educational programme among the citizens through the use of libraries, discussions, educational commitees and public universities.
10. Creating a sense of co-operation among the citizens.

Four Point Programme

The government evolved a four point programme to achieve these targets of social education :

1. Spread of literary.
2. Education in health and hygiene rules.
3. Training in industry and professions for economic progress.
4. Awareness of rights and duties along with sense of citizenship.

9

Social Change

Social Change

Social change is the change in society. Society is a web of social relationships. Hence, social change is a change in social relationships. It is the change in these which alone we shall regard as social change. What are social relationships ? Social relationships include social processes, social patterns and social interactions. These include the mutual activities and relations of the various parts of society.

Jones. "Social change is a term used to describe variations or modifications of any aspect of social processes, social patterns, social interactions, or social organization." Thus, social change is a change in the social organization.

Davis. "By social change is meant only such alterations as secure in social organization-that is, the structure and functions of society." Social change can be observed in every society."

Merril and Eldredge. "Social change means that large numbers of persons are engaging in activities that differ from those which they or their immediate (forefathers) engaged in some time before."

Society is composed of a vast and complex network of patterned human relationships in which all men participate. When human behaviour is in the process of modification, this is only another way of indicating that social change is occurring. Human society is constituted of human beings. Thus, whatever apparent alteration in the mutual behaviour between individuals takes place is a sign of social change. This fact of social change can be verified by glancing at the history of any society. Man is a dynamic being. Hence, society can never remain static. It undergoes constant variation.

Factors of Social Change

What are the factors due to which social relationships undergo constant alterations ? Some writers consider diffusion to be the main factor of social change while some other writers consider invention in a similar capacity. Actually, both diffusion and invention have a hand in the change which besets social relationships. Roughly, the main causes of social change are the Cultural, Technological Biological, Population, Environment, Psychological and other factors.

Cultural Factors. The main cause of social change is the cultural factor. Changes in the culture are accompanied by social changes. Max Weber has proved this hypothesis by a comparative study of religious and economic institutions. Actually, no one can deny that changes and variations in culture inevitably influence social relationships. Culture gives speed and direction to social change and determines the limits beyond which social changes cannot occur. This, however, does not warrant the conclusion that there is no distinction between social and cultural change. Actually, the field of social change is limited in comparison with the field of cultural change.

Technological, Factors. The technological factor has immense influence in social change. To quote Ogburn, "Technology changes society by changing our environments to which we in turn adapt." This change is usually in the material environment and the adjustment we make to the changes often modifies customs and social institutions. In this way, the incessant increase in new machines and methods due to new discoveries has had a very great influence upon social relationships. The form of society is undergoing change as a result of the development and invention of electric, steam and petrol driven machines for production, the means of transport and communication and various mechanical appliances in everyday fife. Even institutions like family and marriage have not remained immune to the effect of these developments. The explicit effects of technological advance are labour organization, division of labour, specialization, high speed of life increase in production, etc. In the modern age technological factors are among the predominant causes of social changes.

Biological Factors. Biological factors too have some indirect influence upon social change. Among the biological factors is the qualitative aspect of the population related to heredity. The qualitative aspect of population is based upon powerful and great men and mutation. Hence, biological factors play a part in social change to that extent. In addition to this, the biological principles to natural selection and struggle for survival are constantly producing alterations in society.

Population Factors. Even changes in the quality and size of the population have an effect upon the social organization as well as customs and traditions, institutions, associations, etc. Increase and decrease of population a change in the ratio of men and women, young and old, have an effect upon social relationships. Decrease or increase in the population has an immediate effect upon economic institutions and associations. The ratio of men to women in a society affects marriage, family and the condition of women in society. In the same way the birth and death rates, etc., also influence social change.

Environmental Factors. The geographists have emphasized the impact of geographical environment upon human society. Huntington has gone so far as to assert that an alteration in the climate is the sole cause of the evolution and devolution of civilizations and cultures. Even if these claims of the geographists are to be discarded, it cannot be denied that floods, earthquakes, excessive rain, drought, change of season etc., have significant effect upon social relationships and these are modified by such natural occurrences.

Psychological Factors. Most sociologists regard psychological factors as important elements in social change. The cause of social changes is the psychology of man himself. Man is by nature a lover of change. He is always trying to discover new things in every sphere of his life and is always anxious for novel experiences. As a result of this tendency, the mores, traditions, customs etc., of every human society are perpetually undergoing change. This does not mean that man always considers the new to be superior to the old. While he is always attending to what is new and unique he also wants to preserve what is old. The form of social relationships is constantly changing in the process of interaction between these two tendencies. New customs and methods which replace the old traditional customs are being formed. Old traditions are respected but time demands change and adaptation to changing conditions. Change is the law of life. When changes do not occur at the appropriate time revolutions take place, wars are fought, epidemics spread and changes are violently introduced.

Other Factors. In addition to the above-mentioned factors, another factor of social change is the appearance of new opinions and thoughts. For example, changes in the attitudes towards dowry, caste system, female education, etc., have resulted in widespread social variations and modifications. In fact, a majority of the social revolutions take place as a result of the evolution of new ways of thinking. Similarly, war is also a cause of social change because it influences the population, the economic situation and ratio of males to females, etc. In the same way, social changes are introduced by the advent of great thinkers as Gandhi and Karl Marx, etc.

Result of Social Change

The form of each aspect of social life is being continually transformed due to the effect of the above mentioned factors which cause social change. New institutions and associations are being formed and destroyed in the social, economic, political, cultural, and verily, in all spheres. The form of family, marriage, state, religion, culture, educational system, and economic and social structures, is continually changing and transforming, as a result of which, a change occurs in the life of the individual and subsequently in his relations with others. To take an example, the result or social change can be well understood and realized by studying the history of the objectives, structure, forms, importance and functions, etc., of the family from the early past to the present day. Similarly, all the changes and differences that can be seen between the tribal society and the present day society can be attributed to social change.

Functions of Education

The functions of education in the sphere of social change are outlined as follows:

Assistance in Adopting Social Change. Whenever some social change occurs, it results in changes in the pattern of doing some work. This change is easily adopted/by some people while others find if very difficult to adjust themselves to this change. It is the aim of education to make all good changes easily accessible to every person. In India, a large majority of people found it difficult to reconcile. themselves to the changes that occurred in the institutions of family and marriage, but the educated only soon realized the advantages of these changes. Later on, as education spread to other sections of society, the importance and value of these changes came to be recognized more universally. For this reason, it is now generally accepted that before bringing about any social change m society, it is necessary to create a receptive temper of mind among the people. Otherwise, there is invariably some resistance to change.

Overcoming Resistance to Change. Certain factors make it easy for some social innovation to be adopted and accepted, but on the other hand, certain factors create resistance to acceptance. The best way of overcoming such resistance is education. Through the medium of education, the importance of social change is convincingly explained to the people so that they are purged of their prejudices and blind faith, and this enabled and also strengthened to accept something new.

Analysis of Change. But society does not progress with any and every change, and neither does the individual. Progress occurs only when the change leads the society to more desirable social values. And for this, analysis and criticism of social change is essential. Only the educated individual can make valid criticisms and offer constructive suggestions, because it is education which invests the individual with the capacity to use his intelligence, to distinguish between right and wrong and to establish certain ideals. Education determines the values which act as a criterion for the analysis of social change. Through this analysis and criticism, undesirable social changes are prevented and desirable social changes encouraged. In every society, this is achieved only through the efforts of rational and educated people.

Emergence of New Changes. Since the educated class is constantly engaged in an analysis of contemporary society, it also makes frequent suggestions for improvement. It is on the basis of such suggestions that social reform movements are set into motion. The flood of social reform movements that was witnessed at the turn of the century was due to modern education. Educated people made a study of western societies and their institutions compared both with our own, and agitated public opinion towards the abolition of many social evils such as child marriage, objections to widow remarriage, unequal rights of women, the custom of women committing sati, etc. Only through education could the importance of such changes be made apparent to the people. It was through education alone that public opinion could be turned in favour of these changes. Hence, it is the educated class in every society which intimates, guides and controls movements for social reform.

Leadership in Social Change. If social change is to be directed properly, it is necessary to have able leadership, well acquainted with the complexity of the problem. Such leaders can be created only through education. For this reason social welfare workers must first be educated before they are unleashed on society. On the one hand, education creates in them a consciousness of social change, while on the other, it teaches them to distinguish between the good and the bad. Education in India must be able to create appropriate leadership at every level if social changes conducive to democracy are to be introduced.

Educating the People of Social Change. Only a properly organized system of education can generate in the people of a society the ability to adopt some social change. As a result of education, individuals learn to analyse their customs and traditions, to criticise them, and to cooperate in movements for social reform. The educational system has played a major role in bringing about revolutionary social changes in England, France, America and Russia.

Advances in the Sphere of Knowledge. New researches and inventions all depend upon education, because only the educated individual can search for new things in every sphere. Only such people can help in the progress of non-material culture. Fresh discoveries in the sphere of knowledge provide the right basis for criticism of society. Then the need for change becomes apparent. Thus, education contributes to social change by bringing changes in knowledge.

It is evident from the above account that educationists,

educators and schools have a tremendous responsibility in social change. Defective education leads to defective social changes. Hence, if society is to change in the right direction, it is essential that attention be paid to the educational system because this alone can create future generation of critics of change and leaders of reform.

Social Change during British Period

Professor A. R. Desai has pointed out the following important features of social change in India during British period.

Functional Differentiation of State-Activity. The British rulers started a capitalist social order with functional differentiation. The administrative machinery was developed on the basis of the principle of functional differentiation of state activity. Thus various departments performing different functions were created such as Revenue, Policy, Justice, Public Health, Excise, Education, etc. These departments were comprised of a complex hierarchy. The bureaucracywas based upon "Legal, Rational Authority" a term used by Max Weber. The qualifications for entering bureaucracy were success in certain types of test and examination and educational training. Bureaucracy was based upon a system of payment of regular salary, promotions, retirement, pensions and transfers.

The Elaboration of the Administrative Machinery. Another feature of social change in India during British period was the elaboration of the administrative machinery as a highly specialized and structured pyramid. Different offices in bureaucracy were provided specific powers, duties, rights, statuses, roles and obligations. Jobs were categorised into convented and non-convented; Indian Provincial or Subordinate Civil-Services : Class I, Class II, Class III and Class IV services. Class I services were equivalent to present All India Services. These were called ICS whose examinations were held in England. Class II, III and IV officers were generally Indians while class I officers were Britons.

Separation of Lawand Religion. The British Rulers separated law from religion. They developed transport. New types of commercial and financial institutions were developed. Jute, cotton, mining and other industries were established and developed. Education was given prestigious position based upon a new value system. The traditional attitudes to caste, family, marriage and the status of women was changed. Caste restrictions started breaking. The institutional joint family disintegrated giving place to nuclear family. The institution of marriage became legal and not only religious. Hindu Code and other rules raised the status of women in society.

Undermining the Traditional Values. The British rule eliminated the categorisation of occupation into clean and unclean, holy and unholy. Formerly, occupations were reserved for different castes. Some occupations were open to all the people having necessary qualifications.

Deindustrialisation. The British rulers ruined old manufacturers, the town handicrafts and the village artisan industries. Production skills were destroyed. On the other hand, the development of new productive skills was prevented. The old economic order was disintegrated. According to Prof. A. R. Desai deindustrialisation created three-fold problems :

(i) The basic productive techniques largely remained traditional and this restricted the growth of wealth.

(ii) The insufficient development of new occupations and employment opportunities, along with the ruin of handicrafts and artisan production, created on the one hand pressure on agriculture and on the other a massive supply of unskilled workers in the labour market.

(iii) Since the need for superior technical skills in the domain of production, did not extensively develop due to the supply of cheap labour, the technical basis of the meagre new industries did not appreciably develop though profit remained the motive of production.

The innovations ushered in modernization of the Indian Economy on a capitalist basis. Private property production for market, money as the medium of exchange and profit as the dominant motive were characteristics of the new economy. Therefore, a new type of education was required to provide skills, techniques, knowledge as well as re-orientation of values for carrying out new functions.

Educational Policy during British Period

In order to establish supremacy of laws and the secularisation on the basis of authority and also creation of new socio-economic order, the British rulers developed specific educational policy. Educational policy started from the time of Warren Hastings as early as 1773. The most important period, however, was that of Woods Despatch of 1854. During this phase the following three schools debated about the aims of education, its pattern and organization, the medium, the method and the extent of education. Educational agencies and educational finance : The Imperial Conservative School of Orientalists, The Liberal-Utilitarian Westemists and a school comprised of 'a section of rulers and missionaries', emerged. According to Prof. A. S. Dasai these three schools agreed on the following major points:

1. British rule in India was justified and had to be strengthened.
2. British rulers required natives to man the lower levels of their politico-administrative organization.
3. British culture was superior to the culture of the conquered Indians and that it was the duty of the white rulers to civilize the conquered people.

Aims of the British System of Education

According to Prof. A.R. Desai the British educational policy was based upon the Liberal-Utilitarian Westernist school. The following aims were adopted by the rulers :

1. To train Indians, with a view to staff the vast politico-administrative machinery, and to imbue the personnel with the underlying principles and procedures governing it.
2. To train educated people to acquire skills and assimilate values arising out of the new capitalist economic system which the British were creating in India, and which had different laws of operation based on a money economy, contractual relations, and production for profit and for the market.
3. 'To win over the confidence of the upper classes of society which had lost their political influence through the British

Conquest,' and make them allies of the British Government, in short, to create a class 'Indian by birth but English in taste, manners and outlook' who could be relied upon as strong supporters of British rule,

4. To inculcate new values among the Indian people with a view to 'civilize' them in the spirit of Western Liberal Christian concepts.

The civilization process was adopted : firstly, for rapid conversion to Christianity and secondly, for development of love for the British Culture and the Christian religion.

The Three Stages of Education. The British rulers introduced in India the pattern of three tier education prevalent at: Primary, Secondary and Higher. The details of these three stages of education however changed from state to state.

Liberal Education. Liberal education was introduced at the Primary and Secondary level. This included in addition to the three R's, Geography, History, Political Science, Economics and other liberal subjects. Knowledge of English Literature, Modern Science, Mathematics, Economics, Philosophy formed the content of higher education.

Job-Oriented Education. However, even the liberal education had a job-oriented bias. The primary aim of the British rulers was to create a cadre of clerks and other subordinate officers for Bureaucracy. Vocational training was however introduced in specialised vocational institutions.

Downward Filtration Theory. The British rulers adopted Downward filtration theory according to which education was limited to a small sector of the population via English. The masses were educated in the native language.

Educational Agencies. We have already pointed out that British rulers considered education as a commodity to be purchased by those who had sufficient needs. The government, however, adopted a scheme of Grant-in-aid to various agencies of education. This resulted in the development of the following five types of educational agencies:

The Government. This was in fact the supplier.

Local Bodies. These provided primary education by government aid and fees from the student.

Christian Missionary Institutions. These were the predominant suppliers of education at primary, secondary and collegiate levels.

Private Indian Agencies. These included Indian religious missions like Ram Krishna Mission, Arya Samaj, Prarthana Samaj, Khalsa, etc.

European Education Centres. These were few and temporary. According to Prof. A. R. Desai the British Policy of Education permitting various types of educational agencies resulted in the following significant consequences:

(a) It resulted in different conditions and facilities in different educational institutions.

(b) It also led to great disparity and unevenness in the provision of facilities to students.

(c) As education became a passport for most of the new jobs, and as the jobs were basically of a non-manual character, they attracted more easily those castes and social groups which were connected with non-manual occupations in the traditional Indian society.

(d) Another feature arising out of education being made a commodity with suppliers deserves to be noted.

(e) The Grants-in-Aid policy of the Government contributed to make education a commodity not freely available to all.

Establishment of Administrative Machinery

The British rulers established Education Departments or Education Boards to inspect and supervise education at various stages given by various agencies. According to Prof. A. R. Desai the British Administrative Machinery for education suffered from the following defects :

1. The machinery was not scientifically planned and its parts were not all well integrated.

2. The Central Government increasingly reduced its own responsibility, financial activity to provincial governments.

3. The provincial governments increasingly reduced their own financial responsibility for education, financing only a few academic institutions.
4. The Government of India and its educational agencies did not elaborate uniform standards for different provinces, leading to problems of eligibility and equivalence.

Social Consequences of the Educational Policy

The British Policy of Education resulted into the following social consequences:

Socialization. Education became the most important socialising agency deciding status and role and over-riding family, caste and religious distinction.

Creation of an Elite Class. The most important social consequences of British educational policy was the creation of a class of WOGS or Western Oriented Gentlemen who had almost no communication with the masses.

Prevention of the Growth of Technocrats. British education was primarily liberal, literary, vocational and non-manual. Therefore, it prevented the growth of technocrat and trained personnel.

Westernization. British educational policy led to fast westernization of at. least the elite educated sections of Indian society. This resulted in Brain-drain, secularisation and creation of All India Education Cadre. It also created consciousness against foreign rule. It strengthened casteism, communalism, linguism and regionalism. It led to reactionary, communal and linguistic movements on the one hand and secularisation and democratization on the other.

Post-independence Social Change

In contrast to the social changes undergone by Indian society during the British rule, the following social changes occurred in post-independent era:

1. The constitution declared all citizens to be equal.
2. The state was governed by quasi form of federal constitution with a strong centre and weak state units.

3. The Indian Constitution laid down fundamental rights and the rights in the directive principles of state policy.

4. As the new state aimed at general welfare, it created a massive net work for the purpose at Central, State and local levels. The educational facilities were expanded in all directions. A new demand for education particularly technical was created. More communication with foreign countries started.

Five Year Planning

The Congress government adopted five-year plans with certain important characteristics:

1. Planning was divided into Public Sector Projects and Private Sector Projects.
2. The state reserved large-scale enterprises for manufacture of necessary goods and amenities.
3. Manufacture of consumer goods was left to private enterprises.
4. Agriculture was left in private sector.
5. Trade, regulated by the government, was left in the private-sector.
6. Financing and money-lending was in the hands of individuals or private institutions.
7. Most of the goods were sold and purchased in the open market.
8. In place of barter system, monetary basis of exchange was adopted.
9. Taxation by the government was mainly indirect.
10. A major source of finance for the plans was foreign aid.

New Educational Policy

The above characteristics of planning under the Congress Government show capitalist social system. This was, however, on the modernised level, while under British rulers it was on the colonial basis. This system however does not suit democracy.

Democracy under *it* because plutocracy or oligarchy. Democracy requires education, social security and employment. All this requires enactment of welfare legislations by the state. It is the duty of a welfare state to provide for the minimum needs of all the citizens. Therefore, most of the thinkers have not supported capitalist system for any under developed country. As Prof. Marshal has pointed out, "In the twentieth century, citizenship and the capitalist class system had been on capitalist system. As Prof. A.R.Desai has pointed out, "The relevance of this point is that the educational system is a part of a wider social system and operates to provide techniques, skills and values which would equip the individual to perform efficiently has adult role in this system." Since India has been a feudal society, therefore, the government will have to make special efforts for the establishment of a democratic society. Realising this responsibility the Indian government framed a new educational policy after independence. This policy had the following characteristics:

Concurrent Subject. Though in theory education is a state subject, in practice it is concurrent since the central government provides a major portion of finance and other facilities. Therefore, both the central and the state government play important role in determining educational policy and its expansion in the country.

Diversification. Every modern country requires diversi-fication of education courses and institutions to provide for a wide variety of specialists, scientists, engineers, doctors and others. Therefore, the government have undertaken the development of vocational institutions particularly. The institutions for the growth of science are mainly grown by the state help while liberal education is partly financed by the state.

Expansion of Special Education. In every country some part of population lags behind others. These are the handicapped, the retarded, the backward classes which require special help and incentive to develop along with others. The Indian government have therefore adopted social education and other special categories for education for the educational advancement of the women, the backward classes, the poor and the mentally and socially handicapped.

Educational Finance. Education is a stupendous task. Therefore, neither public nor the government alone can meet its expenses. Hence, both the private and the public sectors are providing for it. Primary education is mostly governed by local self-government bodies. Secondary education and college education is generally supported by individuals and private trusts. The university education, however,, is particularly the responsibility of the government. Vocational education is also supported by the government. This is helpful in planning the needs and the supply of trained personnel for planned development of the country.

Medium of Instruction. Mother tongue has always been and still is the medium of instruction at the primary level. At the secondary level, Indian languages have substituted English after independence. The central government and the Indian constitution have declared Hindi as the national language. Besides, 15 regional languages have been recognized for development. However, English remains the superior language as it is the medium of technical, scientific and higher education in India everywhere. This has given rise to an English speaking elite class which is separated from the general masses. This is a serious hindrance in the establishment of a democratic society in India. In spite of all government help and vocal incentive to Hindi and other regional languages, English has grown by the leaps and bounds in the last several decades and the present government, having a young leadership of Doon educated leaders, is set to make English defacto *Lingua franca* of India. It is still the language of administration and economic transaction in most of the parts of the country. It is almost the sole medium of instruction in Engineering, Medical and Higher educational institutions in India. So long as this trend continues the gulf between the elite and the masses will be further widened. In fact, whatever may be the avowed aim of the Indian leaders, practically capitalism of the Western type is fast growing in the country. The society is again returning to the old feudal types in new garbs. The public still respects money, power, high breed, the Rajas and the Nawabs. This has been clearly demonstrated in the recent elections to the parliament. Seasoned politicians were defeated by Rajas and filmstars. And this trend is bound to increase its pace. Whatever may be the criticism of English as a medium of instruction the number of English medium primary and even secondary schools is growing fast everywhere. There is a scramble in the moneyed section to get their children educated in public schools and in foreign countries as far as possible. The Hindi text books and general books have no sales in comparison to English text books and general books. Therefore, literature in English language is growing fast and the literature in Indian languages is tagging-behind.

The most strange phenomenon witnessed today is that even in Indian parliament an influential section of leaders communicate through English. All these trends are antidemocratic and not in favour of national interest though some might hail them as modernization. Therefore, there is no wonder that thoughtful persons have severely criticised the present educational policy of the government. It has been rightly suggested that the administration should be transacted in regional language. The regional language or the national language alone should be the medium of instruction of primary and secondary education. The higher education should be limited to few on the basis of merit and they may be given a training in English so that higher education may not suffer. As most of the Indians do not study beyond higher secondary level, therefore, this step will create a wider democratic base. Again, if every child will have primary and secondary education through the mother tongue he will find himself nearer to the general masses and class distances will be minimised. However, whatever may be the rationality of these suggestions the fact is that English as the medium of instruction is being more and more accepted at the primary and secondary level. There is a demand of English medium primary and secondary schools everywhere however costly they may be. Clearly, this is a trend towards westernization. However, modernization requires democratization on indigenous basis and not aping of the West. Therefore, if India has to be a twenty-first century nation, as aimed at by the new government, a nationalist policy of education has to be planned and rigourously followed.

10

Impact of Culture

What is Culture ?

In anthropological literature the term culture is used in many senses, but in general writings it is used to indicate social charm and intellectual superiority. Even some sociologists believe cultured individuals to be the leaders of society. According to Sorokin and Maclver, culture implies man's moral, spiritual and intellectual achievements. In the words of Bogardus, "Culture is composed of integrated customs, traditions and current behaviour patterns of human group. Culture is the stock in trade of group. It is an antecedent complex of value into which every individual is born. It is a midium within which individuals develop and mature." In Indian Society the individual is prepared for performing various functions in society at a very early age by a series of impressions deliberately made upon his mind. For example, the ceremony of marriage places upon the individual's shoulders the responsibility of procreating and thus ensuring the continuity of the race. Culture includes all those elements for which ceremonies and their consequent impressions are required. It is the process of purification. In ancient India Sanskrit was believed to be the language of the educated people, and this too is intimately concerned with culture, because the Hindi synonym is 'sanskriti'

Man and Culture

In the words of Kroeber, "In short, a cultural fact is always a historical fact, and its most immediate understanding, and usually the fullest understanding of it to which we can attain, is a historical one. To a large degree calling culture super-organic or super-individual means that it yields more readily to historical interpretation than to organized or psychosomatic explanations." Thus, Kroeber calls culture super-organic and super-individual in the sense that it is amenable to a historical interpretation or more apt interpretation of culture. This viewpoint makes it amply clear that although human beings create culture, it is not the creation of single individual. The same thing has been stated by Majumdar and Madan in these words "Human beings, it must be realised, are perhaps equally the creator of cultures as they are its creatures and careers." Hence, culture guides mankind, and while it renders him free from many causes, it also, to certain extent, enslaves him It is evident that Majumdar and Madan have also accepted culture as super psychic and super social. Kroeber's viewpoint on culture is considered to belong to the category of cultural determinism according to which culture is the determinant of man's activity, not itself dependent upon man. But this concept of cultural determinism is no less unbalanced and one-sided than biological or geographical determinism Kroeber's belief that culture is super organic and super individual is acceptable only to the extent that culture is not the creation of any one individual but of a community of human beings. But it is difficult to agree with him in the belief that culture is the final determinant of all human activity.

Relation between Education and Culture

The intimate relationship between culture and education is evident from the fact that one of the major aims of education is to impart to the child his cultural heritage, the social heritage. In any human group, the various elements and parts of culture evolve after thousands of years of the experience, and these are handed down as a whole to the succeeding generations. Hence, every individual is born into a particular culture which provide him with definite patterns of behaviour and values which guide his conduct in different walks of life. He has thereby saved the necessity of making fresh experiments every time. Obviously, then, culture plays an important part in man's life. But understanding the nature of its importance, it will be easy to understand how the education of various elements of culture can help man. The main features of the contribution of culture to man's life are the following:

Adaptation to the Natural Environment. Everywhere, man lives in a definite natural environment to which he must necessarily adapt himself. Without doing this, he cannot exist. All the experiments and inventions that he makes in the process of this adaptation form an important part of the culture. Due to differences in the natural environment of different communities, there arise differences in their cultures also, and it is on this basis that a distinction is made between primitive and developed cultures. In all the tribes of India, the members behave in certain distinct and specific ways in order to adapt to their respective environments. These modes of behaviour are taught to the younger generations. It is these modes of behaviour which go to make up culture.

Adaptation to the Social Environment. Culture also includes customs, traditions and the pattern of current behaviour, etc. Inherent in it are our beliefs and ideas, decisions, values and social institutions. All of these help the individual to adapt to his social environment, but it must be remembered that all these elements undergo gradual changes as the social environment itself changes. Culture determines the patterns of social control, through which the individual is subjected to the coercion of the group. Hence, the advantage in communicating the culture of the group to the child through education is that he is thereby acquainted with the traditions, customs, values and patterns of conduct prevailing in his group. This knowledge enables him to adapt to the social environment and thus achieve his socialization.

Development of Personality. The personality of an individual is manifested through his pattern of behaviour. The behaviour is always profoundly influenced by the culture of his group. Anthropologists have established as a fact that one finds differences in the basic behaviour patterns of individuals belonging to different cultures and that differences of behaviour correspond to differences in culture. Some people are more aggressive while others are submissive. One can find the clear imprint of Indian culture on an Indian and the imprint of Western culture on a European or American. Culture influences the physical, mental, social, emotional, moral and aesthetic aspects of the individual. Individual efforts lead to important changes in culture, but the behaviour of the average individual is determined by culture.

Socialization. Culture plays an important role in socializing the individual, and for this reason the quantity and direction of socialization differs from one society to another. Every society has its own ethos, and this is communicated to the individual in many different ways. Ralph Linton has pointed out three ways in which the individual can participate in culture. In the first place he participates universally in culture, that is, he adopts the habits, ideas and emotional patterns that prevail among the adults of that group. In the second place, the individual specifically participates in culture by adopting those elements of culture which are found among some specific organization or specific group of people. And finally, in third place, the individual's participation in culture turns to that alternative elements in which he adapts those elements which are found only in a small number of individuals. It is this participation in the third, the alternative aspect, that leads individuality to the personality of each person. George H. Mead expresses the opinion that in adopting his culture the individual's ego passes through three stages analogous to the three stages of education. In the first stage, the individual imitates other people around himself, normally unconsciously. He is found smiling at others. In childhood, the infant acquires his culture through imitation. In the second stage, the children imitate different individuals in society in their play. Play of this kind introduces many different kinds of qualities in the child's personality. The third stage of acquiring culture is the stage of games where the individual learns to control his behaviour. In the social environment of the playground, the individual cannot behave wilfully, since he has to conform to the social norms. Hence, he gradually begins to adopt the ideals, principles and beliefs of his group, and it is only this kind of individual who is called cultured.

Education in Various Fields

Education of Culture in Family. The child's cultural education begins at home, and it is in the family that he participates in the elements of culture and he passes through the various stages of culture development explained by Mead. The parents and other members of the family educate the child in the various means of culture such as traditions, customs, values, belief, etc. It is in the family that the child first learns to distinguish between right and wrong. The various impressions impinging upon his mind in the family environment help to make the child cultured. In Indian society a variety of religious ceremonies are performed to initiate the child into cultured life. Comparable religious practices are found in other cultures also. Patterns of moral and religious behaviour are also learnt in the family. Good behaviour is imbibed from the behaviour of adult members of the family, because the child invariably imitates the behaviour of the adults and brothers and sisters. One can find the clear imprint of family influence upon the lives of the greatest men who have contributed to their respective cultures. A part of the cultural training in the family is unconscious, but a large part of it is consciously imparted to the child by the adults.

Cultural Education in School. Now-a-days, it is the school which has taken over the function of culturally educating the child, just as it educates him in every other way. Schools in different countries educate the child according to their own cultures because through their text books they seek to acquaint the child with their own values, mores, ideas, customs, etc. Various extracurricular programmes are also intended to impart culture to the child. These programmes take the form of games of various kinds, dramas, community songs, dances, discussions, tours, of various parts of the country, etc.

Cultural Education in Society. Generally speaking, of course, both the family and the school undertake the task of communicating the society's specific culture to the younger generation, but nevertheless one does find minimal differences between the cultures of individuals belonging to different ranks of the same society. Hence, this education in culture is limited not only to training in the culture of the society as a whole, but also of a more limited culture belonging to different strata of society. Hence, cultural education comprehends both the general or extensive culture as well as the numerous sub-cultures existing within the extensive culture. Culture education is important inasmuch as it helps the individual to adapt to his natural and social environment, to develop his social personality, to enable him to conduct himself fruitfully in this intercourse with other members of the society.

Apart from this, the individual is also assisted by culture in his livehood and other important functions of life. Through this culture he adopts social institutions and learns to conform his behaviour to the accepted norm. He finds in this culture distinctive patterns of behaviour designed to meet the various contingencies of social life. It is through this training that he becomes a useful member of society.

Education in Liberality to Other Cultures. Cultural education must supplement knowledge of one's own culture with the liberality of approach for other cultures which is so essential for understanding and sympathising with them. In the absence of this liberality members of one culture believe themselves to be either superior or inferior to members of other cultures, with the result that tension is enhanced. This tension can even find violent expression. This is a major cause of many communal riots that frequently disrupt the peace in India. It is, therefore, desirable that the children should not only be taught their own culture but also be taught to appreciate other cultures. This is essential if the organization of society and world peace is to be maintained.

For this, some attention should be paid to other cultures also while imparting training in the various aspects of one's own culture. While leaching the child about the religion of his own group for example, it is necessary to tell him that despite the obvious differences the same elements arc also to be found at the root of other religions. The child should be made to understand that cultural differences arc the manifestation of the different natural environments, but that this is no reason to believe one culture to be superior or inferior to another. There is no magnificance or denigration attached to differences in the natural environment. It is more creditable for every human group to lead its life according to its own culture. Therefore, it is never proper to foist the culture of one group upon another. When the child comprehends the true causes at the root of cultural differences, he can adopt a more liberal and sympathetic attitude to other cultures, and also avoid the mistake of considering his own culture to be the best one.

Education in the Proper Use of Leisure. One important aspect of cultural education is training in the proper use of one's leisure. That man is a cultured animal can be judged from the manner in which he spends his leisure, and it is only this which really distinguishes between the cultured and the uncultured individual. Hence, children should be educated to use their leisure for cultural attainments, such as literature, music, art, self-development, etc. It is for this reason that educationists have insisted upon supplementing education in science with some education in humanities also.

The relationship between education and culture is clear from the foregoing account.

11

Economic Factors

Economics may be defined as a scientific study of man in reaction to his wealth getting and wealth spending activities. It studies the unlimited wants of man, and the limited resources with which he wants to fulfil these wants. Economics deals with the resources of environment and studies how economic goods satisfy the wants of man, are produced, consumed, exchanged and distributed. Thus, production, consumption, exchange and distribution form the basic aspects of economics. Economics is concerned with land, labour, capital and organization. It explains theories, laws and principles connected with agriculture, trade, industry, banking, commerce, capital, investment, manpower planning and everything that concerns the economic life of the nation.

Economic Aspects of Education

The following points explain the economic aspects of education :

Education as Economic Good. A 'good' can be included under the scope of economic good only when its availability is limited and it is capable of allocation. Following are two types of econoic good :

(i) *Material good.* A material good is physical and tangible.

(ii) *Non-material good.* A non-material good is a service rendered that satisfies a human want.

Education is a non-material economic good. It is service rendered to satisfy a human want. It is limited and capable of being allocated to individuals.

Education is a Producer's and Consumer's Good as given below :

(i) *Producer's Good.* Producer's good is a good used in the process of producing other goods.

(ii) *Consumer's Good.* Consumer's good is a good used by a consumer to satisfy his wants.

Education is both producer's good and a consumer's good. It gives satisfaction to the person who consumed it. It helps in the production of more goods. Education in the form of a producer's good is acquired for the purpose of becoming a teacher, lawyer, engineer or mechanic, or for any other profession or vocation, the main purpose of which is to produce a material or non-material good. At the same time it is consumer by those who receive it in the satisfaction of some of their wants. Again, education becomes a consumer's goods when the purpose of acquiring knowledge is to enrich a person's life by increasing his capacity to use, enjoy or appreciate any material or non-material good that satisfies human want.

Education as Industry. A country's government spends its gross national income on different sectors of the economy such as agriculture, industry and education every year expecting more returns than the previous year. The share for education is increasing every year in both developed and developing economics. Thus education is indeed a 'growth industry' which provides employment and services needed by the total economy as any other industry contributes to the gross national product of the country. It contributes substantially to the total economy of the country, and without it the economy would be all too poor. Again, education produces non-material goods which satisfy human wants. Education, as it produces goods necessary for human welfare, is amenable to demand supply and cost benefit analysis.

Education as Human Capital. Capital is anything that involves costs but yields a stream of income over time. It is the key to the production of income and consequently to economic growth. It consists largely in its power to produce or accumulate income immediately or in the long run. H.G. Johnson classified capital in the following four categories :

(i) *Capital Goods.* These render specific services to production or consumption by the owner.

(ii) *Human Capital.* This is labour. Labour, the important characteristics of which is that both inherently and by legal tradition, control over the use of the capital is vested in the individual embodying the capital regardless of the source of finance or·the investment in it.

(iii) *Social Capital.* This is collective capital, the important, characteristic of which is that for reasons of inherent necessity or administrative convenience its services to production or consumption are not charged to individual users but are paid for by taxation of the community at large.

(iv) *Intellectual capital* This is knowledge, the important characteristic of which is that, once created it is a free good, in the sense that use of it by one individual does not diminish its availability to others.

Essentially, education is human capital as it directly promotes the quality and capability of human beings. It contributes to intellectual and partly at least makes social capital. Economics considers human beings as a form of capital due to following reasons :

1. There are costs associated with development and formation of human capital.
2. The costs of skilled human resources add incrementally to the national product.
3. Expenditure on human resources which increase the national product also increase the national wealth.

Factors affecting human capital formation are investment in formal education, improved health, on the job training, manpower rehabilitation, migration, etc. Formal education raises the economic value of the human capital by raising the future earning power and current asset value of human beings.

Impact of Economics upon Education

Areas of impact of economics upon education are the following:

Aims of Education. Economics determines aims of education. Besides knowledge aim, cultural aim, character aim, spiritual aim, social aim, harmonious development of personality as an aim, vocational aim is one of the important aims of education.

Importance of Education. Economics explains the importance of education is so far as the economic growth of the country is largely based on educational development.

Education as a Means. Economics teaches man to be a better producer: both for his personal good, and for the good of the country. It further points out that education is a means for that end.

Education as an Investment. Education is itself an investment in economic terms. It removes poverty, as it produces skilled labour, and creates right attitude to work and development. It creates awareness for better living.

Education as a Guarantee of Economic Security. Education determines professional values, the wage structure, and guarantees economic security of the people.

Education and Economic Status. Economic status of a person is determined by education. Education helps him in possessing a good earning capacity and leading a good economic life.

Education and Economic Prosperity. Economic development of the country depends on education. Economic prosperity of the country is directly proportional to the educational development of the people.

Education and Economic Growth

Economic growth is identical with prosperity and better life. Faster economic growth helps the people of a country to enjoy higher standards of living. It leads to better social services. It gives more aid to the people of other countries. Economic growth means increase in the net national income during a given period of time. Some economists take increase in per capita income as an indicator and a measure of economic growth. Following are some definitions of economic growth:

(i) *Marshall.* The result of the labour acting on the natural resources of a country which produce within a given period of time a certain, non aggregate of commodities after avoiding double counting.

(ii) *Mayer and Baldwin.* Gross National Product and per capita income.

(iii) *Sclumpeter and Hicks.* Economic growth implies a growth in Gross National Product.

Role of Education

The system of education and the economic growth in a given social set-up are inter-related. One cannot exist without the other. Deterioration in education results in slow economic development. On the other hand, daw economic development will affect educational system and standards. According to B.C. Tilak, the relationship between education and economic growth is a two way process- one of a reçiprocal nature, of mutual contribution. In his book *'The Economics of Education'* John Vaizey has humorously and rightly described this relationship like a "chicken and egg". Harbison and Myers opine that education is both the seed and the flower of economic development. To sum up, the role. of education in economic growth is as follows :

Production of Material Wealth. According to Alfred Marshall, education makes a man "more intelligent, more ready, more trustworthy in his ordinary work; it raises the tone of his life in working hours and out of working hours; it is thus an important means towards the production of material wealth." Education is now universally accepted as a very useful productive activity which promotes national prosperity and national welfare in various fields. Thus it produces material wealth.

Development of Talents and Virtues. An accelerated and higher level of economic welfare depends on bringing about fundamental changes in both the mental outlook and technical knowledge and skills. An awakened mind, right knowledge, appropriate skills and desirable attitudes are the great levers of economic development. Conceived and imparted correctly, education produces these talents and virtues. It yields an automatic bonus in the 'growth process' and the 'change process.' It releases the dynamism and forward flowing energy, which are the assets for a developing country. The constructive urges of man are aroused through education. Better organizational skill and sharp inventiveness are the direct results of education. It aims at the harmonious development of 3 H's (head, hand and heart). This will produce integrated personalities, who are assets to the economic progress.

Development of Human Resources. The development of human beings is the key resource of economic development. Human resource has both quantitative as well as qualitative aspects-quantitative in terms of effective man-hours and qualitative in terms of skills, knowledge and attitudes of human beings, on whom depends the tempo of development of a country. In a developing country every man's outlook and his level of education must change. With more investment in human capital (education) there will be more improvement in skills, knowledge and attitudes.

Karl Marx pleaded for education on the ground that, "It is counter balance to the inhuman results of the division of labour." According to Harbison and Myers the educational process of human resources development is necessary for the transformation of social and political institutions, for which the people of modernizing countries strive. Economic contribution of education could be interpreted in terms of human capital through education. Education improves man-power engaged in production. This improvement achieves higher and higher targets of growth and production in all areas and aspects of industrial development and economic prosperity.

Quantitative and Qualitative Improvement. The role of education in economic growth has both quantity and quality dimensions. Educational innovations and research are necessary and must be encouraged in planning to provide quality labour, efficient administrators, well trained teachers and various other professionals, with dedication and an experimental outlook. The role of education in discoveries and inventions should be supported further with necessary finance.

Education has the power to improve quality. It adapts human

resources and makes them more productive. In USSR in 1920's, "It was estimated that the work of the people who had received primary education was almost one-and-a -half-times more productive than that of illiterate workers of the same age doing the same work; and that the work of those who had received secondary education was twice as productive, while that of graduates was four times as productive."

Japan has been able to make very rapid economic progress in the twentieth century, in spite of the late arrival in the field, large density of population and paucity of natural resources. The explanation may be found-at least partly-in the fact that she has been stepping up her public expenditure on education since World War II. Compared to Mexico and Brazil (rich in natural resources), Denmark and Switzerland (low in natural resources) have higher per capita income because of the effective system of education in the latter. By spending more than half of the national wealth on education, USA has attained great heights of economic prosperity in return. The economic progress of Netherlands is also due to her educational pattern. Thus economic prosperity of modem advanced countries has proved that the most effective means for prosperity is education. By their efficiency and dynamism educated persons contribute to national prosperity and growth of national income.

12

State and Education

Aristotle defined the state as a commune of families and villages whose aim is complete and self reliant life. But this definition was appropriate only to the city state, because the modern state is not limited only to villages. Modern thinkers point out four essential characteristics of the state-population, a definite geographical area, a government and complete sovereignty. Briefly, then, state can be defined as an organised human group living in a definite geographical area and having its own sovereign government.

Role of State

Before going on to a detailed analysis of the relationship between the state and education, one must see the extent to which the state can play a part in social life. In other words, one must see how far education is a subject of state control, guidance and assistance. In modern societies, one finds that education is provided in government controlled institutions as well as privately managed institutions. Many educational institutions are also controlled and managed by religious institutions. And even among the government or state controlled institutions, one finds that some are administered by the central authority and others by state or local self governing bodies. Another aspect of the state control of education is to determine the spheres which the state should take under its own wings and the areas which can be safely left to the control of the people. In the present day, every government, be it totalitarian or democratic, must contribute to education. There is no doubt that in a democracy the government is elected by the people, but it cannot be denied that the people themselves cannot evolve an educational pattern which can look after the educational needs of every individual. And, at the same time, it is also realised that democracy cannot be successful in the absence of universal education. Hence, modern democratic states also play a large part in educational planning and organisation.

Rights of the State

Before elucidating the rights of the state with respect to education, it is necessary to understand that there is considerable difference of opinion on this subject. Most of the theories and opinions on this subject can be divided into the following classes:

Individualism. Hobbes, Locke, Bentham, J. S. Mill and Herbert Spencer attached greater importance to the individual than to the state in the organisation of society. Hence, these philosophers are not in favour of state interference in education. Hobbes favours the policy of Laissez Faire, and suggests that the administration of education should be left to independent citizens. He agrees that state control of primary education is desirable and proper but he objects to state interference in higher education. Bentham is of the opinion that the state exists only to increase the happiness and contentment of the citizens, and therefore the state should interfere in education only to the extent to which such interference will lead to an increase in the sum total of happiness. He suggests that primary education should be compulsory in every country, that the state should provide the schools and colleges, but the state-should not have any monopoly in education. The state must also not try to discourage private educational movements. Spencer believes that social progress is based on the principle of struggle for survival, and from this he argues that it is the duty and responsibility of the state that it should assist the people in their struggle for survival. Yet, even in this assistance, the state must take care not to restrict the freedom of the individual. Raymont has summarised the opinions of the individualist philosophers in these words: "In fine, there has been a strong tendency amongst English political thinkers from Locke to Spencer towards distrusting the intervention of the state beyond the absolutely necessary limits, though opinions have differed considerably as to how far those limits should extend." Putting it succinctly, individualist thinkers favour the adoption of the Laissez faire policy by the state. There is also no doubt that even after putting education in the hands of the people, the state will still have to take special steps for the education of some sections of the people, who cannot make arrangements for their own education. Besides, the state will also have to step in to put an end to the conflict in the sphere of education between various classes of society.

Collectivism. Collectivist thinkers oppose the views of the individualists. This school of thought has been subscribed to by such eminent thinkers as Matthew Arnold, Cărlyle, Ruskin, Edmund Burke and others. Caryle and Ruskin vigorously opposed the concept of laissez faire, and suggested in contrast a complete state monopoly of education. Thinkers of this school suggest that the state's responsibility does not end with protecting the people. It must also contribute to their growth and development in other spheres and for this it has the right to take complete control into its own hands. The state should be given comprehensive rights to protect the nation and its people from external aggression, to apply in practice the national policies, to punish the criminals, to increase and equitably distribute national wealth, to tax the people, to provide means for protecting the health of the people, to emancipate culture by proper control, etc. In the field of education, the state has the responsibility of providing free and compulsory primary education. In this sphere the state has complete rights, and it must exercise these rights. Hence, it is the state which should control the educational system in the country.

Totalitarianism. Collectivist thinking in its extreme form becomes totalitarianism, which theorizes that the state is the most comprehensive form of human communities. In fact, the boundaries of the state and the society are identical, and therefore state should have complete control over education. According to Hegel, complete development of the child is impossible in the absence of an education for citizenship, provided by the state. Totalitarian thinkers are of the opinion that the child should not only be educated by the state, but also for the state.

Pluralism. Propounders of this philosophy want to delimit the powers of the state by a written constitution, for they are in favour of the independence of citizens. It is suggested that the extent of the state's powers should be clearly defined, so that other institutions like the family, church, etc., can make important contributions to education. Thinkers of this school, therefore, favour the establishment of privately controlled as well as state controlled educational institutions. The educand is not merely a citizen but also an individual, and hence his education must represent the combined effort of the family, religious institution and others, in addition to the effort of the state. State monopoly over the education of children is not considered desirable.

Anarchism. Thinkers belonging to this school are opposed to the existence of any kind of governmental or state authority in society, and for that reason the very question of state control of education does not arise. Anarchism argues, from the absence of any central authority, that the individual's development is best achieved in a condition of complete freedom. Such a condition naturally leads to mutual cooperation between individuals, and this is the precondition of proper development. The parents naturally and instinctively educate their children, without being forced to do so. Similarly, the child also does not have to be compelled to receive education. Everything in the field of education can be done by voluntary cooperation, without any external pressure.

Welfare State. Most of the views expressed above are extremist in nature. The concept of the welfare state is an attempt at achieving some balance between the widely divergent views about the authority of the state expressed in these philosophies. In the present age, the state is believed to aim at welfare of the citizens, no view of this, it is desirable that the state should retain some control over education in order to achieve the welfare of the people. For example, it can compel parents to send their children to school, if the parents are not inclined to view this with favour. But state control should be accompanied by state assistance also. The state should arrange for universal and compulsory education, at least at the primary level. It must also provide suitable text books to the students, or encourage other people to produce such books. The state has the authority to impose taxes upon the people to collect funds for educational purposes. It is the duty of the state to determine the proper syllabi for state institutions as well as other institutions controlled by private groups of individuals. Some anarchist and individualist thinkers may oppose state control of education to this extent, but there is no denying the fact that the people cannot successfully put into effect a complete educational programme. Raymont presents a balanced view when he comments, "We observe that education, like the other beneficial influences at work in a civilised community, may be conducted by all or any of three means; first, by voluntary effort with a view to profit; secondly by voluntary effort arising from philanthropic or religious motives; thirdly, by the agency of the state."

The Limitations

Having accepted that the state must exercise control over the educational system, it becomes necessary to determine the extent to which this control should be exercised. Historically viewed, education has been carried on in every state through a variety of means and agencies. On the one hand, one finds colleges and schools run by individuals for profit while on the other one comes across institutions created by religious groups or philanthropists who have collected funds from private individuals for this purpose. In addition, one finds state aided institutions in every country. Even J. S. Mill, who objects to state control of education, has admitted that the state should establish some ideal educational institutions which should serve as models and which should inspire the people to create similar institutions. Mill objects to the state control of education on the ground that the state tries to educate the. People along lines which support its own ideology and thus it controls the ideas of the people. This belief is not completely without logic and supporting evidence, because communist states do try to control the thinking of the younger generations by intellectually feeding them on communist literature. It amounts to slow brainwashing. Much the same tendency has been seen in the past in totalitarian state which also tries to control the thinking of the people by making educational institutions the centres of state propaganda. This is unfair and improper. In fact, state control in education is exercised with the sole purpose of preventing encroachment upon the political and social independence and freedom of the people, because this is essential for a proper development of personality. In the second place, the state has at its disposal unlimited means and resources which enable it to arrange for education on a large scale, something which is beyond the reach of private individuals and groups of individuals. Briefly speaking, it is desirable that state control of education should be guided by the principle of the least possible infringement of the liberties of the people. The welfare state provides for education on precisely this principle. With the establishment of welfare state the responsibilities of the state are increasing. The state imposes taxes on the people in order to finance education and then compos people to send their children to schools and colleges. It also supervises educational arrangements in institutions not controlled by it to ensure uniform standards, and also provides financial aid to them.

Functions of the State

Explaining the functions of the state, Maclver and Page have pointed out that there are certain functions which the state alone can perform, others which can be performed by others but not so efficiently as by the state, and yet others which are best left to other agencies, apart from those which the state does not have the ability to perform. The provision of education falls into the first and second of the above four categories, because not only is the state the best equipped for this task, it is in fact the only agency capable of coping with the educational problems of populations of remarkable size. The state alone can provide universal education to such a large number of people. The functions of the state in the sphere of education can be summed up as follows:

Provision of Proper Schools. The state should establish different kinds of schools-primary, secondary, higher learning and professional colleges - so that the local requirements of the people can be fulfilled. In addition to this, the state must also correlate these various institutions in such a way that the effort at education is not wasted.

Making Primary Education Compulsory. At least at the primary stage, the state should make all education compulsory, free and universal. This kind of education, at least the elementary education, is absolutely necessary for the mental development of the people. Hence, the state should compel parents to send their children to schools.

Providing Finances for Education. The state must plan for and provide the finances required for education. Some people have advanced the argument that the provision of free and compulsory primary eduction will reduce its value in the eyes of the people. While this may be true, the state is faced with the necessity of doing so, because the private sector has failed to provide primary education for the masses. It is now accepted that every modern state must provide free and compulsory education, it has been experienced that private resources are never sufficient to provide proper secondary and higher education to adequate numbers of students. Even here institutions have to seek the assistance of the state. In addition to the creation of primary and secondary school and universities and professional colleges for higher learning the state helps the cause of education by providing scholarships and financial help in different forms to poor but brilliant students. In many western countries the number of students receiving state aid in one form or the other frequently rises to fifty percent of the total number enrolled in the university. In India, this stage has not been achieved, and consequently many brilliant students are deprived of the opportunity to study.

General Control and Guidance. One important aspect of state functioning in the sphere of education is control, inspection and guidance of individual institutions. The state government officials construct syllabi for various levels of education, with the help of educationists and other teamed people. In the same manner, the state does not take independent decisions about educational matters, but seeks the advice and guidance of experts. The state should normally not interfere in teaching methods, but leave it to experienced teachers, researchers and scholars. Besides, the state can also profitably guide the techniques of evaluating educational ability. This, too, is the task of the teacher and the educationist. All that the state can lay down, in the way of guidance, is that some method of evaluating educational ability must be introduced at each level of education. The state may also require this method to be so accurate, dependable and valid that it may serve as a basis for evaluating the individual's fitness for various tasks.

Providing Skilled Educators. It is clear from the preceding paragraph that there is little the state can do in the absence of skilled educators. Hence it is a major responsibility of the state to provide such educators. Even if the national educational policy has been created by brilliant thinkers and incalculable effort has gone into its creation, it will fail to achieve anything if there are no skilled educators to implement it. The responsibility of the state does not end with putting up buildings for schools, filling such schools with educands and making arrangements for the administration of the institution. As Raymont has pointed out, "Educational salvation lies, not in bricks and mortar, nor in sumptuous equipment, nor in paper curricula, nor in elaborate machinery of whatever kind, but in the subtle influence of informed men and women upon the pupils committed to their care. A good teacher, in sympathy with his work, and doing it under reasonably liberal conditions of service will achieve better things in a barn than a bad or dissatisfied one will achieve under the best of external circumstances." Hence, it is desirable that the state should take upon itself the responsibility of providing trained and qualified teachers, and of seeing that their conditions of service create the satisfaction so necessary for the job. The educand's mental health depends very greatly upon the mental health of his educator. More often than not, in most non-government educational institutions one finds conditions of work which are not at all conducive to mental balance, for example, varying scales of pay, physical conditions of work, absence of opportunity to progress, etc. The state should investigate all such conditions and improve them, and also enact legislation which secures the rights of people working in private institutions.

Training in Citizenship. In the sphere of education, one important function of the state is to train young men and women in citizenship. For this, the state must create institutions for training in science, industry, agriculture, etc. The cultural training and advancement of the people can be provided for by creating art galleries, cultural committees, means of recreation etc. Now-a-days, states send cultural delegations to other countries. Another way in which the state can help in improving cultural standards is by facilitating the international exchange of teachers and students. In a democratic society it is necessary for the state to maintain a healthy level of social living, by creating conditions conducive to the physical and mental development of its people, and by assisting all private agencies engaged in similar work. Political training is also essential in a democratic country, because political awareness must be created if proper leadership is to emerge. It is for the state to exploit all means of communications-newspapers, radio, television, cinema, etc.,- in order to acquaint every individual with the latest in political, economic and social thinking, and also to inform him of all economic and industrial progress taking place with in the country. In this way, it can be seen that the political education of people living in a democratic country depends entirely upon the cooperation of the state.

13

Various Agencies

Classifications of Agencies

Sir Godfrey Thomson has written, "The whole of environment is the instrument of man's education in the widest sense. But in that environment certain factors are distinguishable as more particularly concerned; the home, the school, the church, the press, the vocation, public life, amusement and hobbies." Generally, of course, the process of education continues from birth to death, but some specific institutions play a more important part in it. All of these institutions are the agencies of education, and they include all those factors, bases, places or institutions, which have an educative influence upon the child. Hence, the institutions, agencies and bases of education mean the same thing, and should be interpreted as such. These agencies of education have been variously classified by different educationists. Some of the major classifications are the following:

Active and Passive Agencies. Among the active agencies of education are home, schools, religious institutions, society, state, club, social welfare centres, etc. Here the educator and the education, the audience and the speaker, the citizen and the leader, deliberately come into contact with each other and also react to each other. Consequently the process of education forges ahead. Among the passive agencies of education can be enumerated radio, television, films, newspapers, magazines, etc. These are called passive because the process of education set into motion by them is not mutual but onesided, because only the audience, or educand is actively participating. The other element, the agency itself, remains inactive, and hence only the educand is himself influenced without influencing the source of his education.

Commercial and Un-commercial. Brown has divided the agencies of education into the commercial and un-commercial. The commercial agencies have a commercial objective while the un-commercial have social welfare as their objective. Hence, the press, films, radio, television, magazines, etc., are the commercial agencies of education. On the other hand, sports clubs, scouts and guides institutions, adult education centres and social welfare centres, etc., are the un-commercial agencies of education.

Formal and Informal Agencies. The most recognised and well known classification is the division-into the formal and informal agencies of education:

Formal Agencies. In the words of Henderson, "As the child watches, imitates, participates, in the activities of living he is being informally educated. When he is being consciously and intentionally taught, that is formal education." In this manner informal education is unconscious whereas formal education is conscious and deliberately imbibed. Informal education is unsystematic while formal education is systematized. Among the agencies of formal education are those institutions which have a predetermined location, time, plan and curriculum as well as trained educators. The best example of such institutions is the school. Such agencies are brought into existence by the state or society. In such institutions discipline and administration is created by the application of set rules. It is possible to use such agencies to provide education to a large number of educands simultaneously, according to a predetermined plan. At least specific education cannot be provided in the absence of these institutions, but it must be realized that education provided through these agencies is rather lifeless and theoretical, or bookish. It sometimes takes the educant far away from the realities of life. In addition to schools, libraries, lecture theaters, recreation centres, museums, etc. are also enumerated among the formal agencies of education. Pointing out the significance of the formal agencies, Dewey has remarked, "Without formal education, it is not possible to transmit all the resources and achievements of a complex society. It also opens a way to a kind of experience which would not be accessible to the young, if they were left to pick up their training in informal association with others, since books and the symbols of knowledge are mastered." But he is also aware of the shortcomings of formal education. Dewey comments, "Formal education easily becomes remote and dead-abstract and bookish." The importance of formal agencies of education is thus evident.

Informal Agencies. The informal agencies of education are those in which education is provided informally and unconsciously. These lack all formality, rules, systematization, preplanning, premeditation or training. All of them perform the function of educating the educand indirectly. Most of them are independent of the control of any individual or institution. Education provided by them does not follow any set pattern. Besides, providing education, they also perform certain other functions and fulfil many other needs. Education provided by them is devoid of any pretension, formality. It is natural and subtle. Among the agencies of informal education arc family, society, state, radio press, cinema, magazines, television; etc. Dewey believes that the informal agencies of education are more important than the formal ones, for he believes that they are natural. One example of this is education through communal living. Living in a group, the child thinks of many things. The sphere of his experience is bring rapidly enlarged, for he is being subjected to many new stimuli. Under these circumstances his imagination develops and he becomes conscious of new responsibilities which provoke him to think. Even though the influence of these informal agencies is subtle, it is definitely very comprehensive. In the development of the child's personality and character, the informal agencies play a very significant role. The major benefit derived from them is that they do not restrict the child in any way. The child develops naturally. Despite these advantages, the informal agencies cannot completely replace the formal ones, because in the absence of a definite plan of education, much time and energy is wasted over things which ultimately prove useless. Besides, these informal agencies cannot be employed to give specific education or knowledge of a very complex kind. Again, definite and certified education cannot be provided through informal means.

It is evident from the foregoing account of the advantages and disadvantages of formal and informal agencies of education that both are essential for the development of the individual and of society. As social structures become progressively more complex and population increases, the importance of the formal and informal educational agencies also increases. Consequently, it has come to be believed that there is intimate relationship between the formal and informal means and agencies of education. When formal education increases to a great extent, it tends toward abstraction and lifelessness and·then it needs the assistance of the informal agencies to infuse new life into it. For this reason, modern educationists believe that college and family are complementary factors in the child's education. Dewey has correctly commented that in the modern age, "One of the weightiest problems with which the philosophy of education has to cope today is the method of keeping a proper balance between the informal and the formal, the incidental and intentional modes of education." Neither of the two should be stressed at the cost of the other. On the one hand various kinds of schools and colleges should be established to provide formal education, while on the other the informal agencies must also be exploited to make up any deficiencies left in the formal mode. Even in colleges and schools, excessive emphasis should not be upon book learning. It is for this reason that modern schools design their curriculum so that sufficient time is given to extra curricular and social activities. For the same reason, it has been found desirable that educators and parents should meet from time to time.

Formal Education and Schools

The different kinds of schools and colleges are enumerated among the formal means of education. The English word 'school' is derived from the Greek 'skhole', which means leisure. Hence school implies a place of leisure where people gather during their leisure time for the purpose of developing themselves. In Ancient Greece, young men and women used to collect in schools during their leisure time to receive education from famed scholars and philosophers. These same schools later on took the form they have at present. In a school education is imparted to the educand by trained educators, at a fixed time and place, according to a predetermined syllabus.

Example, primary, secondary and higher education, university education, etc. Among professional institutions are medical colleges, engineering colleges, etc. The function of the school is to achieve the physical, mental and character development of the educand, to develop in him a social consciousness, the qualities of citizenship. It must also aim at cultural development and the imparting of professional or industrial training. From this standpoint, it is seen that schools in India suffer from many defects, which have to be removed. If a school is to be successful in achieving its aims in the present age, it must have intimate relationship with the family on the one hand and the state or government on the other. Both must give it their wholehearted support and cooperation.

Major Informal Agencies

The major agencies of informal education are the following:

Home or Family. Pointing out the significance of the informal means of education, as part of the educational system Raymont has commented, "Teachers are not the only educators, and schools and colleges are not the only educational institutions. The other institutions though for good or ill, are unquestionably educational in their effects." This is most true of the family, for the family makes a sizeable contribution to the child's education, irrespective of the quality of this education. In families which provide a defective environment, the child develops many bad qualities of character. On the other hand, the importance of good families as contributing factors to the development of great personalities need hardly be explained. The difference that is seen among all the educands studying in schools and colleges is due to their varying family background. Mazzinni was quite correct in saying that the child's first training in citizenship is in the mother's lap and the father's affection. Accepting the importance of the family as a factor in the child's education, Montessori called his schools the home of children. Locke attached greater importance to education at home than to school education. Comenious opined that the home is the centre of all kinds of education for the child. Forebel is correct when the says that the education imparted at home is both effective and natural. Pestalozzi also felt that the home is the child's first school. Raymont says, "Two children may attend the same school, may come under the influence of the same teachers and the same organisation, may pursue the same studies and perform the same exercises; and yet may differ to came as regards their general knowledge, their interests, their speech, their bearing, and their moral tone, according to the homes they come from." The family looks after the child's physical development, lays the foundations of his character, gives him religious education, acquaints him with the realities of life and provides the right kind of environment for the development of his interests tendencies, motivations, intelligence and other processes. It is the most important agency of the child's socialization. Besides, in many families some kind of professional and practical education is also imparted to the child. It is for this reason that cooperation between the family and the school is considered an important aspect of the child's education.

Community. The community is also an important informal agency for the child's education. Moving out of the family, the child automatically takes up the membership of various groups in community and through them develops various aspects of his character and personality. Playing in the groups, he develops his mind and body. He also experiences moral, social and cultural development. Many institutions in the society provide him with professional and vocational training while different political groups look after his political training.

State. The modern welfare state is responsible for the over all development of all its citizens. That is why modern states pay so much attention to education and formulate national policies for education. The state shoulders the responsibility of establishing different kinds of schools. In many states free and compulsory education is provided, and even where this is not so, almost all educational institutions are aided by the state in one way or the other. The state provides able and trained teachers by establishing training colleges for them. The state also provides military training. Besides, research cannot be carried on without the help of the state. In a democracy, the state trains every individual in responsible citizenship. Although most sociologists oppose complete governmental control of education, every one agrees that without state help education would fail. State also plays an important role by retaining control over literature and encouraging it to evolve along acceptable lines. The state also looks after the education of physically and mentally handicapped children by establishing special institutions for such children.

Religion. From very ancient times, various educational institutions in almost every country have been shouldering the responsibility of educating the populace. In India, most schools were organised either within or very near the places of worship, for example, temples, mosques, etc. All the education was imparted by the chaplain of these places of worship. Although almost all modern welfare states are also secular, it is an acceptable practice to assist religious institutions where they contribute to the educational effort.

Library. There is little need to elaborate the role played by libraries in disseminating education. Libraries are the collection of the knowledge of centuries summarised in books. Many people maintain personal libraries but these do not fulfil all needs. Hence, the state and local self-governing bodies undertake the responsibility of establishing libraries. In almost all countries modern governments spend vast sums of money to establish big libraries.

Reading Room. In most modern towns, one finds reading rooms in addition to the libraries. These are established by the state and other institutions. These reading rooms provide many daily, weekly and monthly newspapers, all kinds of magazine,. which are available to the public which can come there and read them. It is not possible for every individual to subscribe individually to such a large number of magazines. For this reason, the reading room plays a significant role in education.

Museums. Museums are very useful in imparting education in such subjects as history, geography, biology, anthropology, etc. It is for this reason that one finds well stocked museums and zoos in many big cities of the world. The knowledge that an individual can gain by roaming around in these institutions is not available to him anywhere else. It is a psychological principle that the thing seen is remembered longer than the thing heard. For this reason museums can contribute a lot to an individual's education. There are many museums and zoos in many Indian cities.

Cinema. Cinema is one of the important informal agencies of education in the modern world, for it is an important form of audio-visual education. By means of this it is possible to see incidents, individuals and objects as if with the eye itself. It is therefore very useful when one wants to acquaint the educand with things, places and incidents occurring in foreign countries. It can be done by taking the educand to any cinema hall and exhibiting the appropriate film. It is evident, therefore, that this agency can easily be employed for the teaching of history, geography, civics, political science and comparable subjects. The government in India has inspired and financed the production of many entertaining and informative film documentaries concerning the revolution in agriculture and industry that is taking place in the country today. Newsreels also help in the dissemination of news and ideas. For example, the cinema has played an important role in educating the illiterate public about family planning. Apart from newsreels, even the commercial films have a tremendous impact upon the personality, character, behaviour and many smaller things of the young men and women of the country. It has been seen in America that the incidence of crime has gone up after films about crime became popular there. In India also a comparable trend is noticeable. Most films being produced today are concerned with the exhibition of the latest fashions, and this has had a detrimental effect upon the thinking of the younger generation. Hence, the government is faced with the task of encouraging the production of good, illuminating and elevating films, and also with the responsibility of preventing the production of films which cater to the baser instincts of men and women, films concerning sex, crime, etc. In many states, students have been legally barred from seeing films during the matinee, show. This is not a very psychological way of shielding the younger generation from the ill-effects and bad influences of film going. They can see the same films later in the evening, and still imbibe the same ideas. Preventing students from seeing films during college hours will achieve nothing more than to increase attendance in colleges. There is no doubt at all that cinema has a comprehensive influence upon the moral, religious and intellectual development of adolescents. The main cause of this is that in viewing the film, the members of the audience unconsciously identify themselves with the hero or the heroine and hence suffer the same experience through which the hero passes. They can be observed exhibiting the same emotions which are controlling the figure on the screen. It would be no exaggeration to say that if the cinema is exploited to the greatest extent as a medium of education, then there is no other informal agency which can be more influential than the cinema.

Drama. Although the popularity of the cinema has done much to reduce public interest in drama, in fact cinema can never completely replace dramatic performance. In a dramatic performance the actor, through his concrete presence and acting, arouses certain emôtions in his audience. Drama has certain drawbacks in that, unlike the cinema, it cannot exhibit scenes, places and incidents far removed from the location of the theatre. Inspite of this limitation, there is little doubt that the drama can be a very effective medium for the powerful presentation of many ideas and behaviour patterns. But from the educational standpoint, drama is more significant from the point of view of those children who can take active part in it. It does not compare in this respect with films because children cannot participate in films. For this reason, almost all colleges and schools have some or the other dramatic society in which the educands produce plays. Acting is itself an art, and it can only be learnt through drama. Besides, drama also promotes interest in singing and dancing. Participating in drama is useful because it helps a person to outgrow stage fright, or the fear of appearing before an audience. This promotes the ability of work in group. Acting also helps to reflect clearly the differences in the personalities of the actors and actresses. In certain cases, it has been seen that proximity of boys and girls during stage performances has led to certain undesirable consequences, but such incidents can, by and large, be prevented if the educators are conscious of their responsibility and handle the situations psychologically. Drama has also proved to be a useful medium for letting out or expressing many repressed drives and feelings. In the form of psycho-drama, dramatic performances can actually be used to get rid of many of the child's abnormalities. Finally, the teacher himself, in order to be a successful educator, must indulge in some acting, because only then can he present his subject forcefully to the class and influence his audience.

Newspapers and Magazines. The contribution of newspapers and magazines to the education of people in general is far greater than that of any other informal agency because they can be circulated over a far larger area than can be covered by films, dramatic societies, television, etc. Today, the progress of education in a country is completed by the number and quality of magazines and newspapers published there. It is a matter of no little pride that after independence, the number of newspapers and magazines, in English and in local languages has been going up steadily. This has been made possible by the rapid increase of literacy among the people. In the last few years many children's magazines have been published. These play a considerable part in the child's education. Magazines concerning sports and games provide considerable information in that sphere, while certain magazines provide information about health and how it can be maintained. There has been literally a flood of magazines concerning films, although it is difficult to class these among the better magazines. Besides these, a considerable number of weekly, monthly and magazines of other frequency add to the knowledge of the people. Apart form English and Hindi newspapers, newspapers in almost all regional languages are being able to reach the masses living in the villages. And in fact, newspapers play the greatest role in making democracy a success. No other form of informal education can be compared with these as far as political, economic and social education is concerned.

Radio. In the west, the radio has been almost completely supplanted by the television, but in India it is still very much in vogue. It is pleasant to note that transistor radios can now be seen in even the remotest villages, and have become so common that they are carried everywhere, to work, to play, to social gatherings, to travel. The radio amuses as well as instructs. The All India Radio, the national radio network, has conceived and executed a number of programmes to achieve these ends, amusement, pleasure and education. Among their programmes many are aimed at the agriculturists, children, uneducated women, students, those inclined towards light or classical music, towards humour and laughter, towards serious discussions on current topics and scientific subjects, etc. Most of the programmes broadcast over the radio are so full of information and also effective that if one only has the patience to listen to them, one would find unprecedented progress in one's education. Aware of this significance of the part that the radio can play, the Indian government has provided public radio sets for each panchayat so that the villages can collect in the building housing the panchayat and listen to various programmes of interest to them. Radio is a very good medium of political education, in particular. Before the last general elections the All India Radio arranged for the leaders of various political parties to speak on the radio and explain the aims, objectives and 'plans of their respective organisations so that the uneducated people could assess the merits of each party and select the representatives of the party most aligned to their own way of thinking. This was an important step forward in the political education of the electorate. As a consequence, one finds, the opposition parties creating an uproar whenever it seems that the broadcasting system is becoming unduly sympathetic towards the ruling party. Efforts are being made to neutralize the broadcasting organisation, politically, so that it should not become an organ of the ruling party alone, but should develop into an agency for disseminating information, knowledge and amusement. By means of the radio, people who are separated by long distances from the centre of things can listen to all kinds of cultural programmes while relaxing at home. In this it is not even necessary to open one's eyes or to sit up, as is necessary in the case of television or cinema. But if the radio is to be made an effective agency of informal education, there is considerable need for overhauling its programmes. AIR pays considerable attention to the suggestions put forward by its listeners in this connection, and it also consults experts from time to time.

Television. As has already been mentioned, television has become an important means of informal education in most advanced countries. Colour television has also been introduced so that it has now come nearer to reality. Most men and women spend their leisure time in front of the television, and thus absorb a lot of knowledge and information without having to make any great effort. Most of the programmes exhibited over the television are so life-like that one hears of people dying of heart failure while watching boxing matches and other exciting events. Television was extensively used to inform people about man's recent journey to the moon. The launching and various other stages were televised for the benefit of the people. In India, the effective range of television is far too small at present, and most of the programmes put on the screen have a long way to go. Faster development in this direction would be very much desirable, but progress has been hampered by many difficulties. Once these are removed, it will be observed that television is the most effective means of imparting social, economic, political and even professional training. Closed circuit television, a more modern form of television exhibition, is being extensively used in the training of medical students. In this the operation taking place in the operation theatre is televised so that students sitting in the classroom can view it. In this way, more students can be accommodated than would be possible in any operation theatre.

Scouting and Girl Guides. The scouting and girl guide movement has made an important contribution to the education of young boys and girls, for it teaches them social service through giving first aid, swimming, cooking, guiding the physically handicapped, pitching camps, returning lost children to their parents in big fairs, etc. This helps the child to understand the human body, to develop his personality and character and also contributes to his moral progress. Such institutions can be seen in schools the world over. They are even more useful in that they do not indulge in political discrimination.

Social Welfare Centre. In addition to the scouting and girl guide movements, Brown considers social welfare centres as media of informal education. Social welfare centres and social education centres have been set up in India as part of the community development projects. These have been established in rural as well as urban areas. By taking part in it, men and women receive education of different kinds, learn various skills and thus generate the ability and financial independence.

Educational Tours. Now-a-days, much importance is being attached to education tours as means of providing education in history and geography. In such tours the educands accompany the educator to far away places of historical or geographical significance. This has its entertainment value, apart from the information it provides. In many universities, educational tours have been made a compulsory part of education is history so that this education may become more life-like. Educational tours awake in the educand a greater awareness of the various movements occurring within the country, and also help to bring him nearer to nature. Tours are also considered an important part of industrial training, for the educand learns much by visiting industrial establishments.

Other Informal Agencies

In addition to the above agencies of informal education, different societies also have other institutions which are doing valuable work in this direction. Labour welfare committees, women welfare committees, cooperative societies, village panchayats, development block committees, and the like are concrete examples of this. Apart from this exhibitions of various kinds - art, science, industry, railways, postal, etc., do much to increase awareness of these spheres among the public. Now-a-days international exhibitions have also become very popular. In such exhibitions, nations put up their respective pavilions to show their achievements and progress in various directions so that people viewing them can learn how far a particular country has progressed in a particular direction. One such exhibition was organised in Japan in 1970. The cause of higher education is also served by the committees and associations for various subjects-mathematics, history, biology, philosophy, etc., which hold international meetings from time to time in order to exchange views. And, the coffee houses in many large towns are no less important than educational institutions because among their clientele are leading doctors, lawyers, literary figures, artists, impoverished politicians, who gather together to discuss all kinds of things. This helps to disseminate information and improve understanding of all affairs. Many towns also have literary associations which do much valuable work by encouraging and felicitating important literary figures. Professional associations, one example of which is the Indian Chambers of Commerce and Industry, also play a significant role in educating public opinion by holding seminars and discussions. So, in this manner, different institutions contribute to the cause of education in their own way by providing information to the people.

Interrelationship of the Formal and Informal Agencies

Finally, it is necessary to keep in mind that the formal and informal agencies of education are complementary. Those aspects of education which are not attended to in schools are taken care of by the informal agencies. Even educational institutions employ many of the informal agencies for education-reading rooms, libraries, dramatic societies, cinema, films, institutions for military training, scouting and girls guides, etc. Besides, a school education is definitely incomplete if it is not complemented by education at home. For this reason, it is now an axiom of education that parents and educators should be given opportunities to meet each other so that they can consider the problems of their wards and think up ways of solving them. Many schools now celebrate parents day in which the parents of educands come to the school, meet teachers and discuss the various problems that face both the parents and the educators. In addition to this, school must also take the assistance of the community in spreading education, because the school is a special association created by the community which passes its acquired and accumulated knowledge to the younger generation. Without the cooperation of the state, it is difficult to establish or maintain an educational institution. Not only does the state make arrangements for the training of teachers and establishment of various institutions of special education, it also provides financial help to institutions otherwise not concerned with it. Inspectors appointed by the government inspect even the non-government institutions in order to-ensure a uniform standard of education. In the absence of such control, most educational institutions would probably go to the dogs. In the field of higher education, most universities and research school are would probably stop work if the government did not establish national libraries and provide grants for the creation of local libraries. It is therefore evident, that the formal and informal means of education supplement each other's efforts, and both should be exploited to the fullest extent to help the cause of education.

Important Means of Education

The school is considered the most important agency of education on the basis of the following arguments:

Sole Agency. School is the sole agency of education, as this term is generally interpreted. It is difficult to call a person educated if it is known that he has never been through school or college. Even if the individual does not take the trouble of obtaining the highest degrees, had should have been to school to gain elementary knowledge of mathematics and language.

Only Media. Schools and educational institutions are believed to be the only media through which the national educational policy can be put into actual practice. When a national educational policy was laid down after independence in India, main attention was paid towards increasing the number of schools.

School and Family. Without the assistance of the school, the family cannot by itself perform the task of educating the child, and for this reason alone do parents send their children to schools. Earning one's livelihood is one important objective of education, and for this the child has no alternative but to go to the school. It is not at all surprising that family businesses and occupations should have come to an end and that women should also be going out of the home in search of jobs. In consequence, it is no longer possible for the parents to educate their children without external help. It is better therefore to leave this task to the school.

Real Education. Most of other means of education are capable of being turned to-ulterior use, of use as the means of spreading political thought of a particular type, while school is the only one which provides real education. Schools and colleges have no aim but education. Magazines, radio, films, newspapers, etc., can be perverted as; media of political propaganda of a definite school of thought. This reduces their importance as agencies of education.

Aiming Complete Development. School is the only education agency which seeks to develop the individual's body, mind, morale, religious thinking and spiritual contemplation. It aims at complete development. Most of the other agencies can hope to develop any one or the other aspects of a person's personality. Libraries and reading rooms provide only mental, education. The radio does not help in improving the body but school and colleges also provide opportunities for physical, mental, moral and spiritual development.

Conscious and Intentional Media. Schools are also the chief media of conscious or intentional education. Their sole aim is to provide education, just as it is the sole aim of the educators, men and women, who work there. These educators are professional people trained to education. These individuals devote much thought to the objectives and means of education, analyse the novel experiences which fall to their lot during the course of actual teaching, and make use of such experiences to improve their efficiency. No other individual can find or even hope to find so much time to devote to education. Neither is such a person an expert in teaching.

Obviously, the school should be accepted as the best medium of imparting education.

Must for Achievement. In the case of certain specialized forms of education, it is impossible to achieve anything in the absence of schools and colleges, for example, medical, engineering and technical education. Colleges are the only media of providing training in these specialised spheres and in academic learning at the highest level.

Twin Criteria. One criterion of the importance or an agency of education is the extent to which it makes a contribution to education, but another criterion is the possibility of its being substituted by another. If this criterion is applied to the various agencies of education, it will be seen that school is the only one for which there is no substitute, and hence it is indispensable. The state, family, library, cinema, social welfare centres, in fact, none of these agencies can hope to replace the school. Even if the child is educated within the family, such education is limited to primary education or training in the hereditary occupation. The family cannot provide more education than this. On the other hand, even if some agency of education is not available after formal education has been completed, the absence does not constitute such a great handicap. Hence, school is the most important agency of education.

Education within the Family

Every living being feels the necessity of having a home. Even birds and animals experience this need in their infancy. In the home, the parents look after the child and satisfy its needs, for the human child is the most helpless of all living beings. It is not possible for him to exist if he does not have a home. The infant is born in the home and he lives and develops is the home. For a fairly long period in the beginning, the child requires the care, protection and affection of his parents. They look after his physical requirements, protect him from danger, treat him in illness and socialize him into a human being.

Education is interpreted in two ways-restricted and liberal. In its liberal sense, it is taken to mean the comprehensive development of the child, while in its narrower sense it is taken to mean instruction. This instruction is given to the child by the educator, but in either sense, the earliest education is imparted to the child at home. Parents attend not only to the physical, mental, intellectual, moral and spiritual development of the child, but also guide him and give him instructions. All the greatest thinkers of the world have always agreed that the earliest education is given to the child by his mother. One Indian myth concerns the training imparted to Abhimanyu about the breaking of the siege, while he was still in the mother's womb. This myth seeks only to illustrate that the infant's education begins even while he is within his mother's womb. It is said that the foundation of Shivaji's's later greatness and bravery were laid by the stories of heroic deeds related to him in infancy by his mother Jeejabi. Rajasthani are among the bravest people in the world. If one were to analyse the biographies of all the greatest soldiers, religious preachers, philosophers, artists, thinkers and literary figures, one would realize the extent to which their greatness is due to the formative influence directed at them by their mothers. Even Mahatma Gandhi admitted that he owed his religious faith to his mother's religiosity.

Principles of Home Education

It is evident from the above account that the child's earliest education takes place at home. This education within the home has certain principles, although in this case principle implies those general rules on which such education is based. They are the following:

Balanced Physical Development. The aim of education is comprehensive development, an important part of which is the development of the body. Balance is the fundamental principle underlying bodily development. All the proponents of the golden mean wan against excess in any direction, but this statement does not apply to moral, religious and spiritual issues, for it is intended primarily for issues concerning the body. In this, attention must be paid to food, hygiene, exercise and rest, and striking a balance between all of them. Excess in anyone can lead to harm. In the case of food, it is necessary to take carbohydrates, proteins, salt, and most essential of all, vitamins. The child's food should contain a balanced amount of all these elements. Balance implies the need to determine the exact quantity of each element that is required for a particular child. Parents must also pay attention to the child's internal and external cleanliness because he is himself incapable of attending to such things. Hygienic care indulges regular movement of the bowels, cleaning the eyes, nose, ears, tongue, teeth, nails, cleaning the clothes with which the child comes into contact, and washing them at regular intervals. If the child is attacked by some disease he should be immediately taken to some capable doctor. In dress, more attention should be paid to the child's health and comfort than to fashion. Parents must also take care to protect the child from being seriously injured.

Independent and Complete Mental Development At birth, the child's mind does not possess one single trait but a multiplicity of instincts, tendencies and abilities, each one of which he seeks to express. Hence, it is necessary to see that the child, in its mental development, does not develop only on one side. His mental development must be rounded and complete. It is not desirable to repress any one of his tendencies. If necessary, these tendencies should be transformed. To take a simple example, the child expresses his natural curiosity about his surroundings in an unending series of questions which often makes his parents lose their patience and become annoyed. Any irritated and snubbing response to the child's queries will repress his curiosity and thus blunt the development of his mind. It is therefore desirable that the child's curiosity should be satisfied. Independence is also an essential of mental development. Every child has some peculiarities or special qualities, and if effort is made to force these qualities into some traditional pattern, it would inevitably lead to repression. Hence, modem educational psychologists are in favour of giving complete independence to the Child in respect of mental development. As long as the child does not indulge in actually anti-social activities, it is not desirable to shout at the child's smallest actions or words.

Natural Moral Development. Rousseau is of the opinion that the child's moral education takes place naturally. He expressed the view that when the individual adolescent is provided training in communal living and social relations, love becomes a controlling motive and thus moral perfection ana emotional development become the objectives. Hence in providing moral training, parents should avoid the too frequent repetition of negative commands telling the child not to do something. Instead, they should tell the child positively what he should do. Instead of telling the child not to quarrel with others, it is much better to tell him to love others. In this manner, the child's moral development should be natural, independent and not forced. The child instinctively wants the have and affection of his parents, and parents can take advantage of this and train him in doing things they like and teach him to avoid those they dont. But it must also be remembered that much of the child's moral development depends to a large extent upon the model presented to him in the form of the parents' own bahaviour and also upon the moral atmosphere created in the home. Hence, it is most important that these two elements should be improved, to begin with.

In considering these principles guiding the child's education at home, it is necessary to keep in mind that these principles are practical and temporary. In actual fact, child psychology provides the best guidance in this respect, and hence it is desirable that parents should haw knowledge of this. But all knowledge cannot be derived from books alone. The sensible parent will make his own experiment and decide what is best for his child and how the child is influenced by a particular pattern of behaviour.

Methods and Practice

The principles of home education suggest the methods by which they are put into practice. Some of the methods are:

Psychological Behaviour. The single most important factor in providing education to the child is psychological behaviour If one wants to teach the child something, one must know what the child himself is. This can be learnt with the help of psychology. In the absence of psychological knowledge, parents will fail to make an important contribution to their child's development, inspite of the best intentions. Psychological development has an important part to play in the child's mental and moral development. He should be taught the proper use of the various parts of his body only after considering his mental and psychological condition. It requires great patience and considerable knowledge of psychology to rid a chilli of his bad habits and to instill good habits in him.

Discipline. Discipline is an important aspect and method of home education. Since the child is ignorant of what is right and wrong, he cannot be permitted to do as he wishes because, left to himself, he is perfectly capable of playing with fire. Discipline means training the child in such a manner that it arouses in him a desire to obey the rules of the household. Once the child has been conditioned in this, it becomes unnecessary to check him frequently and make life easy for all concerned. The significance of discipline is realized only when one finds a number of children of almost the same age in one house. In the absence of discipline these children make a hell of the house with their constant quarrelling and shouting. If they are trained to be disciplined, each does his own work without interfering with others, and behaves affectionately towards the others. In order to establish discipline, the child should be lovingly persuaded, but such affectionate behaviour should not display weakness. Whatever is said must also be done. Otherwise the child attaches little value to the statements made by *the* parents. Self-discipline is of course best. Hence, the child should be convinced that he himself stands to benefit from discipline, in the absence of which his own independence and satisfaction are likely to be severely sustained. He will thus be ercouraged to discipline himself.

Provision of the Requisite Games. Games play a vital role in the child's development. Froebel has written, "Play is the purest, most spiritual activity of man at this stage, and at the same time typical of human life as a whole, of inner hidden natural life in man and all things. It gives, therefore, joy, freedom, contentment, inner and outer rest, peace with the world; it holds the source of all that is good." In this way games and sports help in the physical, mental, emotional, moral and aesthetic development of the child. Caldwell Cook has expressed the opinion that all the child's creative instincts are best manifested in play. Playing achieves development along with amusement and recreation, and if the child has sufficient and stimulating toys and games at home, there is no reason for him to roam around like an urchin in the streets. Among the games the child can profitably play are ludo, carrom, trade and other similarly stimulating games. In addition to the indoor games, provision should also be made for some games which can be played in some nearby playground, because physical exertion is necessary for the child's physical development. Among such games are cricket, kabaddi, football, kho-kho etc. One can choose from a variety of Indian and western games. When the child gets an opportunity to play he becomes too busy to bother his parents. In fact, if the parents provide him with new games from time to time, the child feels eternally obliged to them.

Systematic Daily Routine. A systematic daily routine does much towards the child's physical, mental and moral development. If the parents can develop in the child the habit of spending his days according to a set routine, this will not only have positive effects on his physical and mental development, it will also lay the foundations of a good moral character. But the child will learn to tive according to a routine only if his parents are also systematic in their behaviour. If they themselves sleep at midnight and get up at midday, there is little chance of their being able to persuade the child to sleep and wake early. It will then become difficult to maintain the child's health. The child should be taught to do things at the right time.

In the context of methods of home education, it must be remembered that almost any method can be adopted so long as it does not interfere with the natural and uninhibited development of the child's personality. Most of the methods recommended above are the result of experiments conducted by educationists, but parents themselves should make experiments in order to discover the method best suited to their own children. The truth of the matter is that the correct principles and methods of home education cannot be learnt from books. If the parents are naturally invested with love and patience, even the absence of theoretical knowledge will not hamper them. But the value of theoretical knowledge cannot be undermined for this reason. It has now come to be believed that people desirous of getting married and having children should first educate themselves in the task of looking after children.

Home Education and School Education

Home education and school education complement each other. The home is the child's first school. Homes in which the mothers are educated are good schools for children because mothers instill good habits in the children and also provide primary education to them. The child's primary education consists of learning the fundamentals of hygiene, exercising his body, listening to stories of good deeds and bravery so that the foundations of his character are laid, learning to live according to a routine, etc. Nursery classes in school also provide the same kind of education. If the mother is herself educated, all this work done in the nursery is done at home, and is often done much better than it can be done in school. The child is educated in his manners, cleanliness, mode of eating, behaving at the dining table, in maintaining a proper routine, etc. Educative stories told to the child have the advantage of stimulating his imagination and also laying a firm foundation for the development of good habits. In some homes the child is taught to develop an interest in gardening and botany. This is done by taking him around the garden. In many houses the child instinctively and unintentionally picks up some knowledge of the various professions practised by members of his family.

On the other hand, nursery also trains the child in hygienic living, in developing a routine, etc. In this way, the educators at home, in the nursery and school supplement the education of the child. Modern educationists are of the opinion that education is a continuous process that begins at birth and continues right through life. Since the child is born into the family, his education also begins there. The moral and religious education that he gets at home lays the foundation for the later moral and religious education he receives throughout his life. The truth of the matter is, that in the absence of cooperation from the family, no school can give adequate moral and religious education to the child. This accounts for the statement that the true aim of education remains unfulfilled in the absence of a home education. All the greatest artists, literary figures, philosophers and thinkers did not become great only on the strength of their school education, because the family also played a significant role in each case and it has some credit for their ultimate greatness. Even the child's spiritual education lacks completeness in the absence of home education because this aspect is influenced very much by the atmosphere at home. Briefly, both parents and professional educators educate the child, and both share the responsibility for his education.

Educators and Guardians

For the above reasons, modern educationists lay stress on cooperation between educators and guardians. In the absence of guardian's cooperation, the teacher, inspite of the greatest efforts, cannot successfully impart moral, religious, spiritual or even physical and mental education to the child. For every one of these kinds of education, he needs the enthusiastic help of the parents. This is explained by the fact that education is not a process which takes place for a few hours every day at a particular place. It continues at all times and at all places. The child receives education in the school, but in fact his education begins much earlier, before he comes to school, and continues even after he leaves school. Hence the extent of influence of the school education will depend largely upon the kind of education that has preceded it and the kind that will follow the school education. Sometimes the parents do not even know whether their child goes to the school after leaving home, or wastes his time loitering around the streets. Before getting the report of the annual examination, they do not know how their child is progressing at school. For this reason they can do nothing to counteract his weaknesses and help him.

Measures to Realise Cooperation. It is evident therefore that active cooperation between the educator and the parents is not merely desirable but essential. This cooperation can be obtained by the following measures:

Regular Reports Prepared by the Educator. Educators should regularly send a report of the child's progress in studies, mental, moral and physical development to the child's parents. Today, many of the modern schools follow this practice. This has the advantage of warning the parent about the weaknesses of his child so that he can make efforts to correct it.

Meeting of Educators and Parents. Many educationists have suggested that educators and parents should get together and constitute teacher-parent committees which should have meetings at regular intervals. During these meetings, problems should be brought forward which need the attention of both parents and educators. Discussion of such problems will create greater awareness of their respective responsibilities and also acquaint both parent and educator with each other's attitude. As a consequence, both will be able to plan how to remove a child's defects instead of merely throwing the blame for such faults on each other.

Parents Invited to School Programmes. Nowadays, almost all schools invite the parents of their students to attend cultural programmes and other collective activities of the students. The presence of the parents on such occasions helps to encourage the child, apart from opening the parents' eyes to their child's talents in the field of extra curricular activities. Besides, on such occasions a small sum can be charged as entrance fee in order to collect funds for the school, or they may even be asked to make contributions on such an occasion.

Personal Contact between Educator and Parents. The methods of educator and parent cooperation mentioned above can be helpful in solving the general problems of the students, but the individual problems of one child cannot be solved in this manner. For this, it is essential that the educator and the child's parents should come into direct, personal and individual contact. Through such contact, the educator and parent can exchange views on how to remove the child's difficulties.

It is evident from foregoing discussion that, in the interests of a proper education for the child, parents and educators should meet each other frequently. While the educators can take the first step in this direction, the active and enthusiastic cooperation of the parents is also essential. Fruitful results can be obtained only if both sides are enthusianstic, because both are responsible for completing the child's education.

14

Role of Peer Groups

According to *Oxford Concise Dictionary* peer means equal. Thus peer group is the group of equals. Such is a social group. A social is that aggregate of persons which is like a unit and whose members have some common aims, interests, stimulations and emotions together with mutual social relations and social interests, stimulations and emotions together with mutual social relations and social interactions. Through the medium of all these, members of a social group influence each other and are tied to each other. According to Bogardus, "A social group may be thought of as a number of persons two or more, who have some common objects of attention, who are stimulating to each other, who have common loyalty and participate in similar activities."

Chief Characteristics of Group-life

Just as to classify the group is a difficult task, similarly to point out the characteristics of group-life is also a difficult problem. Even then some characteristics of group-life can be described. They are as follows :

The Members of a Group are Related to Each Other. Simply a gathering of persons cannot be called a group. The members of the group should be inter-related. In fact, social relation is called a group. Cuber has written, "A group is any number of human beings in reciprocal communication." MacIver and some other sociologists have also admitted the social relations to be the fundamentals of the group-life.

Group Implies a Feeling of Unity. A feeling of unity is essential for every group. By virtue of such feeling, members of a group treat each other as their own and a sense of sympathy between them develops.

Members of a Group have Sense of We-feeling. By a sense of we feeling, the members of group help each other in performing their duties; and they defend collectively against the harmful powers. They treat others as the outsiders and try to make their group prosperous and self-sufficient.

The Interests of the Group Members are Common. A group includes those persons who are related to each other in such a way that they should be treated as one. For it, the interests of the persons of a group should tend to be common because, this similarity promotes unity.

There is Similarity of Behaviour in a Group. As the interests, ideals and values of the persons of a group are common, similarly, the behaviour of the persons also tends to be similar. A social group of persons, but it is a continuation of their behaviour.

Control of Group over the Actions of the Members. The main reason behind the similarity of behaviour in group-life is that actions of the members are controlled by the group. In each group there are some customs, norms and procedures which are acceptable to everyone and the dissenting members of the group given punishment. Even if the group fails to punish a person disobeying these, he shall be severely criticised by public. In this way, every one has to obey the social norms. In fact, without some norms, the existence of group life is practically impossible.

The Members of a Group are Affected by its Characteristics. Each group possesses some social characteristics which separate it from the similar and dissimilar groups. These characteristics affect the members constituting the group. The effect may be of different nature for different persons, but still all the members are affected by the group.

Common Values. Each caste has its own specific common values as help to distinguish it from other castes and also tie its members in the thread of unity. In this way, the social values of the Brahmins and the shudras, the Kshatriyas and the Vaishyas, can be seen differing considerably. The caste panchayats are very vigilant in enforcing the obedience to these social values and people who deviate from them or transgress their bounds are exterminated from the caste. They are subjected to social isolation and ostracism. They cannot again marry into the group. In a similar vein the example of family can also be considered. The social values of the members of a family are common and are traditionally respected and communicated to the succeeding generation ? They are dearly expressed in the mutual behaviour of the members. Thus, members of the social group are bound together in the tie of common values.

Mutual Obligation. The relationship between the members of a social group is-further strengthened through their mutual obligation beside their common social values. The family is a fine example of this. In the family, all the members have complementary obligations to each other. Children obey the orders of parents and try to conform to their desires. Husband and wife love each other. The husband fulfils the needs of the wife, while the wife obeys the orders of the husband besides co-operating with him in all activities. In this way, the members of the family are bound to each other by the tics of mutual obligation.

Mutual Expectations. In a social group, the members are entitled to expect love, sympathy and co-operation from others. In the family the husband expects his wife to love him while his wife expects reciprocation of this affection. When this desire is turned into despair, the family relationship is destroyed and divorce is imminent. In the same way, the parents expect iheir off-spring to accede to their wishes while the children expect from their parents love and sympathy coupled with help to rise in future. The disintegration of the family sets in when these desires are not fulfilled. While the family is a much close knit unit, even the neighbourhood is related to each member through mutual expectation. In all social groups the members have expectations from each other. If the people of one's own clan were not to share in one another's joys and sorrows, then what is the use of any clan.

All individuals hope that in times of joy and sorrow the people belonging to their clan will participate and render the occasion befitting of a social being. And so long as this mutual expectation is being fulfilled, the organization of the group is maintained intact. If in any school, the student were to refuse to show obedience to his teacher and the latter were to abstain from helping the student in his pursuit of knowledge, how long can such a school last ? thus, a social group retains its existence only as long as its constituent members fulfil their responsibility by satisfying the mutual desires among them.

The example of the family as a social group can serve to illustrate the forementioned characteristics of group life. Among the members of the family there are relationships such as husband-wife, father-son, brother-sister, etc., and all of them work for the interests of the family in a mood of a mutual co- operation. Each member treats every other member as his own, and despite all the differences that there may be between their attitudes and tendencies, they share some common ideals and values. It is because of the common interests that the family works as a well knit unit. Family control is exercised on each member. Disobedience of the laws of the family leads to serious altercations between the head of the family and the children while even the senior members do not escape censure. Each member bears the indelible stamp of his family characteristics. The characteristic is so prominent that the study of an individual's behaviour affords some due as to the type of family in which he must have been bred. These characteristics of the group life are to be found in other groups in greater or lesser degree.

Social organization is the organization of social group. And social groups are the units of social organization. Hence the organization and the disintegration of social organization is dependent upon the integration or disintegration of the social groups. The social groups, as is evident from the term applied to it, is a group the basis of which is social relationships. The family, for example, is a social group.

The above discussion of group life maybe useful in understanding how to create group life in school. Social consciousness can be created by arranging social programmes. Guardians may also be invited to participate in several such functions. Group songs and group parade is also useful. Celebration of national festivals in school affects the tone of social life. This tone is improved by means of discipline, cooperation, moral level and mutual relationships. The teachers should present good examples and improve their relations with the students.

Leadership and Education

In the analysis of leadership, the greatest importance, from the practical viewpoint,.is that of the qualities of leadership. While this knowledge of the qualities of a leadership on the one hand reveals the kind of person the leader is, it also, on the other hand, shows the qualities that an individual should possess if he wants to become a leader. Once again, different scholars have attributed different qualities to leaders. Some of the important view will be described here.

Constituents of Leadership. In connection with leadership, Pigors regards the following as indispensable:

1. Common cause 2. Leader 3. Follower 4.Present situation.

Allport's Classification. Allport has included the following in the qualities of leadership: 1. Trait of ascendance, 2. Physical power, 3. High mobility, 4. Erect, aggressive carriage, 5. Tonus, 6. Tenacity 7. Face to face mode of address, 8. Reinforcement of energy, 9. Restraint, 10. Inscrutability, 11. Expansiveness in the field of action, 12. High intelligence, 13. Understanding, 14. Keenly susceptible to social stimulation, 15. Tact, 16. Zeal, 17. Social participation, 18. Character, 19. Drive.

Coffins's Classification. Charles Bird has recounted no less than 79qualities in a leader, but in this long list of qualities, many of the qualities have been repeated. Coffin has tried to place these qualities in some limited classes. According to Coffin, the qualities of a leader can be included in the following classes:

Intelligence. Sharp intellect, insight, intellectual far-sightedness, skill and acuity.

Moral Sensitivity. Honest, just, proper decision, benevolent viewpoint, moral outlook, selfless and idealistic, love of truth.

Imagination. Originality, imagination, foresight, curiosity, comprehensive interests and flexibility.

Restraint. Restraint, self-control and profundity.

Drive and Determination. Inspiration, enthusiasm, mobile or dynamic personality, candidness, aggression, desiring name and fame, bravery, determination, patience, concentration, the tendency to pursue to an end.

Responsibility. Respected, candid, charactered, believable, organized, aware of. duties, lover of work, concentrated.

Self-reliance. Awareness of purpose and direction, self reliance, confidence, the ability to take decision, enthusiasm and unvarying decision.

Dynamic Physical Characteristics. Physical power, shape, ability, tonus, straight body, etc.

Imperturbability. Balance, optimism, benevolence, patience, decisive, energetic and positive nature.

Social Responsiveness. Adaptability of social motivation, taking part in social activities, friendliness, affection, sociability, extrovert tendency and influence of other.

Easy Maintenance of Good Relation with Others. Acuity, sympathy, co-operation, humanity and a knowledge of human nature.

Coffin has further done the job of making these 11 classes even more brief by dividing all the qualities into 3 classes -

Planning. 1. The ability to know problems 2. The ability to evolve plans for solving these problems.

Organization. 3. The ability to organize the necessary objects and individuals to ensure the success of the plans. 4. The ability to organize the entire system and have it function as one unit. 5. The ability to introduce sudden changes.

Persuasion. 6. the ability of distributing responsibility among different individuals for the implementation of the plan. 7. The ability of successfully examining the entire plan.8. The ability of keeping his own control on the entire system of organization.

Traits of the Leader

From the various opinions on the different qualities which a leader should necessarily possess that have been described above, it is evident that it is not sufficient for the leader to be the master of only physical qualities. Here it must be remembered that in the animal world the most powerful animal is the leader but in human society physical power alone is not sufficient. Yet the importance of the qualities of physical power and an attractive personality is not inconsiderable. One can often see intellectual ability and attractive personality is not inconsiderable. One can often see intellectual ability and attractive physical personality going together in the human leader. By his experiments, Partridge has proved that all the individuals who scored the highest in the Army Alpha tests, were tall, attractive and of an independent nature. This view, held by Partridge is one sided, because one often finds a complete lack of physical charm in intellectual giants and leaders. One only need by reminded of Socrates and Chanakya. On the other hand, it would be equally incorrect and baseless to state that in the modern world, only intellectual achievements are enough to bring leadership to an individual. Actually, in order to become leader, an individual should be possessed of many qualities of the personality and in particular skill in behaving, in addition to physical and intellectual qualities.

Education for Leadership

But the mere fact of the existence of these qualities in an individual is not sufficient an insurance of successful leadership. It is true that the leader possesses in innate form the qualities of leadership, but as Plato observed correctly they also require to be educated. In a democracy, leaders can be discovered and created through the medium of education and public programmes. For this, responsible tasks should be entrusted to the men and women of the younger generation. They should be given the opportunity of coming forward and expressing themselves, Youth festivals should be organized in order that the youngsters may be able to display their qualities. In this way, when there will always be new leaders to replace the older and retiring leaders, the society and the nation will be able to progress constantly and at a fast pace.

15

Goal of National Integration

Emotional Integration

The unity of a nation depends upon the extent to which its various members look upon themselves as members of the same group. National unity does not automatically follow upon living within the same geographical boundaries. Emotional integration is necessary for this unity. As is evident from the term itself, emotional integration is the unity. Identity or similarity of emotions. If it exists, then individuals feel related to and concerned with each other, despite any external differences. It is emotional integration which keeps members of a family organised. In colleges, this emotional integration is generated through various communal programmes. It promotes a sense of community and impedes the progress of disorganizing tendencies.

In India one finds marked differences in the living standards, dress, customs, religion, culture, etc., of the various people existing in different parts. India's large size is emphasized by these differences, but one result of this is that when a person goes from one part of the country to another he is almost a foreigner there. This has led to regionalism, expressed in the desire of people of one region to promote their own regional interest at the expense of the interests of other regions. Regionalism has gained tremendous momentum because it has been linked with linguism. Linguism is the prejudice of the speakers of a particular language to develop their language, to the detriment of any and all other languages spoken in different parts of the country. Casteism or racial distinction between the Hindus and Muslims has led to deterioration of social organisation in the country. Untouchability is an offshoot of casteism. Religious communities have been known to come into violent conflict with each other, thus leading to considerable damage to public and private property, and bloodshed on a large scale. Communalism is responsible for the hatred which one religious group fosters for another. Putting it briefly, regionalism, linguism, casteism, communalism, etc., are the disruptive and disorganising influences which have divided Indian society into various groups. It is impossible to hope for a solution of these problems in.the absence of emotional integration. And, if these problems remain unsolved, democracy will also remain a dream.

Unity in Diversity

Generally speaking, the extent of diversity found in India tends to create the impression that it is not a country but a subcontinent. But this does not imply that unity or integration is impossible in such a situation. One finds distinct and different racial characteristics among the inhabitants of different parts of the country, because differences of complexion, size, shape, etc., are dearly evident. It can be clearly seen that there is a gradual decline in the physical stature of the inhabitants as one moves from Punjab to Assam. If other examples are necessary, if can be seen that there are all kinds of complexions in this country. In the north complexion varies from darkly whitish, dark, yellow to red and even runs into mixtures of these colours. Inhabitants of the Andamans are jet black while those of the South Dravidians is a shining black, in direct contrast is the rosy white complexion of the Kashmiris. Turningto languages, one finds that the Indian constitution has granted recognition to Urdu, Bengali, Assamese, Oriya, Punjabi, Gujrati, Marathi, Sindhi and numerous other languages, in addition to Hindi, Besides, Telugu, Kananda, Tamil and Malayalam have been accepted as the four Dravid languages. Sanskrit has also been given special consideration, as the original Aryan language. Differences exist not only at the level of language but also in respect of dress, religion, culture, etc. Tribes of the north east, central districts and the south differ from each other in their modes of life, their social and psychological characteristics, etc., to such a great extent that one can find among them different cultural and social regions. If one travels from east to west, and then back again, one will find clearly perceptible differences in complexion, dress, customs, modes of life, dietary habits and other aspects of culture, even at very short distances. But despite these differences of region, race, language, tribe, etc., the existence of a national unity cannot be questioned. One finds this inner unity or integration in all the people spread over the land limited by Himalayas on the one side and the Indian Ocean on the other, the Burma Hills on the east and Pakistan on the west. This inner unity is the basis of emotional integration. Despite the more obvious and superficial differences, prosperity increases. It is this inner unity which Sir Herbert Rizlcy described when he commented that, at the root of the apparent diversity of physical and social type, language, custom and religion that immediately strikes the observer coming to India, is a definite similarity or identity or inner unity of life from the Himalayas to Cape Comorin. This inner integration or unity is the basis of Indian culture. All the saints of the past were aware of this unity, although they were no less aware of the obvious differences. It is for this reason that India has always been treated as a single unit, even in the remote past. It has been customary to refer to all the people residing in different parts of the country as Indians, even though one could see the differences of religion, culture, languages, etc. In fact, the very name Bharatvarsha denotes not merely geographical boundaries but actually the ideal of a cultural unity. During the Middle Ages, India was always treated as one unit. That India is accepted as the mother by all Indians is only due to a feeling of oneness and identity.

Increasing Emotional Integration

It was this question of integration which inspired the Central Education Ministry in 1961 to organise a committee for integration under the chairmanship of Dr. Sampurnanand. This campaign to increase integration had the solid foundation of belief in the principle of unity in diversity. All that is needed is that the younger generation should be educated in this direction through various kinds of programmes. Speaking at the inauguration of the Indian Integration Committee, Sri K. L. Shrimali, explained the significance of education and commented that if we want to generate a national consciousness in our people, we will have to plan our education accordingly. Education must be so designed as to encourage each participant to think of himself as a responsible part of the Indian nation. Education must take upon itself the responsibility of awakening the younger generation to the truth that, despite obvious external differences, all Indians are the same, emotionally.

Keeping in mind the objective outlined above, the Integration Committee gave the following suggestions:

Reorganisation of Syllabi. In order to reorganise and reshape the syllabi of colleges and universities to accord with the needs of the nation, the committee made the following suggestions:

(i) At the primary stage, stress should be laid upon nationalistic stories, poems, songs, etc.

(ii) At the secondary stage, in addition to the other subjects being taught, special attention should be given to the study of national literature, social studies, moral and religious guidance and extra-curricular activities.

Encouragement to Extra Carricular Activities. Besides imparting formal knowledge to the students, the teachers must provide them with the opportunity to take part in such extra curricular activities which are important from the standpoint of emotional integration. Besides, such programmes, must also represent the entire nation. Such programmes help in the development of 'we' feeling, a feeling of unity and sympathy. One example of such programmes is the Inter University cultural festivals, in which teachers and students participate from all parts of the country.

Improvement of Text Books. It is desirable that text books on various subjects, and especially on history, should be amended and improved. They should be designed to encourage a sense of emotional unity with people living in other parts of the country. This will also help to check the growth of communal feelings. But it should also be remembered that such amendments should not be made at the cost of truth because such violence to truth is not necessary. That the country is one is an undeniable truth. What is required is an expression of this truth.

Improvements Concerning Language and Script. In this connection the committee on Emotional Integration made the following recommendations:

1. The use of the Roman script should be permitted to increase knowledge of Hindi in certain areas.
2. International numerals should be used in every part of the country.
3. Arrangements should be made to teach the Devanagri script where it is not known.
4. Hindi text books should also be provided in the regional scripts. Dictionaries using both Hindi and the regional languages should also be prepared.
5. At the university level, study of Hindi and English literatures should be encouraged so that integration is encouraged and divisive forces checked.
6. The rights of the minorities should be protected in formulating a language policy.

In addition to the above list of suggestions; the committee for Emotional Integration also made certain other suggestions. In schools the daily programme should be started after a community prayer and a ten minute talk, either by the principal or by some respected person, on some subject which may encourage emotional integration. Another way of encouraging emotional integration is to organise a mass meeting of the school once a year and asking the students to take an oath to increase emotional integration. Besides, all subjects and activities likely to lower awareness of differences should be encouraged. In this manner it is possible to create a climate in which all people feel that they are members of one nation. On the negative side, all efforts must be made to destroy all elements which tend to obstruct the growth of emotional integration.

Suggestions for Improving Emotional Integration

A part from the suggestions outlined above, education can be used in the following suggested ways for improving integration in the country:

Development of an All India Language. The first condition for increasing emotional integration in the country is that an All India language should be evolved. Hindi is the only language capable of performing this role. Hence, it is desirable that knowledge of this language be made compulsory for every citizen. Government should extend every facility for developing Hindi literature. The development of a national language will not prejudice the interests of regional languages. They should be allowed to pursue their own course. But all communications between the Centre and the States should be conducted in the all-India language. Applicants for administrative jobs in the government should be required to know Hindi, although they may be allowed to take the examination in their regional language.

An All India Education Policy. Education is the most effective tool for spreading emotional and national integration. For this reason a national educational plan should be devised. This plan should aim at providing every child with knowledge of the ideas of great men, poets, leaders, religious thinkers, etc. Text books should be prepared under the supervision of the Central government and provided by it, so that the younger generation may be brought up in an atmosphere of nationalistic conditions of working should be common all over the country. The same syllabi should be applicable to all institutions in the country at the primary, secondary and university levels. All-India organisations like the N.C.C., Scouting, Girl Guides, etc., should be given appropriate encouragement. University education should be through the medium of the national language, even if the students are permitted to answer questions in their mother tongues. In this manner, the objective of national unity or integration can be achieved by evolving an All-India educational plan.

Programmes for Increasing National Unity. Many kinds of programmes can be devised for increasing national unity. For example, the cinema can be used to spread the feeling of national unity. Radio and television can also be used equally effectively. All-India competitions and meetings can be organised in various parts of the country to increase national unity. Such programmes help people living in different parts of the country to meet residents of other parts and learn through ideas and understand them. Travel facilities should be made more common and delegations and tours encouraged. During the last few years special trains made up of farmers of different areas, students and members of parliament toured the entire country. This helped the cause of national integration. Other programmes similar to these can be organised.

Development of Intercultural Understanding. In all the programmes outlined above, intercultural understanding will be promoted. This helps people to achieve liberality of attitudes to other cultures, an essential precondition of national unity in a country in which there are many cultures.

Role of Teachers. Success of most of these programmes for increasing national unity depends upon teachers. As long as the teachers themselves do not rise above their petty narrow-mindedness and create ideals, there is little hope of the students developing any emotional unity. Hence, it is desirable that national consciousness should first be stirred in the students. For this, teachers from various parts of the country should be encouraged to meet each other. This can be done through the All-India Teachers organisation. Even otherwise, most of the problems may be solved through exchange of ideas. At the same time, a national consciousness will awaken in them. Yet, attention must be paid to forestalling the development of a class consciousness among the teachers. The government can make a positive contribution in this direction by organization of lectures from time to time and distributing literature of this kind.

Government Efforts. Governmental effort, is essential for bringing success to all the projects outlined above, because without official blessing, there is little that education can achieve. This cannot be doubted because there are many agencies which are working against the development of emotional integration. So long as the government fails to check agencies which encourage linguism, communalism, religious bigotry, and other disruptive forces, education will not be able to achieve the goal. One of the first steps in this direction is control over destructive political parties. In every part of the country laws should be enacted to prevent any individual from giving expression to linguism, communalism, regionalism, casteism, untouchability, etc. This should be followed up by a strict application of these laws.

It is evident from the foregoing description of the measures for increasing natural integration that these measures must be both positive and negative. Adoption of all these measure would be a positive step. The negative step of destroying all obstacles in the way of emotional integration is no less important. For this, teachers, administrators and guardians will have to work collectively. Then alone the country will witness solid natural integration inspite of regional pluralism.

Significance of Nation

Nation can be defined as that human group which lives in an area with clearly defined geographical boundaries, united by common traditions, common interests and common sentiments, possessing a desire for unity and common political ambitions. Elements which go to make up the nation are of two kinds - the objective and the subjective. Among the objective elements are geographical unity, of language, unity of race, a common religion, political unity and independence. But the subjective elements are of greater significance. According to Renan and Mill, it must also possess consciousness of a glorious past, feelings of pride and shame, happiness and pain, common experience and sacrifice, true glory, allied to this past. The chief among these emotive elements are common interests and traditions, common political ambitions, and, most important of all, a community feeling, or we feeling.

Nationality and Education

Community feeling or we feeling is such an important constituent of nationhood, that MacIver has defined nationality in terms of this feeling. He defines nationality as a kind of community feeling that has its origin in certain historical circumstances and which is also strengthened by such strong common psychological factors that individuals who experience it desire to form a specific and even an individual government of their own. Oppenheimer has commented that consciousness of nationality makes the nation.

This consciousness of nationality is generated in the younger generation through education, and hence there is a profound relationship between nationality and education. In India, when the revolt against the British government was awakened, all national leaders demanded the formation of a national educational programme. They argued that the educational programme of the country should be modified to suit the requirements of the nation.

In 1921, Mahatma Gandhi expressed his views on this subject in *Young India,* criticising the existing educational pattern introduced by the British people. He too demanded that the educational pattern must be modified to suit the demands of the nation. His reasons for adding manual work to education were sound since he knew that educand must pay its own way in a poor country like India. Rabindra Nath Tagore conducted an experiment in Shantiniketan to produce a novel kind of human society in which the problems of the individual and the community, the nation and the world, could be solved simulataneously. Swami Dayananda insisted upon reforming education to suit the education pattern that existed in ancient times. On the other hand, Annie Besant's educational plan, which included the establishment of primary schools, lower middle schools, higher middle schools, high schools for general education, high schools for general science, commercial schools, technical high schools, agricultural high schools, etc., as more directly in touch with the problems of contemporary India. Madan Mohan Malviya established the Hindu University at Kashi in order to realize the ideals of education which prevailed in ancient India. In addition to these individual and specific efforts, all other educational philosophers of the time, including Sri Aurobindo, Vivekananda, etc., favoured the modification of the educational pattern in order to make it conform to ancient Indian values, ideas and thinking. In more recent times, in his report of the Universities commission, Dr. S. Radhakrishnan pointed out the defects of the existing pattern of education, and suggested that it should be refashioned to fulfil national needs. It is only because of the feeling of nationality that most educationists have objected to the use of English as a medium of instruction in the country. Every one has stressed the need for education to be a character building process, because without this the future of the nation will always remain dark. Dr. S. Radhakrishnan has said that the future of the nation is made by character. No country can be great if its inhabitants have low characters. If we want to create a great nation, we must educate our young men and women in such a manner that they should possess the force of character. We must have men and women who see themselves reflected in other human being. This has been said in our sacred texts.

Stressing the need for an education for nationality the Kothari Education Commission has said that the objective of our system of education be to develop national consciousness. For this we must develop the knowledge of our cultural heritage, but we must also submit this cultural heritage to revaluation. At the same time we must have faith in the future towards which we are moving.

Development of Nationalism

The following suggestions can be given for generating nationalism in the younger generation:

Development of a National Language. The first prerequisite for developing nationalism is the development of a national language in the country. In India, this position can be occupied only by Hindi. When the succeeding generation will learn Hindi and use it, the feeling will gradually take root that India is one nation.

Development of a National Literature. Development of a national language will lead to the development of a national literature. With the propagation of Hindi in every part of the country, a new literature will be created, which will be read everywhere. Apart from encouraging national unity, it will also enable the people to create a literature which encourages national power and protects the cultural heritage of the country.

National Educational Programme. In India the spread of education is the responsibility of both the central and the state governments but as yet, it has not been possible to formulate a national programme of education with the result that one can see considerable disparity in the various parts of the country. In order to evolve a feeling of nationalism the country should have unified educational programme which should be flexible enough, to take within its purview the differences that exist between one region and another. This will lead to a certain similarity in the education in-all parts, and make possible the application of a single curriculum through which national literature on the all India scale can be created.

Observance of National Festivals. The feeling of nationalism can also be strengthened by enthusiastic observance of national festivals, independence day, republic day, children's day, teacher's day and the birthdays of all great men.

Respect for National Symbols. Another way of fostering the feeling of nationalism is to generate and show respect for national symbols such as the national anthems, the national flag, the national bird, etc. Now-a-days the national anthem is played after every film show and people are required to stand at attention to show their respect for it. This also helps growth of national sentiment.

Improvements of Curriculum. In order to help the development of the national sentiment, it is desirable that the teaching of history, civics, etc., should be conducted in such a way that it helps national sentiment. This can be done by preventing the publication of any material in text books and other media of publication which hurts national sentiments and pride. The government seizes all copies of such material and punishes the publishers and authors.

Cooperation of Political Parties. It is impossible to generate nationalism if the political parties fail to cooperate. Many political parties not only hinder the growth of this sentiment, but actively engage in activities calculated to harm the national interest. Such political parties owe their allegiance to other nations, show no respect for national symbols and spread anti national feelings among the people. As far as possible political parties should be prevented from indulging in such activities.

Cooperation of Teachers. Education for nationalism can never be really successful without the active co-operation of teachers. For this. reason the educators must themselves possess this feeling, because then they set an example for the educands. It will then be even easier to foster the national sentiment among the younger generation.

Synthesis of Nationalism and Internationalism

Nowadays many thinkers object to the use of education for fostering the national sentiment because they have come across many bad effects of narrow nationalism in many countries and seen that education for nationalism has stood in the way of the growth of internationalism. The education for nationalism that was given in Italy and Germany, for example, was completely opposed to internationalism. It is in connection with this one-sided education that Bertrand Russell pointed out that children are taught to exhibit complete devotion and worship to the state of which they are citizens. The lesson taught to them is that worship of the state consists in doing as directed by the state. For this they are taught distorted versions of history, politics and economics so that they should not be critical of the blind national faith expected of them. They are acquainted with the evil actions of other nations but not of their own, although the truth is that each nation has been unjust to other nations. It is unquestionably true that if the facts of history are distorted in order to propagate the sentiment of nationalism it is undesirable. But this danger is not peculiar to nationalism alone. It is true of most human relations that as they become deeper and stronger they also become narrower, and that they impede the growth of any liberal attitude. If, for example, an individual has intense love for his family, this may come in the way of his loving his nation, but this does not imply that love for nation can exist only at the cost of love for family. Proper and healthy love for the family does not impede love for the nation, it helps it to grow. In the same way healthy nationalism also does not preclude the possibility of internationalism. As Dr. Louise has said that it is essential to strengthen one's love for one's motherland, but this does not make it proper to violate the canons of humanity, for the external benefit of one's own nation. It is obvious, therefore, that education must not only propagate nationalism but must also encourage internationalism. The plan for national education presented by such eminent educationists as Mahatma Gandhi, Sri Aurobindo, Vivekananda, Rabindra Nath Tagore, etc., has kept this in view, that nationalism and internationalism should grow harmoniously. That is the reason why Rabindra Nath Tagtore's Shantiniketan turned into an ideal institution for education in internationalism. According to Tagore the educand's aim is to reach the level at which there is no distinction between nationalism and internationalism.

Obstacles in the Development of Nationalism

The progress and growth of nationalism in India is being impeded by certain elements and obstacles, the more important among which are the following:

Casteism. Cesteism is the most restricted of narrow interests. As a result of this, not only the country but even Hindu society has been fragmented into small pieces, each one of which is concerned only with preserving its own interests, without caring for those of other groups. In the presence of this casteism. nationalism is a far cry. Even the unity of the Hindu social organisation is difficult to maintain. Hence, it is necessary to get rid of casteism, although it is not necessary for this to destroy the caste system.

Regionalism. In contemporary India, regionalism and regional loyalties have spread so much that even the political unity of the country is being threatened. Some states have expressed the desire to secede from the Union, because they believe themselves to be separate nations. Such tendencies should be suppressed with a strong hand because otherwise unity may be damaged beyond repair.

Communalism. In India today, there are still many Muslims who do not accept India as their country. At the root of this is communalism. and because of their blind faith in their own community they believe the country to belong to Hindus, although it belongs to everybody. It is impossible to evolve nationalism without first putting an end to the mutual distrust of the different communities. For this active steps must be taken in educational institutions.

Linguism. Another expression of the disorganizing influence at work in the country is linguism. With independence came the problem of deciding a national language, because a national language is essential for maintaining the unity of the nation. Compared to other languages Hindi is best equipped to fulfil this role, but many people object to this because of narrow political interests. In addition, the people of some states are not willing to accept any language but their own. This controversy turned violent and led to considerable bloodshed. An early solution of this problem is desirable if nationalism is to foster in the country.

Classism. Most people in India create distinctions among themselves on the basis of economic and social classes. Communist influence has encouraged class hatred to such an extent that various classes fight for their own interest, even at the cost of the national interest. Class interest is also manifested in the form of untouchability. This class struggle is a serious impediment to the growth of national sentiment, and it must be eliminated from the minds of the younger generation.

The purpose behind recounting these obstacles to national sentiment is to point out that both negative and positive steps must be taken. Nationalism can be spread among the younger generation by following the suggestions given earlier and also by removing these hindrances. Mutual cooperation between the people, government and educators is of the essence. It is impossible to improve the country's future without increasing the sentiment of nationalism, irrespective of industrial and scientific progress. The future of the nation is dark unless a high national character of the people is formed.

The Casteism

Casteism is a blind group loyalty towards one's own caste or subcaste which does not care for the interests of other castes and seeks to realise the social, economic, political and other interests of its group. This definition of casteism includes all the preceding definitions of the concept and tends to clarify further the political aspect of casteism.

Causes of Casteism

Now-a-days casteism is at its height in India, the culmination of many causes. Some of the causes follow:

Sense of Caste Prestige. The most important cause of casteism is the desire of people belonging to a particular caste to enhance the prestige of their caste and in so doing see no wrong in adopting even the most downgraded and deleterious methods. But the prestige of the caste.can be maintained only on the ground that every opportunity be availed of in order to improve the social status of members. In order to achieve this objective every caste provides its members with all possible privileges in order to raise their social status. This tends to increase casteism.

Marriage Restrictions. The second cause that encouraged the development of casteism is the restrictions on marriage that prevail in Hindu society. Under the caste system the restrictions that apply to marriage 'turn every caste into a monogamous group in which each individual looks upon himself as related in some way to all the others and for this reason everyone pays proper attention to the interests of others. Such action encourages casteism.

Urbanization. With the advent of the tendency to urbanization, it became possible for all castes to collect in large numbers in towns. At the same time the lives of members of various castes became beset with problems as a result of which it became necessary to provide security for them on a communal basis. Casteism is spreading because of the necessity to fulfil this need for security.

Increase in the Means of Transport and Propaganda. One factor that has assisted the development of casteism is the increase in the means of both transport and propaganda because this improvement has led to the establishment of relations between members of a caste wjp were previously sepated because of distance. And the feeling of casteism is being rapidly propagated through the medium of newspapers and communal magazines.

Remedies of Casteism

The following are some suggestions concerning the solution of the problems arising out of casteism.

Proper Education. The greatest need for a solution of the problem of casteism is proper education. The educational institutions should be able to provide an atmosphere in which caste distinctions are not encouraged while at the same time the children are allowed to develop a distaste for this kind of discrimination. A healthy point of view in the public for casteism can thus be generated. Casteism can be destroyed only by the development of new psychological tendencies and behaviour patterns.

Inter-caste Marriage. A nother way of combating the continuing increase in casteism is the encouragement of intercaste marriages. Intercaste marriage provides an opportunity for two families belonging to different castes to come together not only for two individuals, one male and other female, to do so. In this way, the seed of casteism shall be unable to strike root and even if it does the resulting sapling will be so weak that it will be subsequently wiped out.

Lesser Use of the 'Caste' Name. One way of solving the problem of casteism is to make less frequent use of the 'caste' name so that there may be no traces of it left in the mind of the impressionable children and they should not be imbued with the idea of caste distinction. In this way, at least it will become possible to destroy the notion of casteism in the coming generations.

Cultural and Economic Equality. Another way of facing the problem of casteism is to introduce cultural and economic equality in the minds and the lives of the various castes. Inequality in the sphere of cultural and economic welfare between the races promotes jealousy and competition among them which later assumes the form of casteism. Hence the. restoration of cultural and economic equality of the various castes is an important step towards the abolition of casteism from the society.

India's independence was announced on 15th August 1947 and it was on that day that in every corner of the country Hindus and Muslims shed each other's blood, The inhuman behaivour seen during this communal rioting has probably no equal in the entire history of the world. Entire villages were set on fire and living children were thrown into the conflagration; women were taken in processions being beaten with whips while they were naked. At many places entire trainloads of human beings were butchered. Millions were rendered homeless while millions of others lost their property and earnings; but the worst part of the whole deal is that in spite of such a costly and terrible sacrifice communal tensions have not beėn put to an end. It is only recently that there were communal ritings in Bengal and other states. This spark is one that is apt to catch fire at any moment. There are some particular causes at its root. Knowledge of the ways in which communalism can be removed from the country can be had after these causes are known.

Causes of Communalism

The following are the main causes of communal tension:

Geographical Causes. One main cause of communalism is a geographical one. There is much communal tension wherever the Hindus, Muslims, Christians and others live in separate sections because the modes of life and conduct of the different religious groups exhibit wide differences.

Historical Causes. Another important cause of communal tension is of a historical nature. It is an established historical fact that Muslims religionists came to India as foreigners and started converting Hindus to Islam with the force of the sword. Many of the muslim rulers inflicted much injustice and misery on the Hindus while on other hand, some Hindu kings reacted in an equally violent manner to these activities on the part of the Muslim kings. There came occasions, however, on which the Hindus and the Muslims co-operated with each other. In the war of freedom of 1857, Hindus and Muslims made a combined effort to win the freedom of the country. In the Indian National Congress, and the Indian National Army the Muslims stood by the Hindus in opposing the British but in both the communities many people have been unable to forget the past in which the dictatorship ofAurangzeb posed a threat to the very existence of Hindu religion by his injustice and cruelty. There was a time when the Muslim women of Punjab and Kashmir quietened their children by making them think of Harishingh Nalva. This had the cumulative result of maintaining communal tension. And not only this, some people went so far as to form political parties based on communal interests which indulged in all sorts of petty quarrels! They also inflamed the minds of both the communities against each other. The Muslim League demanded the formation of Pakistan. Pakistan was formed and yet communal tensions were not relieved in any manner of speaking.

Psychological Causes. The main causes of communal tensions are of a psychological nature. Communal rioting breaks out between the Hindus and the Muslims in the country whenever the hatred and disgust that they have for each other reaches fever heat. There are some deceptive and misleading dogmatic concepts at the root of this mutual hatred. Hindus are prone to believe that the Muslim is a born traitor while the Muslims feel that they are in constant danger from the Hindus. Tension increases because of fallacious thoughts based on ignorance.

Social Causes. Some social causes also promote communal tension. Even today there are many restrictions that hinder any profound relationship between the Hindus and the Muslims. The Muslims slaughter cows and this injures the religious feeling of the Hindus while the Hindus find it objectionable to form too close a relationship with the Muslims because they profess a different religion. Many of the customs respected by the two stand in complete contradiction. Hindus grow their religious tuft of hair which the Muslims do not. There respective dresses differ widely. In washing hands the Hindus pour the water so that it proceeds from the direction of the elbow to that of the wrist while the Muslims so pour it that it flows from the wrist to the elbow. These things are insignificant but because of them the two are prone to look at each other as slightly mad. At present intercaste marriages are exceptions in the country and it is unthinkable for the people to think in terms of marriages between different religious groups.

Remedies of Communalism

A study of the forementioned causes of communal tensions provides a clue to the means to their solution. The following are the important ways of eliminating communal tensions:

Propagation of the National History. If communal tensions are to be eliminated it is necessary that those aspects and times in history should be emphatically propagated in which the Hindus and Muslims combined to act in the interests of the nation and made sacrifices to this end. The employment of this measure will serve to vitiate the historical causes of communal tensions while it will simultaneously encourage nationalist emotions.

Mutual Contact. In order to remove the psychological causes at the root of communal tensions it is necessary to improve the mutual contacts between the two communities. Youth organisations should he formed in every village and every town in which the youths of every community should participate and actively take part in different programmes. In addition to this other associations of this kind can also be formed in which members of the different communities get the opportunity to meet and know each other.

Discouraging Communal Parties. The government should keep a vigilant and stern eye on the activities of the communal parties while it should be progressively tried to put an end to these parties. In India many communal parties promote communalism while acting in the guise of cultural and religious association. The government should attend to them, and if found, they should immediately be stopped.

Formation of Healthy Public Opinion. Newspapers, lectures, radio programmes and the cinema should be utilised in forming a healthy national public opinion and for this the instruments of communal propaganda should be declared illegal.

Encouragement to National Festivals. In the country the national festivals and occasions should be encouraged in such a manner as to enable people of all communities to participate to the fullest extent. What can be done in this direction is to declare the important festivals of both communities such as Holi, Diwali, Id, etc., to be national festivals so that Hindus and Muslims should both take part. This mutual contact will help to reduce communal tensions.

From the foregoing treatment of the various method of eradicating or at least lessening communal tensions it is evident that in this direction it is necessary to resort to all social, scientific and psychological methods. It is necessary to make a concerted effort. Both the government as well as the people will have to co-operate if any success is to be achieved in this direction. The element of communalism has been in the country for such a long time that great effort will have to be made if this poisonous weed is to be removed.

The Regionalism

Of course, regionalism has always been present in India in one or the other form but never has it attained such magnitude as it possesses today and neither was it ever as-detrimental to any national interest as it is in the present context. When there were so many states in the country it was not harmful to have regionalism in them but when the entire country has become one nation, regionalism poses a serious threat to national unity and integration.

Regionalism is the sense of affection and attachment for people belonging to one's own region and hatred for those who belong to some other region. As a result of this, people of one region in India have started looking at people from some other part of the country in the same light in which they are prone to regard foreigners. They want that only people of their own area should run the government in their region while they do not want to make anyplace for people who have migrated from some other region irrespective of the period for which they may have been living there. In this way, some people have demanded the formation of a separate state of Nagaland in the Naga area. The Akali party of Punjab has demanded the formation of a Punjabi suba. It was on the basis of region that the state of Bombay was divided into two separate states, those of Gujrat and Maharashtra. In addition to these antics of the politicians some people are demanding that the South should be formed into an entirely separate unit. India is a union of states. The functions of government have been divided between the central government and the respective state governments. All these states are free to act in all domestic matters.

Causes of Regionalism

There are many causes at the root of this regionalism in the country, the major ones being the following:

Geographical Causes. The main cause of regionalism is geographical. There is some essential difference between the food habits, language, life etc., of every region and the people who live there. By virtue of these differences they come to regard each other as foreigners and they acquire an attitude of fear and hatred for each other.

Historical Causes. As has been indicated earlier, there are some historical causes also at the root of regionalism. For example, there have been some differences between the people of the North and South ever since the time of the Aryans and these have continued. Many of the kings of the North have won over the South while there have been few kingdoms in the South which have extended to the Northern part of India. Because of this, many South Indians look upon Northern India as separate from Southern India.

Political Causes. But if the situation is carefully and minutely observed, it will be seen that the main causes at the root of regionalism present in the country are of a political nature. In different regions some people have demanded the formation of regional governments and in this they have been inspired by regional interests and by the aim of gaining power. In this direction, a major part has been played by the revolutionary Naga party of Phizo, the Akali party of Punjab, the D.M. K. party of South India and other political parties. The truth is that the leaders of these political parties are responsible for having propagated regionalism is these respective areas. Not only this, but even some representatives of different areas who are members of political parties give prime importance to the interests of their own regions even in the face of national interests which are disregarded by them.

Psychological Causes. Finally, the psychological causes have contributed no less to the development and stability of regionalism. It is the wish of most of the persons that it be their area that progresses the most. This idea in itself is neither bad nor detestable but when they disregard the national interests and those of other regions for the attainment of this, then this feeling takes on the form of regionalism. Besides this, there are many individuals encouraging regionalism who express the hatred, jealousy, fear, anger and other feelings contained in them in this manner.

Marital and Economic Causes. There are some other causes besides those mentioned above that promote regionalism. For example, it is only rarely that one comes across married couples among whom one belongs to Bengal and the other to Punjab or to Rajasthan or to Madras, for that matter. As a general rule, people belonging to different regions do not marry and hence the occasion for close contact between the two does not arise. In addition to these there are some economic causes of regional tension. In the country there are some regions that are far backward in comparison with some other regions. As a result they are often seen possessed of a sense of inferiority and they become jealous of others. People belonging to some particular sphere are seen to be particularly successful businessmen such as the people of Marwar, Gujrat and Punjab and in this sphere they have a practical monopoly. Due this too they are hated by some people who try to turn them out from their own regions.

Remedies of Regionalism

The following means can help to end regionalism or at least to dilute it to some extent:

Encouragement of Transport and Communication. If regionalism is to be eliminated, the people should be encouraged to indulge in travel and to increase contact with people belonging to different regions of the country, Recently, a train of religious hermits toured the country and similarly many farmers belonging to Rajasthan travelled all over the country. In India, the tradition whereby people are induced to visit places of religious importance is a good one in as much that it helps people to travel all over the country and meet different people. In going to different corners of the country the people realised that India is a large country and regional sentiments can be removed or rendered less effectual by encouraging transport and communication in the country.

Propaganda of National History. The history of the nation should be propagated all over the country so that the people may dearly realise that the history of the individual regions of the country is only a part of the history of the nation to which all the regions have made an important contribution. The propagation of the national history will help to eradicate the sense of regionalism.

Prevention of Regional Political Parties. It is essential for national unity and integration that the political parties propagating regionalism and regional interests should be prevented from doing so. If they indulge in unrestricted campaigns for promoting regional interests they should be declared illegal. Although in a democracy every individual has the right to form a political organization in order to express his views but if it tends to harm the interests of the nation this right should be curbed.

Propagation of the National Sentiment. Finally, in order to remove the psychological causes at the root of regionalism an effort should be made to propagate the sentiment of nationality in the country. It is necessary to resort to all the various media of propaganda to obtain result in this direction. Efforts should be made to remove the regionalistic tendencies from all spheres such as government service, educational institution, etc., and the sentiment of nationality should be encouraged.

Regionalism is a complex problem. If it is to be solved it must be attacked from all sides and furthermore such a task requires cooperation from the government and the people. Only then can this problem be solved.

The Linguism

During the past decade or so, linguism has been gathering momentum and force till now it has become a definite threat to the unity and integrity of the nation. In Punjab, the problem of choice between Punjabi and Hindi has created a lot of conflict and tension while in Assam the language question has even resulted in bloodshed. In Bengal, Bengali has been opposed to Hindi and a serious problem of linguism has thus taken shape. Besides the problems of regional languages, the proponents of Hindi, English and Urdu are creating dissensions in the entire country. It often happens that the language movement is only a disguised political move and on close observation it will become clear that there are not many literary persons but mostly politicians who cause lingual movements. For example, the movement for the Punjabi language in the Punjab is attached to the demand for a Punjabi suba.

Causes of Linguism

What are the causes at the root of linguism ? At it is, linguism is a complex problem and it is difficult to make a complete analysis of all its various causes. Nevertheless, the following are some of the important causes briefly stated:

Geographical Causes. Linguism is like the other tensions inasmuch that it too has a geographical cause. Different languages are spoken in the different parts of India and these individual languages also have a lot of varieties since the dialect differs from one reason to another. Language is the medium through which people express their thoughts and feelings and make them known to others. And it is through language that they come to know each other. Hence, it is natural to feel a bond of intimacy with one who speaks some other language than one's own. Every language has its own literature. This literature is everywhere influenced by the local geographical conditions, rivers, plains and mountains, local vegetation, animals and local culture. It reflects the life of the people who speak that language. Hence, literature bears a very definite relation to its geographical demarcation. The familiarity that a person finds in the literature of the language that he speaks is used by the person to wish for the development and progress of the language of his own region and he does not appreciate it if the language of another region is forced on him. When this mental tendency grows more vicious and strong then the individual acquires a sense of hatred for the other language and the people who speak them and lingual tension is created.

Historical Causes. Some of the causes of linguism are also historical. India has been attacked by one foreigner after another. These foreigners came equipped with their own respective language. The Moghuls came and brought along Persian which mixed with the local language and became Urdu. The Britishers put in their appearance with the English language up their sleeves. These languages found the Indian soil suitable and they prospered and grew, and their Indianization also occurred. Many Hindus wrote in Urdu. If the people had recourse to reason there need have been no occasion for the problem of Urdu or Hindi to have arisen but people who turned to ancient history for their inspiration did not accept the Indianization of Urdu and kept the language as it was, with an abundance of Arabic and Persian words. It was not only confined to this because the literature that they created had a foreign soul.

Psychological Causes. And yet, the most important and the primary causes at the root of linguism are of a psychological nature. At its root is the hatred for the other language and those who speak them, in addition to the respect and admiration of one's own language. At its root is the narrow minded self-respect of the individuals. If the prejudice concerning the other language is removed from the mind and a comprehensive and sympathetic viewpoint is adopted, it becomes possible for any number of languages to proper.

Political Causes. Linguism is also inspired by the political interests and aspirations of different politicians and political groups. Many communal political parties raise the language issue, instigate their people and want to win their votes during the election. The problem of linguism has gained in complexity because of its affiliation with politics.

Economic Causes. There are some economic causes that also inspire linguism. Some languages are financially assisted by the government which aims at their progress but people speaking other languages object to this and thus linguism increases.

Social Causes. Linguism is encouraged by some social factors also. Some myths and legends, customs and traditions prevail in every society. That language is respected in society which provides communication, it also is the language that is adopted by the society. On the contrary, the language that does not respect and accept these or the language that caters to contradicting presumptions are objected to. In this manner linguism spreads.

Remedies of Linguism

Having studied the causes that create linguism, it is now possible to turn to the means for its solution and elimination. In this context the following suggestions can be made :

Development of the National Language. In the event of there being one national language and literature, that may be developed, people speaking the different languages will have an opportunity to come in contact with each other through the medium of this national language and the tension existing between them will be sensibly lessened.

Encouragement to all Major Languages. In addition to the development of one common national language and literature the main regional languages should also be encouraged. No language can be forced upon any region and neither can a language be developed by putting stress upon it. The language automatically develops through the medium of usage. One this fact is clearly understood much of the tension caused by linguism would come to an end. In this way, the government should encourage all the important regional languages. The government should see to it that Punjabi is developed in Punjab, Bengali in Bengal and Assamese in Assam and so on in addition to which Hindi should be propagated in all parts of the country.

Opposition of Communalism. In order to obliterate the political causes of linguism it is necessary to vigourously oppose communalism in the country.

Comprehensive Development. Finally, it should be remembered that in order to solve the problem of linguism it is necessary to adopt a comprehensive viewpoint. Each language should be encouraged by the government and in every region particular attention should be paid to the regional language and its development.

16

Role of Secularism

The Definition

The word 'secularism' was first used in the nineteenth century by George Jacob Holydake. He derived it from the Latin word 'Saeculum' meaning "this present age". He used it in the context of social and ethical values or system. Thus, secularism came to be known as a social and ethical system. The following principles were evolved by Holydake to mark this system ;

(i) Primary emphasis on the material and cultural improvement of human beings.

(ii) Respect for and search for all truth, whatever be its source, which can be tested in experience leading to human betterment.

(iii) Concern for this age or world and its improvement.

(iv) An independent rational morality, which does not base itself on faith in divine commandment.

Bradlaugh observed that secularism was hostile to religion and maintained that either secularism or religion should survive.

Western Secularism

Chambers Dictionary. "The belief that the state, moral, education, etc., should be independent of religion."

Oxford Dictionary. "The doctrine that morality should be based solely in regard to the well-being of mankind in the present life, to the exclusion of all consideration drawn from belief in God."

Webster's Dictionary. "The belief that religion and ecclesiastical affairs should not enter into the functions of the state." The limited sense of the word secularism is often placed in contrast to religion. Thus Webeter gives us an alternative definition of secularism - "A system of doctrines and practices that rejects any form of religious faith and worship."

In the deeper sense of the word, secularism is not concerned with what is religious and spiritual, and is surely opposed to everything that is irrational.

Indian Concept of Secularism

Indian conception of secularism required that there shall be no state religion and the state shall treat all religions equally. In the words of Mahatma Gandhi, "My veneration for other faiths is the same as for my own faith." "We believe in Sarva-dharma-samabhava having equal regard for all faiths and creeds."

Characteristics of Secular Education

Secular education is identified because of the following characteristics:

Moral Outlook. Secular education results in development of moral outlook. It is the foundation for development of character and moral development. It inculcates in students humanity, truthfulness, tolerance, honesty, courtesy, sympathy, spirit of service and sacrifice which form a noble character of man and develop his personality.

Development of Wider Vision. Secular education makes a man dynamic and enlightened. It develops in him a wider vision towards life, and he takes interest in social service by sacrificing his selfish motives. Education makes him courageous enough to face the problems of life and solve them to the best of his efforts and intelligence.

Pluralistic Outlook. Secular education leads to the emergence of a healthy pluralistic outlook which fosters the growth of science, art, philosophy and even religion. A pluralistic outlook is the very essence of democracy.

Democratic Values. Secular education helps man in developing democratic values like liberty, equality, fraternity and co-operative living. True secularism stresses the dignity of the individual and the sacredness of human personality. Secular education helps to establish and incorporate democratic process. Every person is treated as an end and never as a means only.

Cultural Development. Secular education helps in fostering scientific spirit. It releases the individual from the bonds of blind faith. Scientific spirit implies a spirit of free enquiry, a spirit of looking at things objectively and rationally, freedom from an obsession with the past, and a more humble attitude towards one's own history and achievements. Secular education promotes scientific values of rationality, objectivity and open-mindedness. It also promotes humanistic, values like tolerance and compassion.

Synthesis of Spiritual and Material. Secular education glorifies material needs and promotes reverence for earthly life, without rejecting spiritual values. Secularism is based on fundamental human values. It looks upon science not merely as a means of material progress but as a quest for truth and a search for harmony with nature. It helps to strike a healthy balance between the spiritual and the material.

Humanitarianism. Secular education leads to humanitarianism. It stands for peace, good-will and understanding. It helps in fostering the brotherhood of man and the unity of the world. Absence of secular education causes exploitation, corruption, disaster, selfishness, aggression and hatred, chaos and disorder. Betterment of society depends upon secular-based education. It raises man to a high level, it encourages the policy of live and let live. It provides the basis for true humanitarianism. It helps in replacing hatred by love, selfishness by self-sacrifice and violence by non-violence. Secular education leads to happiness, order and contentment in the society by cultivating faith in truth, beauty and goodness.

Education for Secularism in India

India's present educational system promotes secular attitudes and values through its broad-based aims, curricula, enlightened teachers and appropriate activities, all emphasizing open-mindedness, progressivism, rationality, freedom from bigotry and superstition, and equal respect for au religions. The following traits characterise education for secularism in India:

Secular Aims. The aims and objectives of such a system are secular. They seek to develop India as a rational, democratic, progressive and modern state. The philosophy of humanism guides such educational objectives. The well being of all the citizens of the country is the goal towards which India's educational energies are directed.

Democratic Organization of Educational Institutions. The organization of most of Indian educational institution is based on secular principles. It is necessary to observe secular, democratic, rational criteria in appointments, promotions, admissions, and all such matters,

Multiple Curricula. The educational curricula at all levels in India lay special emphasis on the promotion of secular values. Lessons in text-books are free from religions bigotry and prejudice while the good ideas and values emphasized in different religions are presented in appropriate forms. The co-curricular activities aim at promoting harmony and cooperation among different groups and respect for each other's culture in the students. It is not permitted to condemn or unduly praise any one particular religious or cultural system or institution. It is the usual practice in all schools, colleges and universities to celebrate fairs, festivals, birth anniversaries, etc., relating to different religions. While imparting moral education equal importance is given to different faiths.

Science Teaching. Secularism stands for scientific rationalism. It stresses logical thinking, and abhors superstitions and irrational things. Therefore, Indian education today puts much emphasis on science teaching. Science is taught in a practical manner at all levels of schooling, so that it might influence the attitudes and values of the pupils. The spirit of science with emphasis on inquiry, experimentation, proof and critical outlook, permeates the teaching of other subjects also.

Enlightened Teachers. In the education for secularism in India the teachers today-are expected to treat their pupils in an impartial manner. They eschew all caste, community and class considerations in dealing with students and colleagues. Equal respect in given to all students and to all religious groups. Every conscientious teacher behaves in a truly democratic and fair manner.

Thus the present Indian secular educational system is trying to create a social climate in the country in which secular values are sought to be promoted effectively and enthusiastically.

Difficulties in Secular Educational System

In a country like India, in which traditional institutions like religion, caste, untouchability, and dowry have been prevailing for thousands of years, the building up of a secular state is a very challenging task. Despite the best intentions of our constitution makers and great leaders, it is difficult to establish and promote a really functional climate of secularism in India. The main difficulties in secular educational system are as follows:

Traditional Bias and Narrow Outlook. In our country today denominational schools are allowed to function with a lot of freedom. There are D. A. V. Schools, Jain Schools, Vaish Schools, Ahir Schools, Kayastha Pathshalas, Shia Schools, Catholic Schools, Rajput Schools, etc. In these institutions the children of the respective communities or castes are admitted on preferential basis, and also teachers of the same communities are preferred. This creates a serious difficulty in the functioning of Indian education as an integrative and secular force in Indian Society.

Too Much Emphasis on Theoretical Learning. Our educational system presents many things only in theory. Very little effort is made to change the values and attitudes of education. Many highly educated people do not hesitate to demand big dowries. They are too much fastidious about gotras and sub-castes in deciding marriage. They ill-treat women-folk and do not show respect to other religions. The lack of tolerance and courtesy on the part of educated persons towards villagers, women, poor people, minority, community members, old people, etc., in buses, trains and at other public places reveals that our present education has failed to change our value system in a desired manner.

Neglect of Secular and Cultural Celebrations. Schools and colleges observe holidays on the days of important religious fairs, festivals and birth-days. The result is that the students do not get enough opportunities to understand or imbibe secular values.

Neglect of Group Activities. Educational institutions do not encourage group activities. Group activities and group methods of teaching and learning the neglected. This is a serious difficulty in the promotion of secular and free ideas and values.

17

The Modernization

Education and Modernization

Modernization Function of Education : S. N. Eisenstadt has rightly pointed out, "Perhaps the best starting point for the analysis of the characteristics in the educational institutions in modem societies is the pattern of demands for and the supply of educational services that tended to develop with modernization." In the words of Yogendra Singh, "...education has been one of the most influential instruments of modernization in India. It has fed to the mobilization of people's aspiration for nationalism, liberalism and freedom. It alone has been responsible for the growth of an enlightened intelligentsia which carried forward not only a movement for independence but also a relentless struggle for social and cultural reforms."

Meaning of Modernization

The most important function of education is modernization. Modernization is a comprehensive concept aimed at capturing, describing the transition of a society from medieval to modern culture. It stands for progress beyond tradition. Modernization, according to some sociologists, is based upon European and American models. As compared to urbanization, Industrialization, Westernization and Europeanization, modernization presents a more complex process and a more complex result. In the intellectual sphere it is an awareness that it is possible to see a rational explanation of physical and social phenomena. Thus, it is represented by positivism and empiricism and rationalism. In the field of religion it is expressed in secularism. It approach is multiple. In philosophy it is expressed in humanist thought It includes social mobilization and differentiation and specialization in individual and institutional activities. In political field it stands for democratization. In ecology it is characterized by advancing degree of urbanization.

Culture of Modernization

But the most important feature of modernization as related to education is cultural. In cultural sphere its symptoms have been pointed out by A. R. Desai as follows:

1. Growing differentiation of the major secular or cultural system, The spread of literacy and secular education: a more complex intellectual and institutional system for the cultivation and advancement of specialized roles based on intellectual disciplines.
2. Emergence of a new cultural outlook characterized by emphasis on progress and improvement, on happiness and spontaneous expression of abilities and feelings, on the development of individuality as a value, and efficiency.
3. Emergence of a new personality orientation, traits and characteristics revealed in greater ability to adjust to the broadening societal horizons: some ego-flexibility; widening spheres of interest; growing potential empathy with other people and situations; a growing evaluation of self-advancement and mobility, a growing emphasis on the present as the meaningful temporal dimension of human existence; a growing awareness of dignity of others and an increased disposition to respect them; a growing awareness in the individual that his world is calculable, that other people and institutions around him can be relied on to fulfil their delegation and responsibilities, growing faith in sciences and technology and a growing awareness that, 'rewards should be according to contribution and not according to either whim or special properties of person not relating to his contribution.'

4. Finally, modernization implies, the ability of society to develop an institutional structure capable of adjusting to continually changing problems and demands. The emergence of such a challenge is the result of modernization.

Modernization through Education

Education is the most important instrument of modernization since modernization includes the following:

1. Directed change in the system of attitudes, beliefs and values and also in the institutional complex, to enhance the acceptability of modern technology and its organizational and operational framework.
2. Growth of the infrastructure essential to the adaptation to technology of foreign origin to specific national needs.
3. Laying the foundations of institutions and organizations which could, in time, assume responsibility for independent innovation and technological growth to the country's needs and problems.

Functions of Education

In view of the above mentioned changes required by modernization the functions of education in this direction may be achieved by the following

Alternatives to Tradition. By enlarging the cognitive map of those exposed to it, education suggests alternatives to attraction, bringing into focus the rewards implicit in them, and indicates roughly at least -the paths through which the new goals with their attendant regards can be achieved. It broadens mental horizons, raises expectations and predisposes people to make experiments.

Socialization. As an instrument of socialization it can project new images and values. Purposively used, it can be a help in obliterating attitudes and behaviour patterns that are dysfunctional programmes of modernization.

National Consciousness. By providing ideological articulation it can promote the development of national consciousness and can help people see their needs and their problems in a national perspective. This can stimulate the creation of a national consensus at least on major issues.

Educated Elite. Education provides a highway to elite status on the educated. The educated provide a reference model to the masses, who, in imitation of the former, take the first steps away from tradition. Modernizing elites are almost always the products of modem or semi-modem school/ university systems.

Problem-solving Leadership. Scientists and technicians, management experts and administrators with the requisite knowledge and skills, can only be expected to emerge out of the educational system. Large-scale programmes of modernization demand specialists of several types at different levels, and look to the eduction system for a steady How of technocrats, planners and managers to operate them.

Mobility Multiplier. Although its impact is on the immobility of thought-ways, in the long run it does alter rigid forms of social stratification. Modernization requires both types of mobility.

In sum, with proper planning and under efficient direction, education can make a meaningful contribution to the attainment of modernization. It can be harnessed to diffuse attitudes and ideologies required for the adoption of modem technology and its associated values and organizational premises, to provide personnel to operate and sustain the programmes of modernization, and to create capabilities for adaptation and origination of new technology.

Modernization of Institutional Education

Researches have been conducted in West and India about the role of educational institutions in bringing about modernization. Most of them have shown a positive correlation between the two. However, Saunders in his study *Education and Modernization in Brazil* has found that it undermines modernity. He remarks: 'Brazililian schools, especially at the primary level where their impact on personality development is greatest, tend to stifle rather than develop the personality traits on which modernization depends, and from which the society must draw its innovators.' Learners in his research work *The Passing of Traditional Society; modernising the Middle East* (1963), on the basis of his study with adult samples of six developing countries, asserted that literacy is the basic personal skill underlying the modernization process. Joseph A. Kahl in his research. *The Measurement of Modernism:* A study of Values in Brazil and Mexico (University of Texas Press 1968), pointed out significant correlation between education and modernization. Reporting results of the Harward's project on the social and cultural aspects of economic development, covering Argentina, Chili, India, Pakistan, Israel and Nigeria, Inkeles concluded that, 'Education is the most powerful factor in making men modern'. In their study based on 5 national probability samples of adult age, 20 and older, drawn from the U. S. A., Finland, Japan, Mexico and Costarica, Waisanen and Kumata, concludeo positive co-relationship between education and various indicators of modernity.

School and Modernity

Examining the immediate effects of schooling on people's modernity Armer and Youtz conclude, "Western education leads to the modernization of perspective in traditional, non-industrial societies." After a study of 591 seventeen years old males in Kano City in Nigeria they maintain, "Western education does, indeed, have a definite effect on value orientations of youth that is largely independent of test factor." This has been collaborated by S. L. Sharma in his work *Modernizing Effects of University Education* published by Indian Council of Social Science Research in 1979. This conclusion has been again supported by articles in a special number *of International Journal of Comparative Sociology* (1974, *XIV*, 3-4). In this special number, researches conducted independently in various parts of the world, showed remarkable uniformity in concluding that schooling promotes attitudinal modernity in developing societies.

Higher Education and Modernization

Besides the relation of schooling and modernization researches have been conducted about the effect of higher education on modernity. Williamson studying university students in United States, Germany, Japan and Columbia concluded that while Americans and Columbians are at the conservative the Japanese are on the other end of the scale of rationalism -traditionalism developed by Kahl. Similar researches were conducted by some other notable sociologists in the West including Silberman (1970), Greer (1972), Smith and Inkeles (1966), Sack (1973), etc. In India studies concerning schooling and social change were! conducted by A. R. Desai (1952), G. S. Bhatnagar (1972), and Margaret L. Connack (1961). Cormack made a full length study of Indian students concerning social change. She concluded, "They are not considering values, attitudes and attitudinal change. They are concerned with certificates, degrees and employment." Thus, Cormack maintained negative correlation between higher education and social change in India. She found little evidence of change orientation, among her respondents. Similar conclusion was reached by B. V. Shah (1964), in his study *Social Change among College Students of Gujarat* (Baroda: Maharja Sayaji Rao University). Y. B. Damley in his study *College Youth in Poona*, however, found some positive correlation between higher education and individuation, a trait of modernization. But he himself admits, "It is not a study of the nature of the student's behaviour or thinking." M. S. Gore, I. P. Desai and Suma Chitnis found encouraging evidence of the relation between education and modernization. According to them, "The state, sex, and educational level of the respondents were all important variables in determining the modernity of student sample." Similar conclusion was reached by Malik and Marquitte in their study *Changing Social Values of College Students in the Punjab*. They concluded that, "...an overwhelming majority of Punjab youth favours the abolition of such traditional institutions as caste and untouchablity and strongly approves of a general social revolution in India." In his book Education in *Social Change* Sullivan found that, "Factors other than experience at a particular training college appear to be operative in changing that students outlook towards traditional social practices."

Modernizing Effects of University Education

The latest study in this connection was however made by Dr. S. L. Sharma published by ICSSR (1979) under the title *Modernizing Effects of University Education*. On the basis of a study of 3437 students in the 34 teaching departments of Punjab University during the academic year 1973-74 Dr.Sharma reached the following important conclusions concerning the relationships of modernization and education:

1. The level of higher education is of no consequence as an explanatory variable of student modernity.
2. There is the lowest percentage of modems in the humanities, followed by social sciences and professionals with the highest percentage in the science faculty.
3. Males are more modem than females.
4. High status students are more modem than low status students.
5. There is a significant and positive correspondence between level of student modernity and that of their reference teacher, provided the latter preferred character-building role, over other roles, favoured no social distance in their relations with students and reported greater interpersonal interaction with students.
6. There is a weak though positive relationship between years of hostel exposure and modernity course.
7. Age is found to be inversely related to student modernity. Boys out scored girls in modernity.
8. Caste has no bearing on modernity.
9. A significantly larger percentage of high modernity cases hails from medium size families with 4 to 6 numbers.
10. Family type has no association with modernity.
11. Socio-economic status of the family has a significant though weak positive relationship with modernity.
12. Father's education and occupation are only weakly related to student modernity.
13. Father's income has a moderately strong positive association with modernity.
14. Students with early urban background are not more modem than those with rural background.

16. Those who have lived longer in urban setting are more modem than those with fewer years of urban dwelling.

17. The initial exposure to cosmopolitan city like Chandigarh makes not much difference in modernity.
18. Duration of urban exposure is positively associated with modernity.
19. Early residential background and modernism of the city have no influence on student modernity.
20. There is a significant and positive relationship between media exposure and modernity.
21. There is a strong positive relationship between extent of exposure to other cultures and level of modernity.
22. Constant exposure to other culture significantly increases the negative effect of education on modernity.
23. The convent and or public school educated students are more modem than the government and or aided school educated.
24. The type of schooling is the best predictor of modernity with the convent or public school educated being most modern.
25. Early socialization variables account for greater variance in student modernity than the later socialization variables.
26. Developmental variables are more powerful than structural variables in explaining students modernity.

On the basis of the above conclusion Dr. S. L. Sharma points out inverse relationship between the level of higher education and the student modernity. He gives the following reasons for this suprising fact:

1. The present higher education leads to mere transmission of information to the neglect of inculcating ability to think of one self. It stresses mere skill acquisition to the neglect of generating this position, for skill formation. It neglects character training and stresses mere certification for white-collar jobs.
2. The system of higher education in India lacks an articulate social ideal.

3. The present educational system has not changed in the light of goals set by the constitution of free India.

4. The present system of education is not a source of characteriological transformation.

5. The course content of the present higher education does not lead to modernization.

6. The cognitive and value content in conjunction with the social context of the present higher education is not relevant to the cultivation of modernity.

7. Our teachers are not so modern as to influence the student. They are not interested in character-building and social training. They are unsure of what the community expects from them, The persistent authoritarian orientation limits the power of teachers to act as agents of student modernity.

8. The objective conditions in our educational institutions such as over-crowded classes, low teacher-pupil ratio, impersonal character of teacher-taught relationship, render the task of change orientation on the part of the teacher the more difficult. Small classes are better for such influence than large and unwieldy classes.

9. The lack of freedom for the teacher to design his own courses restrict considerably his potential for induction for social change. In the words of Dr. S. L. Sharma, "*Our* teachers thus presented a case of double failure as socializers of student modernity; first, they lacked strong modernity orientation, and second, they failed to modify their role orientation so as to bring in line with modern norms."

10. The extra academic component of campus climate restricts its relevance to modernity.

11. Routinization of educational experience is a possible reason for the failure of higher education as a modernizer.

12. The overgrown structural formal at of higher education is a significant reason for its failure to modernize.

13. The built-in-traits of present higher education such as under

emphasis on the value element in its course content, are responsible for its poor performance.

Dr. Sharma suggests the following three objectives as the aims of higher education to make it a better instrument of modernization.

1. To prepare skilled manpower for a developing economy,
2. To re-socialize people in the values conducive to socio-economic development; and
3. To inculcate in man a creative self-awareness, and ability to think for himself and a sense of critical judgment.

He suggested that three areas should be particularly modernized: the re-orientation of the content, the recasting of teaching-learning nexus, and improving the quality of education. The quality of early education should be improved. Group extra-curricular activities should been couraged. Asecular-rational and egalitarian man should be created. To conclude, "Besides providing the highly skilled man-power to a teachnico-industrial economy, higher education in our view can lay down the foundation of socio-economic development in the following ways : (1) by imparting to the younger generation the requisite psychological dispositions which are regarded as helpful for development; (2) by instilling in students a reflective ability and a capacity to make rational decisions."

Two Patterns of Modernization

In his paper *Social Change and Educational Policy* published in *The Sociology of Education in India* (NCERT 1967), Professor A. R. Desal accepts two patterns of modernization of a traditional society pointed out by Don Martindale-exogenous and endogenous. He defines these two patterns by pointing out that, "An exogenous factor is one arising outside the social system." both these factors initiate and shape soda! change. They determine the nature of leadership and its basic aim. These in their turn determine the objectives of education the structure of the machinery of education, technical and other means of spread, the allocation of finances of education and the nature of personnel executing it. Historically, the modernization process worked differently in the capitalist and the non-capitalist countries. In U.S.A., it grew in three phases merchantilist, *laissez faire* and-monopoly.

It developed a massive formal education system. This system, though basically the same, changed according to changing circumstances in each country. Not only in Europe but also in Africa, Asia and Latin America the modernization process transformed the politico-economic and socio-cultural structures. However, the colonial hold on these nations was maintained. Thus, modernization in colonial countries was brought about by the foreign rulers, an exogenous factor. In communist countries, on the other hand, modernization developed on non-capitalist lines aiming at the establishment of a social structure based upon collective ownership and meeting the assessed needs of the citizen. After the Second World War these countries developed a modem educational system different from that evolved in capitalist countries. The countries liberated from colonial subjugation engaged in modernization according to their specific conditions aiming at over coming backwardness by rapid industrialization and social institutional reconstruction. According to Professor A. R. Desai, "The two patterns of modernization, viz., modernization on the capitalist and the non-capitalist basis have the following implications for their educational system :

(a) They provide different aims and approaches to the content of education and to the communication process.

(b) They result in different attitudes towards education.

(c) They determine different methods of providing finances for education.

(d) They also generate different patterns of organization of education.

In capitalist countries education was considered as a commodity purchased by the consumer at different prices in the market. Thus, it depends on the purchasing capacity of the family and group that the individual gets a particular type of education. In non-capitalist countries, however, education was considered a vital need and a fundamental right and therefore provided as free communal service by the society. Besides the aims and approaches and attitudes, the methods of providing finance for education also differed in capitalist and non-capitalist countries. In capitalist countries finances for education were provided by individual, private societies, endowments and the government. Thus, the government is one of the competing financiers though being the supreme it frames laws to regulate education market. It reserves certain aspects of education which are essential for the community. It also takes such measures as are required to safeguard the educational interests of the handicapped and backward groups. In non-capitalist countries, however, the entire responsibility for educational finance is the burden of the state. Finally, there are two partners of organization of education in capitalist and non-capitalist societies. In the former it is made of an amalgam of the heterogeneous bodies and groups providing finances. In non-capitalist countries there are no diversities and conflicts in several agencies controlling education as the total control is in the hands of the state in the name of the society.

18

Human Values

Values relate to the aims of human life. For the achievement of the aims men frame certain notions and these notions are called values. In the words of W. H. Kilpatrick, "That out of man's capacity for goal seeking behaviour arise his wants and efforts and out of these come in consciously chosen ends (goal) and means. Because ends conflict, man is led to weild his goals against each other. When this is done critically enough values emerge. According to Mr. Henderson, "It has been pointed out that man acts to satisfy his wants, anything which satisfies a human want becomes thereby a value. To say, that our conduct is motivated by our values is another way of saying that we act to satisfy our wants."

Theories and Values

Educationist have propounded the following theories about the determination of values:

Hedonistic View of Life. The value of a thing is due to the fact that the thing has power to satisfy our wants.

Perfection Theory. Any thing has value if it relates to the perfection of life for which a man endeavours in his life.

Utility Theory. Anything which has utility is valuable.

Order Theory. Anything which is helpful in organizing society is called value.

Existence Theory. Value is helpful in existence.

Experimental Theory. Values are experiments in present and past as well.

Part and whole Theory. Values are felt sometimes partly and sometimes wholly.

Objective and Subjective theory. Values are determined by the notions of individuals and also by the circumstances in which he lives.

Emotive Theory. Man's emotions are expressed by his nature. These emotions change according to the circumstances. Thus by virtue of his emotion man determines his values.

These values have certain characteristics like subjectivity, objectivity, material or abstract, elasticity, etc. These values aim at perfection; self-realisation, satisfaction, development, integrity and cohesion etc.

Education and Values

According to Reid, "Education is part of life, and clearly our questions about values and education are insuperable from questions of values in life. Values are embodied in educational practice." Thus education develops a sense of discrimination between good and bad. This discrimination is based on values. And these value are tested in schools.

To quote W. H. Kilpatrick, "The teacher must have an essential part of his professional equipment, which is here called "map of values". Such a map consists of his hopes, aims, ideals, all the cherished values which he will use as aims in guiding those things. Teaching should aim continually on keeping this aggregate of values alive and growing but especially it should include all that the teacher hopes for students to learn so as life for them becomes as rich and fine as possible." In other words, "Aims are an end in themselves and values are the product." Values of education are the same as of life. These educational values are individual as well as social.

Contribution of Educational Values

Educational values contribute the following advantages for individual and social life:

1. Development of healthy and balanced personality.
2. Capacity to earn livelihood and acquire prosperity.
3. Development of vocational efficiency.
4. Creation of good citizenship.
5. Reorganisation and reconstruction of experience.
6. Adjustment with the environment and its modifications.
7. Fulfilment of the needs of man.
8. Development of character.
9. National integration and national development.
10. Leaders and skilled workers.
11. Promotion of social efficiency.
12. Cultural values.
13. Utilisation of leisure.

Therefore, educational values play a significant role in the life of man. Through them one is able to lead his personal and social life successfully. To sum up in the word of J.. S. Brubacher, "Hence the ultimate aim of education is self-realization, the fulfilment of potentialities, for many in addition to the realization of eternal life. All proximate aims of education take their direction from the aim which itself stands imperishable and eternal."

Need for Religious Education

The aim of contemporary education is not only the mental, physical and social development of the individual, but also his religious and moral development , which is why modern educationists have stressed the importance of moral education for the country. Vivekananda said that religion is the basis of education, although here he does not imply his own or some one else's religion. This comment also implies that the aim of religious education is not to propound the theories of any one particular religion but to create faith which helps the individual to face all kinds of adverse conditions with the belief that he can progress at least a little, irrespective of the darkness of the outlook. Hence religious faith helps man in his progress, raises him to a high level, and also assists him in developing democratic qualities. Religion is the foundation of all moral character, because without religion man cannot have faith in truth, beauty and goodness. The freedom that we want to grant the child through education is not possible without religion. Besides, even culture has no meaning in the absence of religion which also acquaints us with the final goal of life. Without knowing this goal, education cannot progress. Religion is the basis of true humanitarianism.

It is evident from the foregoing comments that religion should be given its appropriate place in the curricula for education. Vivekananda has recommended that modern science should be used to awaken the educand's knowledge. History, geography and literature should be taught to the educand along with the teaching of religion which must be used to teach them the greatest truths. Dr. S. Radhakrishanan also supported the teaching of religion at the various levels of education. He said that we will have to plan for a rational religion for our conflict ridden emerging humanity, a religion that does not ridicule man's soul filled with unrestrained individualism and hesitation born out of conflict. We have to present a new philosophy of God with which we can fight against those doubting communities of men who are fighting against each other to establish their supremacy on men's souls. Rabindra nath Tagore also expressed sympathy with this viewpoint in granting the greatest importance to a humanitarian religions. Tagore said that these religions differ from each other in moral value, but each one is inspired by the same tendency. In these religions, man looks for his highest ideal, which he calls God. They try to discover it in some personality of human character.

Mahatma Gandhi has also attached the greatest significance to religious education and he has advocated that educands should be acquainted with the basic elements of all religions. Sri Aurobindo has considered religious education to be the most important aspect of education.

Aims of Religious Education

The introduction of religious education leads to many-advantages. It also has some objectives, the main ones being the following:

Moral Development. James Ross has opined that without a religious education, the highest moral development of the educand is impossible because religion is the foundation of moral development and character. All the religions of the world have stressed the need for developing moral qualities, and for this reason religious education is essential for developing the educand's moral character.

Refinement of Human Values. One aim of religious education is to distinguish between the divine and material, and to give a divine touch to human values. In this way, religious education refines human values and thus puts humanity on the path to higher ideals.

Socialization. Social service is recommended by every religion of the world. In the Gita, people are advised to act with a view, not to personal gain, but to add to the prosperity of the humanity. By inspiring man to forget his own narrow interest and to think of humanity at large, religious education continues the process of socializing the individual.

Development of Democratic Values. Religious feelings relates man on one side with God and on the other with human beings, and by showing that the same God exists in every human being, it encourages the development of the democratic qualities of liberty, fraternity and equality. In the absence of this sense of fraternity, equality has no meaning. It only remains a legal concept, not reality.

Cultural Development Religion is an important part of culture, and for that reason religious education contributes to man's cultural development. In fact, cultural progress of a group is measured by its religious development. Dr. S. Radhakrishnan has laid special stress on the contribution of religious education to the cultural development of the individual.

Sense of Respect for Man. Another objective of religious education is to induce a sense of respect for humanity in the educand. The basis of religion is the synthesizing element, and this is the basis also of education and culture.

Proper Attitude. The aim of religious education is to achieve the complete development of the child's personality and to induce in him the correct attitude to life and the universe. In the words of V. T. Thayer, "The school must therefore concern itself with the whole child and no child can become whole without instruction in religion."

Mode, Form and Subject Matter of Religious Education

The method and form of religious education is clarified by its objectives mentioned above. The question is how religious education can be imparted and what should be its subject matter. In this connection it is essential to remember the principle that religion is acquired, not taught, for it is not a subject to be learnt, but to be realized and translated into life. That is why Vivekananda has suggested that religious education should be proceeded by an account of the ideals of great men such as Rama, Krishna, Mahavir, etc. Religion means continued progress on the path to service and worship despite the greatest handicaps and obstacles. According to Vivekananda, one example of this is the ideal of Hanuman. He has advised the young men of the country never to let weakness fall upon the mind. In such a situation they should think of Mahavir and Mother Goddess and they will find that this weakness vanishes immediately. Vivekananda felt that the country needs a kind of religious education which achieves synthesis with science on the one side and teaches the lesson of patriotism, sacrifice and service, on the other.

According to Sri Aurobindo, there is little to be gained by paying mere lip service to religious education unless religious education is actually transferred to real life and a tendency to worship, contemplation, self-control and abstinence does not grow. Spiritual development can be helped to a certain extent by worship, prayer and the celebration of various religious festivals. The educand must be educated in his religious duties, prayer and contemplation, and in every school the educands must be initiated into the ideals of service to and living for God, humanity, the country and the nation. Religious education does not necessarily imply that the child should be forced to read all religious texts, as suggested by Mahatma Gandhi, Vinoba Bhave and other thinkers. This is also not necessary for religious tolerance. Study of different religions is not as important as actual application of the various principles of religion, and it is equally undesirable to foist any particular religious practice on every individual. Hence, the curricula of religious education should centre around the basic elements of religion.

Role of Religious Education in a Secular State

Some people opine that religious education should not be encouraged by the state in a secular country like India, and they argue that religious education should be given by religious institutions and society, not by the school. This attitude has no justification because education must aim at the complete development of the individual, an aim that cannot be fulfilled in the absence of religious education. A secular state does not imply a state which is hostile to or indifferent towards religion, because all that the term secular implies is that the state shall not insist upon the adoption of any particular religion, because there is no state religion. It is correct to assume that the government should not try to spread any particular religion, but it should also be remembered that religious education cannot be equated with the deliberate campaigning for some particular religion. All that is required in religious is that the educand should be taught the basic elements which are at the root of every religion, thus developing the educand's faith in moral character, religious values and humanitarianism. And, since India is also a democratic country, it has a great stake in the development of democratic values, which also depend upon religious education. Hence, religious education has its significance even in a secular state because it is the most powerful medium for developing democratic values. But religious education in a secular state must be carefully planned so as not to injure the sentiments of any particular sect of religion and also to avoid giving undue importance to any one religion. Every educand must be given the freedom and opportunity to profess his own religion, but he should be accompanied by acquaintances with other religions^ since this alone is the way to religious tolerance. True religious feeling can be evolved in the educand by telling him about the lives of all the great religious leaders and founders. The subject matter of religious education should be designed to conform to the level of training and intelligence of the educands. A religious life is a life with a purpose, the same purpose which religious education has.

Moral Education

The aim of education is the complete development of the child, a development in which moral development occupies an important place. Man's greatest characteristic is his character. Vivekananda has defined character as the sum total of an individual's instincts, the inclinations of his mind. Man is made by his thoughts. One finds that children develop characters according to the ideas presented to them during their growth. For this reason they should be initiated into the ideals of sacrifice, hard work and contemplation. Good thoughts lead to a sound determination and this is turn puts the man on the path to good life, and he is filled with strength of soul which inspire him to adhere to this path. In order to form character, it is necessary to pay attention to subtle and small things, for the character manifested through habits. Character can, therefore, only be improved by the habits of the individual. For this both determination and courage are required. Vivekananda had said in a resonant voice that one must form one's character and express one's true nature, the enlightened pure element in oneself. On must also look for the same element in every other individual.

According to Sri Aurobindo, moral education is the education of the heart, without which no individual can be completely human. But this moral education cannot be imparted though lectures and text books because the basis of this education is proper feelings, proper conduct and the development of proper habits of thought, feeling and action. The task of education is to guide, direct and suggest to the child, without interfering with his activities in any way. Teachers should present the highest ideals but must also remember that moral education is imparted through imitation and setting examples rather only by imitating his teacher. The modern teacher, therefore, must also have the highest ideals. In addition, moral education takes place through moral conversation and behaviour. Senior educands should be required to read literature which encourages the purest emotion in them and inspires them to attempt at the highest ideals. In order to give moral training to the child, the latter should be acquainted with the means of distinguishing between the right and the wrong. The various emotions of the child are not to be suppressed but sublimated. Mahatma Gandhi, like Sri Aurobindo, believed that the development of character is the aim of education, for which, in his opinion also, moral education is essential. Dayananda believed that education of any kind is impossible without the practice of abstinence. Dr. S. Radhakrishnan also said that moral education is absolutely necessary for any education. In Indian culture very great importance has always been attached to moral character. No education is complete without moral education, and this morality is the foundation of man's future and therefore the seed of this must be sown in the school. Dr. S. Radhakrishnan said that we must create the proper social order but we must also keep in mind that the individual does not become complete only by achieving economic prosperity. In order to become a complete individual the pleasure and beauty of the soul is essential. This soul must be brimming with love, faith, and the willingness and ability to serve humanity re-born.

From the foregoing account of the opinions of various philosophers, it is evident that moral education is as much a part of education as religious education is. In this connection, it is stated in the report of the Secondary Education Reorganization Committee for U.P., that "moral and humanistic education should form an integral part of our education; students should be taught the fundamental truth from all religious and ethical movements with a view to emphasizing their essential unity".

19

Purposes and Aims

Aims and Functions

The aims of education are determined by human life. Putting it differently, the aims of education are formulated after deciding the kind of life we want human beings to lead. In addition to this, the aims of education are also determined by the kind of life human beings live. It can thus be said that the aims of education are based upon human nature. Since the basic form of human nature has remained unchanged over many centuries, the aims of education have also remaind the same while humanity has passed through many centuries. For example, the human being is constituted not only of the reason and intellect, but also of emotions and the body. Any system of education which seeks to fulfil its aims must provide for the development of all these aspects. In view of the complex social and economic structure of human society, every adult human being is faced with the necessity of earning his bread and of fulfilling his various needs. In view of this permanent necessity of human life, one of the aims of education has always been to equip the individual to earn his livelihood. Man has to fight with nature to ensure his own existence, and in this process he needs his physical abilities and powers. For this reason children are taught to maintain their health, not only in civilized societies but even in the most primitive ones. Education is also made to conform to the changing environment of a particular social group so that its later generations may be able to adjust better.

Human beings always live in groups because they cannot fulfil many of their needs alone. Without a family group a human child cannot be born, and neither can it survive. Social life of some kind is essential for everyone. Social life is based upon the fulfilment of certain duties and obligations and upon facing certain responsibilities. Hence, one of the most common objectives of education is to train the individual to lead a fruitful social life.

One finds some form of political organisation in civilized as well as in primitive societies. These serve to control and to systematize the life uf individuals. Most political systems aim at the greatest good of the greatest number and it is considered essential that individuals should obey the rules of the state and be aware of their responsibilities towards, it. Most of the modern political states have taken the responsibility of education upon themselves. For this reason, the state plays a prominent part in the individual's life, and training an individual to become a responsible citizen is one of the aims of education.

Universal Aims

Roughly speaking, education has two kinds of aims - the universal aims, and the specific aims. Universal aims tend to remain the same, irrespective of the time and place. One of the universally accepted.objectives of education is the comprehensive development of the human personality. From the earliest times to the present day and in every country of the world education has aimed at developing the abilities and tendencies of human beings in such a way that they may be able to achieve maximum adjustment, both personal and social. Human nature does not change with time and latitude, and for that reason education has some universal aims. To take one example, the principle that a healthy mind needs a healthy body is a universal maxim, and a universal aim of education. For this reason, education everywhere includes mental and physical training. Similarly, everywhere individuals make families after entering adult life, and in order to ensure their survival, they have to adopt some means of earning their livelihood. Consequently, another commonly accepted aim of education is to train the individual so that he can occupy himself usefully and profitably. And, since man lives in society, it is essential that there should be adjustment between one man and another because without it society cannot survive. Education, therefore, must ensure that men and society develop in such a manner that occasions of clash and conflict are reduced to a minimum. Clearly, then, there are certain objectives of education which remain the same in all places and at all tunes.

Specific Aims of Education

But, the aims of education are also conditioned by the social ideas, circumstances and changes that occur at a particular place and time. Hence, the aims of education also change with the circumstances. This change and adjustment between one man and another because without it society cannot survive. Education, therefore, must ensure that men and society develop in such a manner that occasions of clash and conflict are reduced to a minimum. Clearly, then, there are certain objectives of education which remain the same in all places and at all times.

But, the aims of education are also conditioned by the social ideas, circumstances and changes that occur at a particular place and time. Hence, the aims of education also change with the circumstances. This change and adjustment is essential because education is the tool with which the society, and the individuals in it, can be made more efficient, satisfied and adjusted. And this can be possible only if the aims of education are changed to suit the circumstances. The example of India will clearly establish this.

Humanitarian Aims

The attitude prevailing in ancient times was 'that education should indicate the ways and means of defeating the pains created by man's passions. Self-knowledge was believed to be the only way of becoming independent of one's passions. Yajnavalkya, one of the greatest philosophers in the period of the Upanishads, believed that education must aim at developing a moral character. This attitude is best explained by Shankaracharya who believed that only that which brings liberation or salvation is education.

The old attitude outlined above cannot be applied to the present period in India. One reason for this is that the contemporary political, social and economic conditions differ completely from those existing in the past. In the past, the schools then the monasteries of the saints, situated outside the towns. Such schools were helped by the state and the society, with the result that the scholarly educator could devote his entire life to mental and spiritual development. Today, India is one of the backward countries in which there is a shortage of the means of survival. Before worrying about achieving complete literacy, the nation is more concerned with arriving at a stage of economic independence. Almost everybody has to wage a terrible battle against others to satisfy his own physical needs. If education does not prepare the man to earn his own bread and that of his family, and to fulfil the common needs of his dependents, his education will be useless, however, spiritual it may be.

The modern individual is less concerned with salvation and liberation than his ancient counterpart because he is more engrossed in solving the more material problems of life which surround him. Survival is his fast concern. If he does not survive, the problem of development will not trouble him at all. The modern individual has to exert his mind and his body to ensure his own survival. Thus, it is evident that, as far as India is concerned, it is essential that education today must aim at training for livelihood Mahatma Gandhi's comments on this subjects are very illuminating. He pointed out that India's most immediate concern was to win liberation from slavery by making the greatest possible efforts, be they educational, economic, social or political. Three-fourth of the battle lay in making this effort. He did not object to higher education; in fact, he supported it. But he objected to the kind of higher education which was being imparted in the country. He said that he had provided for the best libraries, the best laboratories and research facilities in his plan. He felt that an entire army of chemists, engineers and other specialists would be dedicated to the task of fulfilling the various needs of a people who were growing daily more conscious of their rights and their requirements.

It is evident from the above description that the aims of education are intimately connected with human life. The following points can be made in this connection:

Livelihood. As has been already pointed out, livelihood is essential for human life everywhere. Hence, one of the main aims of education is to train men and women according to their abilities so that they can earn their own livelihood.

Development of Personality. A balanced development of personality is essential for the individual's private and social life, for without this he can neither satisfy all his needs nor lead a successful life. Consequently, all modern educationists unanimously agree that education must aim at the complete development of human personality.

Intellectual Development. Man is distinct among all living beings because of his intelligence. It is on the basis of his intelligence that he has become superior to all other forms of life. Through his intelligence he has developed the sciences and by using them he has gamed mastery over nature. It will, therefore, be quite in order to state that all his future progress depends to a great extent upon his intellectual development. This, too, has become one of the major aims of education.

Physical Development. In the struggle for survival, man needs a healthy and strong body, for without it, he cannot either live or satisfy his requirements. Hence, education must also aim at developing the individual's body.

Moral Development. Ethical and moral values are considered the most important in human life. Character is the most valuable thing an individual can possess. Success in human life in every sphere, be it the family, the neighbourhood, society at large, depends very much upon the possession of moral qualities and upon obedience of moral laws. The importance of moral values is even more evident in the modern world since the unprecedented improvement in the means of transport and communications and the remarkable power of destruction possessed by modern weapons. In the absence of ethical values there would be little to prevent the world from being destroyed in catastrophic wars. For this reason, moral and ethical development has also become an important object of education.

Aesthetic Development As other living beings are, man is not satisfied merely by maintaining his existence. He seeks to raise his life above the level of survival, and the things he needs for his requirements must not only be useful but also attractive and aesthetically satisfying. Cultural development includes development of sensibilities, awareness of the aesthetically satisfying in art and literature. Education also seeks to develop the aesthetic sensibility.

Social Development. Most of man's life is spent in a social environment, and in order to accommodate to this environment, the individual requires many social qualities. Education tries to develop these social qualities to facilitate the child's social adjustment.

Cultural Development. When human beings are to be-distinguished from other living beings, they are said to be cultured. Culture is man's prerogative, since it is not found among other animals. It is culture which maintains a man's relationship with his ancestors and ensures his own connections with the succeeding generations. He gets it as his social heritage and passes it on. Cultural development is also an important aspect of education.

Spiritual Development. Another distinctive feature of human life is the presence of the spiritual element. It is for this reason that Indian religious texts state that human life is granted to the soul after it has lived the life of other living beings. Man's superiority is thus the result of his spirituality. He is not merely a more efficient animal. He even seeks to identify himself with the divine power. His future depends to a large extent upon this spiritual development. Thus, spiritual development is also accepted as one of the aims of human education. Religious education is introduced solely for this purpose.

Total Development. Man is a complex being, made up of such physiological parts as the motor organs, sense organs, nervous system, etc., such processes as intelligence, emotions, feelings, etc., the social, cultural and other aspect of personality. In view of this complexity, it is believed that education must seek to develop every aspect of the human individual. He is trained to make the best use of his body. Efforts are made to develop his intellectual, moral, aesthetic, social and cultural aspects. Some people believe that this is the ideal of human perfection.

Training for Civic Life. It has already been explained that, in civilized societies, human life is identical with social life. Hence, education seeks to train the individual to live as a citizen and to fulfil all his obligations to society.

Training in International Living. The individual of today is not restricted in his movement by the boundaries of his country. In the West, in particular, people commonly move from one country to another. It is now commonly felt that if man is to rise above his present level, he must be prepared to discard his narrow nationalistic leanings and adopt a more universal or international attitude. Since this is a new situation, another objective has been imported into the mandate of education, and that is, it must prepare the education for international living.

Interrelationship of Education and Social Life

Aims of Vedic Education. A single glance at the history of education in any country will reveal that the aims of education have invariably gone hand-in-hand with the aims and ideals of social life. One can take the case of education in India. In ancient times, the Aryans believed that the objective of human life was to lead a prosperous and varied life in a natural environment and to aim at total development. In the Upanishadic period, salvation was believed to be the ideal of life and hence it was felt that anything which led to salvation was educative. Thus, spiritual development was the objective of education in ancient India because it was also the social ideal of the time. Clarifying the aims of Vedic education, Altekar has commented that the aims of Vedic education were worship of God and a feeling of religiosity, building of character, development of personality, training in the fulfilment of civil and social duties, improvement in social skills, the protection and further propagation of national culture.

Aims of Buddhist Education. Gautama Buddha established a new set of religious ideals which differed from the Brahman ideals. He placed the greatest emphasis upon religion, and consequently one of the main aims of education in the Buddhist monasteries was religious training. In other educational institutions the students were also given training in other-skills necessary for life. Buddhist education was more practical and useful than Brahmanic teaching but it did not include military training. Education was open to men and women both. It was imparted by the Buddhist monks, whose only aim was to spread their own religion.

Aims of Muslim Education. During the Muslim period, the social education and mode of life in the country underwent considerable change due to Muslim influence. The Muslim system of education sought only to instill respect for their own religious principles, laws and traditions. Most of these aims were borrowed from their religious texts. At the same time the Hindu schools provided education on the lines of the ancient educational system.

Aims of English Education. The arrival of the English in India led to further changes in the social life and ideals. The British administration was keen only on strengthening its hold in the country. Consequently, Macaulcy commented that the aim of their education was to create a class of individuals who were Indian only in colour and blood, but who were English in their interests, opinions, morality and intelligence. Schools following the British pattern of education turned out individuals good only for white collar jobs. Besides, they were also subjected to indoctrination in Christian principles.

Aims of Education in Free India. After India had won independence, the pattern of social life and its ideal underwent another change. Education no longer aimed at the propaganda of a particular religion or at strengthening the roots of a foreign administration. The establish end of democracy helped to import democratic ideals into education also. Education was given the aim of achieving the all round development of the nation. It therefore sought to provide education in the arts and sciences, business and commerce, law and medicine in fact, in every sphere of activity calculated to promote the nation's interests. Education at all levels, primary, intermediate and college levels, was reconsidered and reformed in order to help in achieving the national goal. It was oriented to the needs of the nation. Various committees were set up to examine the pattern of education and to redefine its aims and objectives in the light of the new aims of the society and the nation. All the notable educationists-Sri Aurobindo, Mahatma Gandhi, Rabindra Nath, vivekananda, Radha Krishnan, Dayananda, and others-suggested the need for a comprehensive education based upon human psychology. Education in India today represents a synthesis between utility and idealism, keeping in view the needs and aims of modern India. The present pattern of education allows the presence of various kinds of syllabi. It stresses the importance of national values, and aims at a synthesis between the individual and the social good. This casual survey of the history of education in India is adequate to illustrate that the ideals of education are linked with the social ideals, and hence they change when the social ideals change.

Aims of Ancient Greek Education. All that has been said of Indian education also holds true of education in every other country. Any study of education from ancient Greece to present day Europe will show that the aims of education change along with variations in social life and its ideals. Ancient Greek society laid great emphasis upon physical and mental development, and hence education also concentrated upon these two elements.

Aims of education in Napoleon's France. In Napoleon's France education aimed at instilling knowledge of the Christian moral principles, respect for the authority of the state, and obedience of the rules of the university.

Aims of Education in America. Before the First World War, American education was primarily oriented towards training in body, mind and character. Present day American education is concerned much more with training the individual in responsible citizenship, to earn his livelihood, to spend his leisure profitably and to develop his personality to the fullest possible extent. It is obvious, then, the educational ideals change with changed social life and ideals.

Aims of Education Due to Political Organisation. In the modern era, it is the political organization which determines the pattern of social life. Life and social ideals under communist government differ from those under democratic or despotic governments. J. F. Brown astutely remarks, "Education in any country and at all periods reflects values of the ruling class." It cannot be denied that, at times, educationists have raised their voice against educational patterns set down by the state, but all such efforts have been futile until the social ideals themselves have changed and accommodated the ideas of the rebels. Irrespective of the form of the government, it is the state which lays down the objectives of education. One main reason for this is that, in any case, the state exercises considerable control over education in most countries. In fact, without such control and governmental assistance it would be impossible to provide all kinds of education. This is true of India also. Here, too, the objectives of primary, intermediate and university education have been determined by committees formed and empowered by the state. Education in America, for example, is oriented towards propagation of the democratic ideal while education teaches the individual to prepare for democratic citizenship while education under communist or dictatorial regimes is concerned primarily with instilling in the individual a healthy respect and obedience to the rules and mandates of the government.

It is clear from the foregoing discussion that social life and ideals influence educational objectives to a very great extent. This subject will now be subjected to more detailed analysis - effect of social life on the aims of education, and effect of social philosophies on the aims of education.

Social Life and the Aims of Education

In the history of human civilization, one can see considerable changes in the pattern and form of social life, as new attitudes and scientific and technological developments made their impact. Social life today is so different from the primitive social life because of technology. The recent remarkable developments in science and technology have led to important changes in human values. As a consequence, one of the aims recently given to education, in most civilized countries, is to provide technical and professional training. In addition to the technological developments, economic changes have also influenced social life considerably. Industrialization and urbanization have also influenced economic change. Increases in population have only added to the complexity of economic problems. For this reason education is faced with the problem of providing such training as will improve the practical and vocational skills of the individual so that he may be able to earn his livelihood and also make his contribution to national development.

The democratic values of equality, fraternity and liberty are now part of social life almost in every country of the world. The social instinct of most people today refuses to discriminate between one another on the bases of caste, class, creed, community, sex, etc. Everyone wants freedom and demands an equal share of the opportunities in every sphere of life. It has been experienced everywhere that true liberty and equality are impossible without spreading the feeling of fraternity. Consequently, one of the chief responsibilities of modern education is to generate a character which will help the education to become a useful member of a democratic society.

Social Philosophies and the Aims of Education

In any country the social ideals are determined by the form of government and the ideas of its great individuals. In modem India, social ideals have been formed by the ideas of such great individuals as Aurobindo, Vivekananda, Rabindranath, Mahatma Gandhi, Dayananda, on the one hand, and by the suggestions of various government committees on the other. Much the same can be seen in the case of other civilized countries as England, America, Germany, France, etc. The objectives of education are formulated by the ideas of leading thinkers and the plans of the government. The influence of social ideals can also be seen in the form of the prevailing social philosophy. This social philosophy is seen in the form of materialism, utilitarianism, fascism, communism, democracy, and other philosophical attitudes. These attitudes are seen not only in the thinking of a few people, but also as a powerful force, in the form of an ism, when it influences and sways entire societies. These social philosophies influence and change the ideals of education.

Idealism. In idealistic societies, of which one example is ancient Indian Vedic society, the greatest emphasis is laid upon the propagation of religious, moral and spiritual ideals. In this case, the more permanent objectives are considered more important than the more immediate ones. Efforts are made to achieve a complete development of the human personality, and also to create the best possible synthesis between the basic elements of the individual and the society. Most of the objectives of this kind of education tend to be universal.

Realism. The philosophy of realism suggests that in determining the objectives of education, the immediate needs of society should be .kept in view. This attitude encourages technological, economic and scientific education which can help in the material development of the nation.

Materialism. A society which accepts the materialistic philosophy sets on store by moral, religious or spiritual values. Consequently, education is fashioned to achieve the physical and mental development of the individual.

Pragmatism. Pragmatic thinking encourages a pattern of education in which every individual gets the opportunity to develop all his abilities and capabilities to their fullest extent.

Fascism. Fascism accepts the complete authority of the state, and argues that the state is the end, and the individual only the means to that end. Consequently, education is designed to train the individual merely to serve as the instrument of the state. In this case, he is taught to wo... ... the interests of the state and to be prepared for the greatest sacrifices he is called upon to perform.

Communism. Communist societies normally stress the value of the realistic aims of education. Labour is accorded the greatest importance. The aim of education is concerned with labour from every aspect, the economic, political, social and even aesthetic. Educational institutions are mere instruments of state policy. The ideas of the state are propagated among the educands everywhere, and no one has the liberty to oppose or to criticise them. Consequently, the objective of education is to propound communist ideals to the educands.

Democracy. One example of a democratic society is the modern American society. The two fundamental principles of democracy are that the individual is an end in himself and that he should comfort himself in such a way that his conduct promotes the welfare of all. Liberty, equality and fraternity are the ideas of democracy. Such a society allows the greatest possible freedom to its members and tries to provide equal opportunities to all. The aim of democratic society is the maximum good of the maximum number. Consequently, education has the following objectives in a democratic society:

Respect for Human Personality. Creating respect for human personality in the new generation.

Control over Means. Assisting the people to obtain control over the means of education and, according to the time and ability available, to gain control over the greatest possible extent of social heritage.

Welfare. Helping the people to pay attention to general welfare and to learn the difficult art of self-development.

Ability to Think. Developing in each individual the ability to think in terms of the established categories of truth.

Democratic Progress. Assisting the people in understanding the nature of democracy and in aiming at the progress of society as the goal of life.

It is thus seen, that educational objectives in a democratic society are framed to assist in the spread of democratic ideals. India is a democratic republic. Here, also education aims at instilling the ideal of democratic life in the educands at every stage of education.

Changing Aims of Education

From the foregoing account of the various forms of social life and social ideals, and the objectives of education conforming to each one of them, it is evident that the aims of education are not permanent but changeable. Hence, it follows that if we want to create a particular pattern of social life and social ideals in a society, it is necessary that the educational pattern should conform to that kind of social life. Most educationists level criticism at the existing pattern of education for this reason. As long as the ideals and objectives of education continue to stray away from the social ideals, it is necessary to offer criticism to guide them back. This is necessary because, in the final analysis, the one single aim of education is to try and make every individual the ideal member of an ideal society.

Vocational Aims of Education

The aims of education have been variously defined by different educationists, depending upon the time and situation. Majority of the modern educationists suggest that the aim of education is to prepare the individual for life by developing in him qualities and abilities which he will require in future life. If this preparation for life is taken to mean development which will fulfil all the needs of adult life, it may lead to complications. Most of the modern thinkers interpret this preparation for life as the development of capabilities which enable the individual to earn his livelihood. This is true of India and of most other modern countries. Education aims at preparing a man to earn his livelihood.

Dewey, an American educationist, has commented that education is meaningful only when it aims at some vocation or employment. In the present age, some kind of educational qualification is essential for almost every job. As a result, very extensive educational qualifications become necessary for good jobs which carry big salaries. Economic independence is essential in the present day world and for this reason parents are determined to educate their children so that they can become economically independent.

And, in fact, there can be no reason for denying this. Every individual should depend upon himself for his means of support. In the case of developing countries like India, technical and professional training is of the greatest importance. If the investments made on education do not help the economic advancement of the country, such expenditure cannot be justified. Every young man is faced with the question of earning his bread. If his education does not prepare him for this, there is little reason to commend such an education. In India, the earning of one's livelihood is not merely an economic necessity, but a spiritual duty.

The Advantages. It is clear from the above description that the vocational objective of education is an important aspect of it, and it has the following advantages:

Solution of Economic Problems. India is today facing such grave problems as unemployment, poverty, famine, etc. Our economic problems are our greatest difficulties. On the other hand, most Western and Asian nations accept the vocational aspect of education, and it is seen that these nations are self- dependent and prosperous. They enjoy great respect and power in the world. Hence, technical and vocational training is of the greatest importance, since only such training can help to solve the economic problems of any country.

Dynamism. The principle of activity applies to the vocational aim of education. Dewey has commented that education imparted in this way makes use of the child's tendencies and habits, pays attention to their interests and awakens their minds.

Moral, Intellectual and Cultural Development. As far as the vocational aspect of education is concerned, it is connected with earning money. For this reason, one can expect a high moral, intellectual and cultural level from an educated individual. If the educated individual fails to win economic independence, he tends to be immoral in his behaviour, degenerate in his intellectuality and indifferent to the arts and sciences.

The Disadvantages. In view of these advantages of vocational objectives, most educationists in India are in favour of it. Efforts are being made to expand the facilities for technical and professional training in the country. Even the kind. Of basic education suggested by Mahatma Gandhi aimed at making the individual financially independent. But if the earning of one's bread is considered the sole aim of education, it leads to many difficulties. The major ones are the following:

Absence of Liberal Education. Liberal education plays an important part in the individual's development, since it alone is responsible for his intellectual and cultural development.

One-sided Attitude. Although vocational guidance and professional training aimed at economic independence are important forms of education, it cannot be denied that education must also be responsible for the individual's character development, spiritual development, cultural development, development of his personality, etc. If education aims only at vocational proficiency, it represents a one-sided approach.

Materialism. If education has vocational proficiency as its only objective, it becomes materialistic, at the cost of religious, moral and intellectual values. Materialism also leads to an increase in self-interest, violence and cut-throat competition which are detrimental to society and individual both.

It is evident from the foregoing discussion of the vocational objective of education that although it is an important objective, it cannot be considered the sole aim of education, even if it is considered the most important.

Character Development as Aim

Philosophers of education have always considered character formation as one of the most important objectives of education. Among these Philosophers are Plato, Aristotle, Herbart and Pestalozzi. Herbart has gone to the length of saying that the very fundamental nature of education is implicit in morality. He argues that education is essential for moral development since the moral individual must be free. Independence is bestowed by reason, and reason is obtained by education. The educational system in ancient India laid great stress upon forming the character of the student. Yajnavalkya suggested that only that is education which enhances the individual's usefulness for society and provides him with a good character.

At that time, the education was compelled to obey the rules of cleanliness of behaviour, self-control and regularity. Education in ancient Greece had the same objectives. Even today, educationists agree that education must aim at forming the character of the individual.

Meaning of Character

But it must be remembered that no two thinkers have defined character in the same way, McDougall, the psychologist, defines it as an organization of sentiments, in which one particular sentiment governs all the other sentiments of the individual. From the psychological point of view, an individual whose sentiments are not governed by a governing or driving passion, has a disorganised personality. The higher the governing passion, the higher is the individual's character. It must also be kept in mind that, basically, character does knot imply moral character. It has been interpreted in this sense only after Immanuel Kant, the German philosopher, who explained it in this way. In ancient Greece, the word character was taken to mean the moulds used for making coins. In order to prevent the minting of false coins, each one of these moulds was designed to avoid possible forgery. The word retains this meaning even in modern English usage. For this reason, some people use the term ethical character to distinguish between good and bad characters. Skinner has commented that the character of an individual, as the word character has been defined by history, implies all that which renders a man or a woman unique, unlike all other human beings. Accordingly, then, character includes all those qualities and peculiarities of a person which help to distinguish him from all others. Nevertheless, in actual fact, character can be seen only as an organisation of sentiments. The Hindi equivalent of this word refers, to a great extent, to the qualities of the personality. Values which a person considers important are concerned with his sentiments. For example, the sentiments of patriotism, love for mother or philanthropy are concerned with the values of sacrifice, service or kindness.

Process of Character Formation

The sentiment of self-respect plays an important part in

character formation. Most of the qualities concerned with the, development of character are acquired by the individual, as he lives his life in society. This process of character formation starts in childhood. The child's environment, made up of his family life, the society and culture to which he is exposed, plays an important part in his character formation.

Character Formation through Education

There can be no two opinions about accepting character formation as the objective of education. Now that the world has been made much smaller by rapid transport and communications, the obedience of ethical rules is important not only in an individual's conduct but also in the behaviour of nations. With the development of nuclear weapons, man possesses fantastic destructive power, which has endangered the existence of the very rate. In the absence of morality he may be inspired to use these weapons. Wars can be avoided not by the rules of the more powerful nations. In these conditions, it is imperative that education in every part of the world aims at the development of moral character.

Even if character is interpreted in more liberal terms, without limiting it to the concept of a moral character, it remains one of the major aims of education. Man cannot develop if his character is the basis of his individual qualities, since he expresses his individuality through his character. Character is thus an essential characteristic of a developed individual.

It is evident from the foregoing discussion that the major objectives of education should be the formation of character. But in India's present condition, education should also aim at enabling the individual to earn his livelihood. Education cannot aim exclusively at character formation. A fool cannot be ethical. Knowledge is essential to morality. For this reason, education must also aim at imparting knowledge. In the same way, one cannot survive on good deeds and good words alone. The educated individual must also be capable of earning his bread. Education must also aim at developing the individual's personality. If character formation is accepted as the major aim of education, it would benefit society, but education must also seek to enhance the individual's individuality.

It is evident from this that character formation is an important objective of education, but by no means the only one.

Individual Aims

Individual aim of education does not imply that it is intended for the individual alone, because, in view of the close relationship between them, the individual and society cannot be dissociated from each other. But when we talk of the individual aims of education, we imply those objectives of education which seek to benefit the individual alone. It is possible that these may even go against the interests of society. The first individual aim of education is to fit the individual to earn his livelihood so that he can earn money and satisfy his own and his family's moral needs. The second individual objective is the individual's mental development. Without this, he finds it difficult to understand and to solve the problems of his life. Mental development includes education through a formal syllabi. Knowledge of language enables the individual to exchange ideas with other people and to take advantage of the social heritage, secure in the form of books. It is said that the body is the only means of achieving fulfilment. Hence, another aim of education is to develop the body. In addition to mental and physical development, education must also allow for moral and spiritual development because without these no individual can even dream of complete development.

Social Aims

Man lives in society, acquires socialization through his contact with his family, his relatives, his neighbours and friends. He learns the ways of moving in society, of talking to people, of mutual behaviour. Through these contacts with others he satisfies his own physical and psychological needs. Hence it would not be out of place to say that if education does not fulfil the social aims, it is incomplete. What is this social aim of education ? From the social standpoint, education must aim at developing those qualities in the individual which will help him; to adjust with other members of society. Such qualities are sympathy, service, kindness, love, brotherhood, equality, etc. By developing such qualities, an individual can become a useful member of society.

A college is a prototype of society, on a very small-scale. From one viewpoint therefore, education is the most important means of establishing social control over the individual. The civilization, culture, ideas and traditions of society are kept secure and transmitted from one generation to the next, through education.

The former American President, late Roosevelt, once commented that the criterion of a man's education and ability was the role he had played in the progress of his nation and society. It is the duty of every educated individual that he must use his abilities, his intelligence and power to benefit his society and his country. Only that society progress which has such individuals among its members.

Another social objective of education is the safe-keeping and transmission of culture from one generation to another. It is education which makes a man cultured, for through education he acquires the culture of his society. Education not only safeguards the culture of the society but also tries to develop in individuals the ability to criticise and root out the evils and malpractices in society. Education should not only teach individuals to be controlled by society but also teach them to change the society because social change can be brought about only through individuals. In democratic societies, social progress depends upon the leaders of societies. Education, therefore, must also aim at creating this type of constructive leadership. To put it briefly, the aim of education is to guide the progress of society.

Functions of Education in Human Life

Whatever is acquired in human life is the result of formal or informal education. When the child is born, he has no knowledge of his surroundings. Gradually he comes to recognise his environment by using his sense organs and by coming in contact with other people. Many ideas and habits he learns merely by observing others. But in no civilised society is it believed possible for degree of formal education. For this reason, one finds arrangements for education everywhere. Not only in civilised societies, but even in primitive societies the adults try to educate adolescents in the ways of adult life. Among the tribals of India, this social education of the young girls and boys takes place at the dormitories. To put it briefly, the individual's character, personality, culture, thinking, commonsense, skills, habits and even the other less significant things of life depend upon education. The importance of education in human life is thus evident. This importance is further clarified if we look at the following functions of education.

Development of Natural Abilities. When the child is born, he is already possessed of many kinds of natural abilities. As the body grows the mind also grows, but the innate abilities and qualities do not develop quite so naturally and without aid. It is often said that if the mind is not exercised its abilities cannot be developed. Hence, the first aim of education is to try to develop such abilities as power of imagination, of thinking, etc., by providing appropriate opportunities and stimuli. It is for this reason that, as a part of child education, one of the first steps is to put various kinds of instruments and apparatus before the child so that he can learn to use his sense organs. This is called education of senses.

The child is also made to improve his power of thinking by presenting many different kinds of problems. His imagination is allowed to develop through the medium of various arts and skills. He is taught to concentrate by using many kinds of techniques to attract his attention. The various methods of learning are brought to his notice by letting him do different kinds of work. He is also taught to make adequate use of the different parts of his body by various games and sports. Such basic requirements of life as eating, sleeping, sitting and walking, moving around, are taught to the child by family it self. All these activities are part of the child's early education.

Character-building. Psychologists contend that the foundation of the child's character is laid in the first few years of his life. The impressions about behaviour and conduct that fall upon the infant's mind are later exhibited in the form of his character. The importance of character is hardly a subject to be discussed. It is developed by education, mainly informal education. Putting it differently, the infant's character is built up not so much by lectures and lessons as by the examples presented to him in the family, school, neighbourhood, group, etc. Character is the organization of various sentiment. The focus of this organization is the sentiment of self-regard. And it is up to the teacher and the child's parents to develop this sentiment of self-regard in the child. Once this is developed, the child can then move further on the road to self-development. Education is of particular significance in the development of moral character because the child is not naturally endowed with the power of distinguishing between the right and the wrong. The difference between right and wrong is taught by adults. This is aided by story-telling, setting good examples and providing education of social life. In fact, many educationists believe that the aim of education is to develop a moral character. As Herbart has expressed it, the development of a good moral character amounts to education.

Development of Personality. The patterns of behaviour that a child choose in his adjustment with the individuals and objects in his environment depend upon his personality. It is the development of personality which leads to a development of individuality, which is an inevitable characteristicofan educated individual. The informal development of the personality takes place through his family, neighbourhood, the conditions of work, etc., but educationists believe that one important objective of education is to develop personality. Hence, the child is given opportunities of performing different kinds of work so that his personality may develop. Games play an important role and in personality development. His personality achieves integration and strength in facing the many kinds of problems which make up a game. The social aspect of his personality is developed in the communal life of the school. Social customs, traditions, the forms of social control, cultural elements, etc., also play an important role in personality development. His personality achieves integration and strength in facing the many kinds of problems which make up a game. The social aspect of his personality is developed in the communal life of the school. Social customs, traditions, the forms of social control, cultural elements, etc., also pay important part in developing the personality. It is for this reason that distinct differences can be seen in the personalities of individuals belonging to different cultures and societies. The first and most permanent influence upon the child's personality development is the family such things as his order of birth in the family, the parents' behaviour towards the child, the mutual behaviour of the parent's themselves, their profession, influence their personality. It is said that parental education plays a large part in building the personality of great men. Apart from this, the child's personality is influenced by many kinds of literature such as biographies of great men, stories, novels, essay, etc. It is believed that it is the duty of the teacher to prevent his wards from developing bad habit and also see if the wards are developing balanced personalities. The teacher can take the assistance of the psychologists and also of the parents in ensuring a healthy development of personality. If the child does not develop a balanced personality, it can be said that his education is incomplete.

Preparation for Adult Life. Livelihood is believed to be the aim of education. Economic factors controlling life in the present day world have become so complex that no one who is not properly educated can hope at successfully earn his living. In the past, most people pursued agriculture, which does not demand such a high degree of specialization. For them education was not so essential. But the recent developments in science and the increasing specialization of all professions has made it impossible for one individual to perform any job without training and education. As a general rule, highly paid jobs require specialized training of a very high calibre. The ability to earn enough is not the only factor to be considered in the preparation for adult life. Earning money is one of the aspects of adult life, another is marriage and children. Once this stage is reached, the individual has to face all the attendant responsibilities. Education aims at training the individual to earn his livelihood and society in general. In fact, if the child is helped to develop a balanced personality and a good character, there can be no better preparation for adult life. If education can perform this task, then men and women become highly responsible and useful citizen.

Control and Fulfilment of Basic Instincts. Every being is born into the world possessed of certain basic instincts. There may be difference of opinion about the instincts that the child is born with, but there can be no doubt about the presence of some instincts, the child's mind is not a blank tablet on which any thing can be written. Psychologists have demonstrated that not only does the human infant possess some instincts, but also that there are individual differences in respect of these instincts. If a human being lives alone, he can give expression to his instincts in any manner that he likes. But human beings live in groups, and hence it becomes necessary for them to control some instincts and to change the mode of expression of other instincts in such a manner that they do not injure other people. Besides, there are certain instincts which can be fulfilled only with the co-operation of another human being. Sex is one such instinct. Since, from the moral standpoint, the individuality and the humanity of every individual must be respected, it becomes necessary for people to control their instincts in all forms of communal life, such as marriage.

Sublimation of Human Instincts. Civilized life would become impossible if such instincts as aggressiveness and sex were not sublimated. Education helps in the control, sublimation and change of instincts. Various kinds of arts are used is a medium of sublimation. Education in social life helps the child to learn how to control his instincts. The same end is served through the system of reward and punishment found in the family, college or society at large. Rules of administration and the means of social control also help in this work.

Creation of Useful Citizens. Although many thinkers have dreamt of a society without government, in actual fact no such society exists. Individuals who have been deprived of their citizenship or have never been granted this, make all kinds of efforts to get the citizenship of one nation or another. If they cannot obtain it, they have to face all kinds of difficulties. Hence, the relationship between the individual and the state is universal. In this relationship, the status of the individual is called the status of citizenship. Hence, it is desirable that the individual should be trained in behaving as a citizen so that he can fulfil his duties to the state. In the present age, this function of education is emphasized very much because most states themselves are responsible for providing education. In democratic systems, public also plays a hand in guiding the educational system. But in communist countries, the state has control of the educational system. Despite this, it is believed that education must provide capable citizens, because in the absence of such citizens the adjustment between the individual and the state would suffer. The thinkers of ancient Greece believed that this is the most important function of education. Now-a-days almost all thinkers agree that true democracy in any country is possible only when almost all its citizens arc properly educated. Education in responsible citizenship is also given through the medium of political parties, radio, television, newspapers, magazines, etc.

Development of a Sense of Community. The statement that man is a social animal means no more than that he lives in society. It does not imply that the human child is possessed of social qualities at birth. These social qualities are acquired and taught. One major objective of education, therefore, is the teaching of social qualities and development of sense of community. This community feeling urges the child to co-operate with his fellows, to make sacrifices if they become necessary, to rise above the considerations of caste and creed and develop a sense of oneness with the nation, etc. The development of this feeling depends upon opportunities provided in family life, play groups and schools and colleges. For this reason educational institutions pay particular attention to this. The student is given the opportunity of collectively running the administration, of organising extra-curricular programmes, of devising consecutive programme which help in developing this sense of community. This feeling is the basis of national unity. The efforts being made in India to-day to evolve an emotional unity are in fact efforts to develop this feeling of community.

Protection through Culture and Civilization. As compared to other animals, man has progressed more because human society has succeeded in protecting its knowledge and in conveying it to future generations. This has been done through the medium of culture and civilization. A child born in the present time does not think of everything from the beginning. His thinking and modes of behaviour are determined by customs, traditions and social institutions, which are repositories of the experience and thinking of his ancestors. For this reason, societies which have a more ancient culture shows signs of greater organization and systematization, greater stability. Hence, it is now universally accepted that culture and civilization should be protected and allowed to grow through new developments. This is mainly achieved through education. The child receives the social heritage in the form of education. Then, through education. For this reason many contemporary thinkers in India have suggested that teaching of Indian culture should be made compulsory in all universities.

Encouragement to Social Welfare. Both formal and informal education helps the individual to evolve a critical attitude which helps him to analyse everything presented to him. If he fmds any faults in it, he exercises his mind to find some ways of removing the faults. In this manner education has been the basis of all social welfare programmes. When English education was introduced in India, it brought along with it the western tendencies of individualism, rationalism, etc. As a consequence all educated people in the country were impelled to re-examine ancient Indian traditions and institutions. This led to the development of such institutions as the Braham Samaj, Arya Samaj, Prarthana Samaj, Theosophical Society, etc. Each one aimed at social welfare. And the inspiration for each of these institutions came from highly educated individuals. Education thus leads to a continuous evaluation of the various constituents of society, its institutions, modes of social control etc. and inspires efforts to make improvements where they are needed.

National Development. The overall development of all national groups is essential for the development and progress of human society, but this is not possible without universal education. It is for this reason that the U.N.0. is making efforts to provide education to the backward countries. In every country, efforts are made to develop a feeling of belonging among its citizens, the sense of nationality. It helps to induce the individual to do his best for the nation. Besides almost every nation has its own plan of national education which seeks to fulfil the aim of that nation.

Use of Leisure. One of the main aims of education is to teach an individual to make the best use of leisure. Using leisure time in educational activities is itself useful. On the other hand, education itself guides the individual to utilise his leisure time properly. Educated people can use their leisure time effectively by devoting themselves to magazines, arts, etc. Even the standard of their normal conversation, discussions etc., is higher than that of the uneducated persons. Education helps to develop various kinds of interests so that leisure itself does not become a burden.

Increase of Consciousness of Other Cultures. In countries in which many different cultural groups co-exist, education helps to increase consciousness of these other cultures and of cultural exchange. This helps individuals to understand each other, thus increasing national unity. There are many different cultures in the world today. As long as education cannot create a feelings of cooperation and of mutual love, the ideal of a unified world cannot be realized.

Improvement in Emotional Unity. At the present time, many disintegrating forces such as regionalism, casteism, communalism, linguism, etc., are working towards complete disintegration of the country. If the nation is to be saved from complete fragmentation, it is necessary to generate a sense of emotional unity in all men and women. Then individuals can be expected to feel that they are members of the same nation and to behave in the interests of the nation. Education can help to create this emotional unity. Many educationists have given valuable suggestions for achieving this.

Development of an International Feeling. As a result of the unprecedented improvements in the means of transport and communications, people of different nations are constantly coming into contact with each other. All kinds of people are realizing the importance of internationalism, after having witnessed the havoc caused by the two world wars. All contemporary educationists in India, including Sri Aurobindo, Rabindra Nath, Vivekananda, have stressed the importance of creating this feeling of internationalism in all educands. In the present context, therefore, one of the main tasks of education is to generate this feeling in the student community.

From the foregoing description of the functions of education in human life, it is evident that the functions of education are the same as its objectives. To put it differently, the objective which have been assigned to education by various thinkers are the tasks it has to do. It need hardly be stressed that the functions of education change when ideals governing it undergo changes. Nevertheless, the fundamental elements of human life are the same today as they were in Plato's and Aristotle's times. Hence, such aims of education as character-building, development of personality, social welfare, proper use of leisure, protection of culture and civilization, development of innate qualities, etc., are permanent objectives which will remain the same in future also.

Functions of Education in National Life

The functions of education in national life differ somewhat from its functions in normal life because human life is possible even without a nation. Primitive societies still do not possess any kind of nation. Nations are found in more civilized societies. Before examining the role of education in national life, it is necessary to discover the nature of a nation. Nation is a group of human beings which lives in a country delimited by geographical boundaries. This group is possessed of a desire to be bound by common traditions, common interests, similar political ambitions and political unity. The important aspects of national life can be understood from this description. For national life to be possible, it is essential that its members should have common traditions, interests, sentiments and political ambitions, and an emotional unity. Education aims at creating and maintaining all these various elements, and thus contributes to national life. The following points are to be considered in this connection :

Maintaining Communal Interests and Tradition. The main objective in applying a uniform system of education to an entire nation is that a similarity of interests and traditions may be generated among the people. For India, this is of even greater importance, because the nation is composed of many different cultural and linguistic groups. Education achieves this similarity and identity through its prescribed syllabi and various kinds of extra-carricular programmes.

Similarity of Political Ambitions. If different groups within a single nation are found to possess various and contradictory political ambitions, it becomes difficult to maintain that nation's independence and unity. One chief objective of education, thus, is to propagate similar political ambitions among all classes and groups of people. In India, young men and women who received English education studied the history of Western nations and concluded that India must also win its freedom. Once this political awakening spread among the educated classes and led to similarity of political ambitions, national movements took shape and the demand for a free India was put forward. In the more recent context, education should aim at creating a desire for complete and comprehensive development of the nation so that people may rise above their own narrow interests and work in the interests of the nation as a whole.

Diffusion of Emotional Unity. It is obvious that one task of education is to diffuse a feeling of emotional unity in the younger generation so that all its members may feel identified with the nation and be inspired, to work for its improvement. Such forces of disintegration as communalism, casteism, linguism, regionalism, etc., can be countered only when emotional unity is increased. For this the educational programme should insist on the teaching of the same history, same cultural heritage, etc. Sense of community is an essential part of nationalism and the foundations of sense of belonging to a community are laid in schools. Hence, efforts should be made to create such an atmosphere in schools that the students may have a sense of belonging, not of alienation.

Development of a National Language. Although the development of many different languages and the common use of them does not hinder national unity in any way, the absence of a single common language hinders it considerably since language is the medium through which thoughts and emotions are expressed. Just as thoughts and language are intimately connected, nationalism and language are also intimately related to each other. Hence one objective of education is the development to a national language. In India, the Constitution has laid down Hindi as the national language, and it has been accepted in principle that this language must be spread over the entire country. But it is regrettable that the work of giving this status to Hindi is not progressing as fast as is desirable. If greater efforts arc not made in this direction, it may create a danger to national unity in the country. Hence, it is desirable that the teaching of Hindi should be compulsory at all stages of education.

Respect to All Religions. India is a secular state in that it grants equal status and importance to every religion, and refuses to discriminate between citizens on the basis of their religious beliefs. But despite the provision of the Constitution, the poison of communalism is found in greater abundance in the country, and it has been impossible to remove it despite the greatest efforts. One way of achieving this is to indoctrinate the children through education that every religion deserves equal respect and that one's own religion is not necessarily the best. Education must seek to eliminate all such prejudices. Hence, in a country like India, one task of education is to generate respect for all religions.

Training for Leadership. Proper development in any sphere can be achieved only if there is adequate leadership. A country can progress only if it has able leaders in the social, economic, political, literary, cultural, artistic, industrial and moral fields. Education can provide such leaders. Hence, one of the objectives of education is to bring forth leaders in various spheres and to train them to perform their tasks efficiently. This can be done by encouraging students participation in various kinds of extracurricular programmes in the college so that the student's capabilities can find expression. This also helps to train them in leadership.

Fulfilment of the Need for Skilled Workers. Every sphere needs the dedication and cooperation of skilled and efficient workers. Such workers arc required not only in industry and commerce, but also in the social and political spheres. This need can be fulfilled by education. During the process of education it is possible to discover the sphere for which a particular individual is best suited. Once this has been found out, he can then be trained in his particular profession.

Consciousness of Duties. If a nation is to progress, it is essential that its citizens should be aware of their duties and responsibilities. Education can spread this awareness among the people. In schools the students are told of their responsibilities as members of the nation. This awareness of their duties is created in them, and they are also taught how they can fulfil these duties. This role of education is of the greatest importance in democratic states.

Evolution of National Feeling. The strength of national feeling in an individual is judged by the extent to which he can subject his personal and narrow class interests in favour of the wider national interests and the extent to which he is prepared to work for the national interests. For this it is essential that the individual should be conscious of his duties to the nation as well as capable of rising above narrow interests of regionalism, communalism, casteism, etc.. Both these can be made possible through education. National feeling is generated among the students in the colleges through various extra-curricular programmes and syllabi. But in fact the informal mode of education, such as family, newspapers, magazines, radio, television, etc., play an important role in generating a national feeling. National education programmes should pay particular attention to these and to the creation of a national literature.

It is evident from the function of education in national life that the members of the nation should be educated in such a way, through the teaching of national history, the national language, different kinds of programmes, etc., that a national feeling is created in them. They should begin to consider national interests as higher than any other interests, and they should he prepared to make any sacrifice for the nation. It is education which provides efficient leadership in the various spheres of national endeavour, and it is education which maintains the nation's heritage.

20

The Curriculum

The Definition

Liberal Meaning. The term curriculum is of Latin origin and it implies an athletic ground, thus indicating that curriculum is the ground through which the educand has to pass in order to reach a definite goal. In the past the term was taken to mean a collection of knowledge and skill. It did not then imply to educand's needs, but instead the knowledge and skill of the specialists working in different spheres.

Modern Interpretation. Bent and Kronenburg suggest that the curriculum is the organized form subject matter, specially prepared to meet the requirements of children. Hence, now curriculum includes those experiences and activities which provide the student with the knowledge and the skill he will require in facing the various situations of real life. Obviously, the term 'curriculum' cannot be restricted to a list of books, because it must include other activities which provide the student with the knowledge and the experiences and activities which provide the student with the knowledge and the skill he will require in facing the various situations of real life. Obviously, the term 'curriculum' cannot be restricted to a list of books, because it must include other activities which provide the student with the knowledge and the skill he will require in facing the various situations of real life. Obviously, the term 'curriculum' cannot be restricted to a list of books, because it must include other activities, the environment of the schools and numerous other elements not taught by books. In the words of Bent and Kronenburg, "Curriculum, in its broadest sense, includes the complete school environment, involving all the courses, activities, reading and associations furnished to the pupils in the school."

Curriculum as Experience. In the words of Munroe, "Curriculum embodies all the experiences which are utilized by the school to attain the aims of education." Thus, the various subjects included for study in a curriculum are not intended merely for study or rote learning but to convey experiences of various kinds. The concept has been defined in more or less the same terms in the report of the Secondary Education Commission in traditionally taught in the school, but it includes the totality of experiences that a pupil receives through the manifold activities that go on in the school in the classroom, liberty, laboratory, workshop, playgrounds and in the numerous informal contacts between teachers and pupils." Another definition of curriculum as experience is provided by Crow and Crow, "The curriculum includes all the learner's experiences in or outside school that are included in a programme which has been devised to help him develop mentally, physically, emotionally, socially, spiritually and morally." It is obvious, then, that the aim of a curriculum is to provide experience to the educand so that he may achieve complete development. By calling the curriculum an experience, the fact is made explicit the it includes not merely books but all those activities and relationships which are indulged in by the educand, both inside and outside the school. Hence, the syllabi specified by the authority should not be taken to mean curriculum.

Curriculum as a Means or Tool. It is apparent from the foregoing definitions that curriculum is not an end in itself, but a means to an end because it is created in order to achieve the aims of education. That is why one finds that different educationists have suggested different kinds of curricula to conform to the aims and objectives ascribed to education. Explaining the concept of curriculum as a tool of education, Cunningham writes, "The curriculum is the tool in the hands of the artist (the teacher) to mould his material (the pupil) according to his ideal (objective) in his studio (the school)." Here the educator is compared to an artist and the curriculum as one of the instruments of tools used by him to develop the educand according to and in conformity with the aims of education. It is evident that the curriculum will change with every change in the aims of education.

Curriculum as Environment. The most comprehensive definition of curriculum is given by those who conceive it to include the total environment of the school. In the words of H.L. Caswell, "The curriculum is all that goes on in the lives of the children, their parents and their teachers. The curriculum is made up of every thing that surrounds the learner in all his working hours." In fact, the curriculum has been described as "the environment in motion." In modern times, the term is interpreted in this more liberal sense because there is no questioning the fact that the child's education is influenced by not only books but the playgrounds, library, laboratory, reading room, extra curricular programmes, the educational environment, and a host of other factors. In the school both the educator and the educand are part of the curriculum because they are part of the environment, while in the family the child is expected to progress and achieve the goals of education.

Curriculum Includes all Activities. It is stated in the Twenty-ninth Year Book of the National Society for the Study of Education. U.S.A. that, "The curriculum may be defined as the totality of subject matter, activities, and experiences which constitute a pupil's school life." Elaborating the same concept further, H.H.Horne says. "The curriculum is that which the pupil is taught It involves more than the acts of learning and quiet study, it involves occupations, production, achievements, exercise, activity." Pragmatists, too, have included the entire range of the educand's activities in the curriculum because according to them the child learns by doing.

In the light of the various definitions of curriculum given above, it is possible to arrive at a definition of the term which includes all the points mentioned in these definitions. Briefly, then, curriculum is the means of achieving the goals of education. It includes all those experiences, activities and environments which the educand received during his educational career. Such a definition of curriculum comprehends the educand's entire life, a contention borne out by all modern educationists who believe that the child learns not only inside the school but also outside it, on the playground, at home, in society, in fact, everywhere. That is why there is nowadays so much insistence on the participation of the parents in the child's education and on not restricting the environment of the curriculum to the school environment but taking it mean every possible kind of environment encountered by the child. Besides, it includes all those activities which the child does, irrespective of the time and place of these activities. It also includes the entire range of experiences that the child has in the school, at home, in the world at large. Considering from this liberal standpoint, one finds that in preparing the curriculum one has much wider background than would otherwise be possible.

Aims and Objectives

Clarifying the aims and objectives of curriculum, it has been pointed out in the report of the Secondary Education Commission that, "The starting point for curricular reconstruction must therefore be the device to bridge the gulf between the school subjects and to enrich the varied activities that make up the warp and woof of life." Hence, the curricula should be so designed that it strains the educand to face the situations of real life, a curriculum can be said to have the following major objectives :

Synthesis of Subjects and Life. The aim of the curriculum is to arrange and provide those subjects for an educand's study which will enable the educand to destroy any gulf between school life and life outside the school. The opinion of the Secondary Education Commission has already been quoted.

Development of Democratic Values. In all democratic countries, the curriculum of education must aim to develop the democratic values of equality, liberty and fraternity, so that the educands may develop into fine democratic citizens. But the development should not only aim at national benefit. The curriculum must also aim at introducing a spirit of internationalism in the educand.

Satisfaction of the Educand's Need. In defining curriculum many educationists have insisted that it must be designed to satisfy the needs and requirements of the educand. It is seen that one finds a great variety of interests, skills, abilities, attitudes, aptitudes, etc., among educands. A curriculum should be so designed as to satisfy the general-and specific requirements of the educands.

Realization of Values. One aim of education is development of character, and what is required for this is to create in the educand a faith in the various desirable values. Hence, one of the objectives of education is to create in the educand a definite realization of the prevailing system of values.

Development of Knowledge. In its most common connotation, the term curriculum is taken to mean development of knowledge or acquisition of facts and, very frequently, this is the aspect kept in mind while designing a curriculum. But it must be remembered that it is not the only objective, although it is the most fundamental objective of a curriculum.

Creation of a Useful Environment. Another objective of curriculum is to create an environment suitable to the educand. Primarily, the environment must assist toe educand in achieving the maximum possible development of his facilities, abilities and capabilities.

Addition to Knowledge. In the contemporary educational patterns that curriculum is believed to be suitable which can create a harmony between the various branches of knowledge so that the educand's attitude should be comprehensive and complete, not one sided.

Harmony between Individual and Activity. In a democracy, such social qualities as social skills, cooperation, the desire to be of service, sympathy, etc., are very significant because without them no society can continue to exist. On the other hand, development of the individual's own character and personality are also very important. Hence, the curriculum must create an environment and provide those books which enable the individual to achieve his own development at the same time as he learns these social qualities.

Curriculum and Syllabus

The relationship between curriculum and syllabus is made very dear by the foregoing description of the aims of curriculum. Curriculum is not merely syllabus, because the latter is only verbal, book oriented and theoretical, while the former is not. Syllabus places more stress on learning and memory. On the other hand, the scope of the curriculum is much greater for it comprehends every aspect of the educand's life, seeks to satisfy all'his requirements and to develop every aspect of his personality. Hence, the syllabus is part and parcel of the curriculum but the two terms should not be treated as synonymous. In addition to the syllabus, the curriculum also includes various kinds of extra-curricular programmes, community relationships, various kinds of experiences, and all the various parts of the educational environment. Despite this the syallabus is treated as the basis of curriculum in the school, although it is improper to restrict the curriculum in this manner.

Bases of Curriculum

It is everywhere seen that the form of the curriculum undergoes a change whenever the aims of education are altered to suit changed conditions in society. For this reason, it is necessary to define the various bases of curriculum, of which the more important ones are the following:

Aims of Education. One finds differences of curriculum according to the differing aims of education determined by the different philosophies of education such as idealism, realism, pragmatism, etc. If the aim of education is to bring about an industrial revolution then the curriculum will place more stress on industrial activity but if education seeks to build the character of the educand, the curriculum will naturally lay a heavy emphasis upon the study of those subjects which help in character formation. If the curriculum aims at preparing the educand for future life and enabling him to earn his livelihood, it must include those subjects which give the educand some professional skill.

Philosophy of Education. Another basis for the formation of curriculum is the philosophy of education. Difference in philosophic concepts leads to changes in the curriculum. Philosophy considers such fundamentals and profound questions as man's place in the universe, the aims of nature, the aim of society, the relationships between man and society, etc. In every philosophy the answer derived for these questions is different and this difference lends colour to the curriculum.

Sociological Basis. In recent times, the curriculum has always been profoundably influenced by the discoveries in the various social sciences. This constitutes the sociological basis of education.

Psychological Basis. But the most important basis of

curriculum formation is the psychological one. In modern times so much research has been conducted in the sphere of educational psychology that it has become an independent branch of psychology. These researches have had great impact on the shaping of curricula and this is only natural since the curriculum is only a means to the educand's development. Hence, it should be shaped according to the psychology of the educand.

Basic Principles of Curriculum Construction

Different educationists have expressed their own views about the fundamental principles of curriculum construction, the difference being created by their different philosophies of education. Briefly, the main principles of curriculum construction are the following:

Principle of Utility. T.P. Nunn, the educationist, believes that the principle of utility is the most important principle underlying the formation of a curriculum. He writes, "While the plain man generally likes his children to pick up some scraps of useless learning for purely decorative purposes, he requires, on the whole, that they shall be taught what will be useful to them in later life, and he is inclined to give 'useful' a rather strict interpretation." As a general rule, parents are in favour of including all those subjects in the curriculum which are likely to prove useful for their child in his life and by means of which he can be made a responsible member of society.

Training in the Proper Patterns of Conduct. According to Crow and Crow, the main principle underlying the construction of a curriculum is that through education the educand should be able to adopt the patterns of behaviour proper to different circumstances. Man is a social animal who has to constantly adapt himself to the social environment. Therefore education must aim at developing all those qualities in the educand which will facilitate this adaptation to the social milieu. The child is by nature self-centred, but education must teach him to attend the needs and requirements of others besides himself. Once criterion of an educated individual is that he should be able to adapt himself to different situations with which he is confronted. In this context, the term conduct must be understood in its widest sense. Only then can this principle of curriculum construction be properly understood. "All our activities in social, economic, family and cultural environment constitute behaviour or conduct, and it is the function of education to teach us how to behave in different situations."

Synthesis of Play and Work. Of the various modern techniques of education, some try to educate through work and others through play. But a great majority of educationists agree that the curriculum should aim at achieving a balance between play and work. In other words, the work given to the educand should be performed in such a manner that the child may believe it to be play. There is a difference between work and play. That is why parents want to engage the child in work instead of allowing him to play all the time, but the child is naturally inclined to spend his time in playing. Keeping this in view, T. P. Nunn has written, "The school should be thought of not as a knowledge-monger's shop but a place where the young are disciplined in certain forms of activity. All subjects should be taught in the 'play way', care being taken that the 'way' leads continuously from the irresponsible frolic of childhood to the disciplined labours of manhood."

Synthesis of All Activities of Life. In framing a curriculum, attention should be paid to the inclusion, in it, of all the various activities of life, such as contemplation, learning, acquisition of various kinds of skill, etc. In the individual and social sphere of life, every individual has to perform a great variety of activities, and his success in life is determined by the success of all these activities. Hence, the curriculum should not neglect any form of activity related to any aspect of life. A curriculum constructed on this basis will be both comprehensive and closely related to life. In other words, it should include all the activities that the enducand is likely to require in later life.

Principle of Individual Differences. Modern educational psychology has brought to light, and stressed the significance of individual differences that exist between one individual and another. It has been discovered that people differ in respect of their mental processes, interests, aptitudes, attitudes, abilities, skills, etc., and that these differences are innate. All modern education is paidocentric, that is it is centred around the child. Psychologists insist that the curriculum should be so designed as to provide an opportunity for complete and comprehensive development to widely differing individuals. One of the basic qualities of such a curriculum is flexibility, for it must be flexible in order to accommodate educands of low, average or high intelligence and ability, and to provide each one a chance to develop all his abilities to the greatest possible extent.

Constant Development. Another basis for curriculum construction is the principle of a dynamic curriculum, based on the realization that no curriculum can prove adequate for all times and in all places. For this reason the curriculum should be flexible and changeable. This is all the more true in the modern context when new discoveries in the various branches of science are taking place everyday. Hence, it becomes necessary to reshape the curriculum fairly frequently in order to incorporate the latest developments.

Creative Training. Another important principle of curriculum construction is that of creative training. Raymont has correctly stated that a curriculum appropriate for the needs of today and the future must definitely have a positive bias towards creative subjects. And, one of the aims of education is to develop the creative faculty of the educand. All that is finest in human culture is the creation of man's creative abilities. Children differ from each other in respect of this ability. Hence, in framing a curriculum attention must be paid to the fact that it should encourage each educand to develop his creative ability as far as is possible.

Variety. Variety is another important principle of curriculum construction. The innate complexity of man and many facets of his personality make it necessary that the curriculum should be valid, because no one kind of curriculum can develop all the facilities of an individual. Hence, at every level the curriculum must have variety, it will, on the one hand, provide an opportunity for development of the different faculties of the educand, while on the other, it will retain his interest in education.

Education for Leisure. One of the objectives ascribed to education is training for leisure, because it is believed that education is not merely for employment or work. Hence it is desirable that the curriculum should also include a training in those activities which will make the individual's leisure more pleasurable. A great variety of social, artistic and sporting activities can be included in this kind of training. Besides, educands should be encouraged to foster some or the other hobby so that they can put their leisure to constructive and pleasant use.

Related to Community Life. Curriculum can also be based on the principle that school and community life must be intimately related to each other. One cannot forget that the school is only a miniature form of community. Hence, the school curriculum should include all those activities which are performed by members of larger community outside the boundaries of the school. This will help in evolving social qualities of the individual, in developing the social aspect of his personality and finally, in helping his final adaptation to the social environment into which he must ultimately go.

Evolution of Democratic Values. The construction of a curriculum in a democratic society is conditioned by the need to develop democratic qualities in the individual. The curriculum should be so designed that it develops a democratic feeling and creates a positive faith in democratic values. The programmes devise in the college qualities in the educand so that he may be able to participate usefully and successfully in democratic life. In all the democratic societies of the world, this is the chief consideration in shaping the curricula for primary, secondary and higher education.

It is evident from the foregoing account of the various bases of curriculum construction that this should be duly conditioned by careful thinking on all aspects individual and social life, variety, play and work, earning of livelihood, leisure, etc.

21

Significance of College

So many brilliant boys and girls have to stop their studies after high school due to lack of facilities. Therefore, who will go to college also depends on the facilities offered by the government and the colleges. Besides, the poor parents cannot meet the expenses of college education. Therefore, who will go to college depends upon the financial condition of the family. Again, the employment situation is also important in this connection. In India most of the girls are married after passing through the schools. Therefore, few go to college. Again, in rural areas most of the young men take up their family occupation after high school or intermediate and therefore do not go to college. Thus, the colleges are mostly attended by urban youths and the unemployed men from the suburban villages. This situation may be changed by governmental measures such as provision of scholarship to all the meritorious students particularly those coming from poor families.

Types of Colleges

The most important types of colleges may be categorised as follows:

Degree Colleges. As is clear by the term, these colleges provide education up to degree level in arts, sciences and technical subjects.

Post-Graduate Colleges. As is dear by the nomenclature, these colleges provide education inhumanities, sciences, commerce, engineering and medicines up to post-graduate level. These colleges have independent departments for every subject, organized under a head of department and two or more lecturers. The time-table of each department is framed separately, particularly as the post-graduate colleges include degree education in the subjects offered by them.

Categorisation according to Types of Education

Arts Colleges. These colleges provide education in arts subjects such as literature, economics, political science, geography, history, psychology, sociology and languages, etc.

Science Colleges. While the arts colleges prepare for B. A. and M. A. degrees, the science colleges prepare for B. Sc. and M. Sc. degrees. The science colleges provide teaching in physical sciences, such as Physics, Chemistry, Botany, Geology, Zoology, etc.

Commerce Colleges. These colleges provide commerce education to B. Com. and M. Com. students.

Medical Colleges. These colleges provide education in different branches of medicine, organized in separate and independent departments under a head, one or two professors, one or more readers and several lecturers, well equipped laboratories and libraries and the attached out patient departments with all the facilities for practical medical training. These require huge grants from the government. The admission is made through competitive examinations on a highly selective basis. Sufficient provision is made for scholarships to deserving and poor students. Most of the student; are hostellers. Therefore, facilities for hostel accommodation are available on a good scale. The colleges prepare for M. B. B. S., M. S. and M. D. degrees.

Colleges of Education. These colleges prepare for B. Ed., M. Ed., and other degrees required for trained teacher. These are also known as teachers training colleges. Admission to these colleges is made on a highly selective basis depending upon academic merits of the candidates. The Government provides special aids to these colleges.

Law Colleges. These colleges prepare for LL. B. and LL. M. degrees. Most of them work in the evening because a good number of students are employed during day time. Most of the law teachers are allowed to practice as advocates in the Courts. The law colleges in India are generally part and parcel of arts or science colleges and governed by their management. Therefore, establishment of independent law colleges will be a progressive step.

Technical Colleges. Colleges of engineering are the most developed, richest and the most important colleges in a country. Their staff is highly paid and well qualified. Each department is located in big buildings with suitable workshops and all facilities. The government not only gives huge grant for buildings and equipments, books and libraries but also for scholarships to deserving and needy students. Admission is made on a highly competitive basis. The campuses are usually extending to several kilometer since almost all the "students are hostellers. The hostels of engineering departments, like the hostels of medical students offer better facilities of boarding and lodging. These colleges prepare the students for B. E. and M. E. or B. Tech. and M. Tech. degrees in various branches of engineering and technology.

Specialized Colleges. Besides the above categories of the subjects of the teaching, there are some specialized colleges, teaching special subjects such as management, home science, performing arts, music, dance, acting, photography, painting, etc. These colleges may be private, governed by some Trust or established by the government. They prepare the students for diploma in the field of their specialization. They provide practical training and sometimes even arrange for employment of their students.

How many should go to College ?

Different committees surveying the quality and quantity of the students of the colleges in India, complain about the low quality of the students with the consequent result of growing educated unemployment. As most of the urban youths have no courage to take up self-employment ventures, most of them go on adding one degree after another to their qualifications. This makes them unable to take up any vocation other than white-collar jobs, which are not sufficient to cope with their growing number. Beside the boys the highly educated girls also do not find employment easily nor are they easily adjusted· in matrimony. In no progressive country education is so much lop sided with such a large number of students in the colleges. In most of the countries the youths take up vocations and employment after finishing their high school education and getting in specialized institutions. In India, on the other hand, most of the students passing through high schools thoughtlessly and almost spontaneously seek admission to the colleges. Failing to get admissions to specialized medical and engineering colleges they flock to the colleges of arts and sciences and stay there sometimes for half a dozen years seeking this or that degree. These degrees do not brighten their employment prospects. Therefore, one finds a lot of frustration among educated youth in India. This is due to lack of proper planning.

Only those should be admitted to colleges who have necessary physical, mental and financial equipment for the purpose. Failing this they only create problems for those who have these with them. Therefore, the government should restrict admissions to colleges through different measures, this will improve the quality of education and reduce so many problems. On the other hand, initiative from the teachers and the college managing bodies is equally necessary. Delinking of jobs and degrees will help this process.

Growth of Community Sentiments

Modern psychology does not credit the existence of any group mind distinct from the mind of individual, but in group situations the laws of group behaviour are freely employed. A college is a sociological group. Qualities such as discipline and co-operation can be evolved in the students only after some community feeling has been injected into them. William Me Dougall has pointed out several conditions that are necessary for the development of a group mind. They can be put to good use in development of community sentiment in colleges. They are:

Permanence of Group. A college, in its role as group, should possess certain degree of permanence or physical stability. Naturally, some students join the college every year while others leave it, and some change is always going on in the shape of additional buildings, staff members changing their colleges, etc. But despite this change there is some permanence for the average student who spends two to four years in one college while in exceptional cases this period even extends from ten to twelve years.

If the teachers is a college are not unnecessarily changed at a rapid rate and some of the college rules are maintained, the students derive a sense of permanence and the realization that the college has a distinct nature. This can help them to develop a community sentiment, which is part of their greater community sentiment comprehending their society as a whole.

Study of the Form of the Group by Members and the Member's Understanding of its Duties and Functions. Each student is a member of the college group. He can have community feeling for it only if he learns to regard it as a group, realizes the duties that he has to perform as a student, and has knowledge of the college's rules and methods of working. For this reason it is desirable for the teachers to introduce their new students every year to the institution as it is, what it stands for, how things are run in it what is expected of the newcomers. It is only in these circumstances that the student will be able to play his role in achieving the ideals of the college.

Contact with Other Groups. Community sentiment does not develop only by taking part in the functions of one's own group. It is necessary that members of different groups should intermingle. Occasions for such contact can be developed by organizing debates, discussions, dramatic performances, games and sports. But on all such occasions it is necessary that the feeling of the contestants for each other should be those of friendliness and respect. Should these feelings be lacking, the healthy development of any community feeling is not easy. In all such programmes students come to regard themselves as representatives of a particular college, with which they identify themselves. It is for the honour of this institution that they have to fight. Community sentiment will inevitably result.

Development of Community Tradition. In college, as in every other group, the members keep on changing every year but the community life of the group can be maintained for years at a time if a community tradition is developed. Old students who keep up their contact with old college play an important role. Old Boys Associations can perform a useful function by renewing contact with the newer generation of students and by holding meetings and thus keeping alive the traditions of the colleges. Many colleges and universities are famous for some particular tradition. Some colleges can boast of a fine tradition of discipline while another college may be producing the best students. If the old students and teachers are successful in keeping up these traditions every year the newcomers are encouraged to do their best.

Division of Labour Among Members. In every group different individuals are entrusted with the performance of different duties. Without this division of labour the life of the group cannot run smoothly. In a school or college, in particular, it is desirable that individual students should be entrusted with the task of looking after the discipline, the gardens and lawns, the classrooms, the library and the reading room, etc., and of organizing cultural programmes. If the student is compelled to perform such functions he learns to shoulder responsibility and to take decisions on his own. Beside, he feels some personal interest in the functioning of the college and this gives vitality to his understanding of the community spirit.

College and Social Structure

In the social structure of a society the college occupies a very important place. It provides trained personnel and developed males and females to the society. The technical colleges prepare the students for occupational roles. Thus the colleges are connected with the general social structure. Immediately after finishing the college studies the boys and girls enter matrimony and professions. The success in these is initially guarantied by the training at the college. Therefore, the college students should be prepared for adult roles. Various types of colleges such as arts colleges, science colleges and technical colleges occupy slightly different positions in the structure of the society. The technical colleges particularly prepare for vocations while the colleges of humanities prepare the students for general roles. The college is a forum not only for the discussion of intellectual matters but also for analysis of social and political affairs. Discussions and debates on all these develop critical attitudes among the coming generation. It encourages independent thinking and the demand of social and political reforms.

Contribution of College

The college promotes development of autonomy and the formation of identity. The college provides opportunities of the development of these traits. After leaving the college as a person gets married and establishes his own family he is helped by his training in the college. Sometimes the colleges open opportunity for knowing and selecting life partners. This depends on the disciplined and free atmosphere in the mixing of males and females in the college.

Social Structure of the College

The Principal. The social structure of the college is organized by the Principal at the apex, the professors, the tutors, the administrative staff and finally the students. The everyday affairs are run by the principal with the help of a council of management. As the government gives financial grants therefore it exercises control over the expenditures and general functioning of the college through inspectors and officers of the education department of the state.

Teachers. There is a hierarchy of statuses and roles among the teachers according to seniority and administrative matters. While in smaller colleges the principal may directly interfere in the functioning of a teacher, in bigger colleges, this is done through the departmental heads.

University Government. While most of the colleges are governed by rules framed by the university to which they are affiliated, the autonomous colleges are free in their selection of syllabi and mode of examination. However, most of the colleges are affiliated with some university. The nominees of the university occupy an important place in the management of the college. During examination the nominee of the university watches the conduct of the examination and reports to the university. The curriculum is framed by Boards of Studies of the University in order to ensure uniformity among the colleges affiliated to the university. However, each university organizes its own boards of studies and enjoys autonomy in this connection. As the colleges are governed by the rules framed by the university they are part and parcel of university education.

Students. The students are the most important part of the social structure of the college. They are divided into two categories. Those who live in the hostels are called or hostellers, while those staying outside the college are known as day scholars. Hostels are governed according to the college rules. The warden maintains discipline and supervises all sorts of activities in the hostel.

Therefore, the hostelers are more strictly governed than the day scholars. The college provides facilities for the development of skills and abilities through different types of teaching. It develops general abilities and leadership qualities thorough extra-curricular activities such as study circles, debating unions, discussion groups, sports councils, N. C. C. and other provisions. It provides facilities for activities started in the various parts of the country. The social structure of the colleges of arts, science, law medicine, engineering, agriculture, technology, education and commerce, may be a bit different in their routine activities but the general traits described so far are applicable to all these.

College as a Social System

Functionally, the college is a social system. It selects and differentiates the students on the basis of achievements in different directions. It puts a premium on academic excellence. It promotes development and exposes the students to various activities. It encourages creativity and critical faculty. It develops responsibility and provides occasion for taking up independent decision. It promotes qualities of team work as well as initiative and leadership. It provides opportunities for development of friendship among same sexes and also among different sexes. The friendship among different sexes provides opportunity to select life partners and lays the foundation for a successful marriage and happy family. Thus, in the modern societies each male and female passes through the college life to become an adult prepared to accept various roles and statuses in the wider society outside.

Factors Related to College Attendance

A good college must be well attended. The attendance in a class is the index of the success of classroom teaching. If the attendance in a class is poor it is a reflection upon the teacher and his teaching method. Besides the interesting teaching method, attendance is also influenced by relevance of the matter taught to the students. If the lecture delivered is not relevant to the curriculum most of the students decide to play truant. Therefore, the management and the principal must look to college attendance and analyse the factors related to it. The most important factors are as follows:

Quality of Teaching. As has been already pointed out,

attendance is an index of the quality of teaching. Therefore, one finds a higher percentage of attendance in a better college and in a better class in the same college.

Facilities Offered. Attendance also depends upon facilities offered to the students. If the class rooms are congested and small so many students will not attend lectures. If the college does not provide minimum facilities such as canteens, drinking water, suitable places to sit, reading rooms and libraries, common rooms for girls and boys, mixed and separate, and neat and sufficient buildings and open lawns and attractive natural environment, most of the students will not like to pass their time outside it. On the other hand, if these facilities are ample the students will be within the campus even in their spare times and sometimes even in holidays.

Teacher-taught Relationship. The college is a social system. Therefore, the most important single factor governing college attendance is the teacher-taught relationship. If this relationship is informal and warm there is better attendance. If it is formal and rude the attendance is thin. It is common observation that some teachers are more loved and respected by their students who do not want to miss any class and therefore, attend almost centpercent. On the other hand, teachers whose method is uninteresting, formal and lacking warmth have a thin attendance in their class. Besides the differences among colleges in the attendance rates, there is difference in the attendance rates in different departments in the same college. As a rule, as the number of students grows the rate of attendance falls. The teacher-taught ratio should not be allowed to rise beyond a certain level as it adversely affects the attendance. The size of a class should not be bigger than the prescribed limit necessary for good teacher-taught relationships. The subjects which are more interesting are better attended. The teachers who are better psychologists and better scholars attract more attendance to their lectures.

Time-table. An important factor related to college attendance is the time-table, lit should be suitable for the day scholar both boys and girls. It maybe modified if a good number of students are working in offices during day time. It should not be late in the night particularly as this may cause difficulties in the changing weather and climate of the region. It should have sufficient provision for leisure, particularly during the lunch hour. It should have sufficient spacing so that the students may easily attend the next class after finishing the present work.

The Curriculum. An important factor related to college attendance is the curriculum. It should be moulded according to the needs and tastes of the educands. It should be made interesting and involve practical work. It should be made more attractive by provision for extra-curricular activities.

22

The Measurement

The aim and object of education is the comprehensive, overall development of the child. This development and progress is gradual. Hence, it is essential to examine the child at regular intervals to find out the extent to which he has progressed. In the school, students study a number of subjects. To test one in respect of these subjects from time to time is essential as it makes clear the success with which he is studying and understanding them. It is the examination that makes it possible for one to know the child's achievement in terms of ability in learning these subjects. Hence, in almost all schools some mode of examining the children, in respect of their attainments in learning and retaining all that is taught to them, is prevalent.

Present System of Examinations

Under the present system of examinations in this country, all the students are put in a single hall, at the end of each session, and answer books are distributed to each of them. At the appointed time, the question papers are distributed to them, following which during the space of two or three hours the student is expected to answer a required number of questions. Finally, the answer books are gathered and sent to an examiner whose appointment in that capacity is previously confirmed. Sometimes, the examiner is other than the person who sets the examination paper. If the student's attempt in the answer books is considered worthy of being awarded

33 percent marks by the examiner, he is deemed to have passed the said examination. It he fails to secure these marks, in the eyes of examiner, he is deemed to have failed to pass the examination. The individual who does not succeed is compelled to spend another session in the same class.

Defects of the Present Examination System

There is hardly any need to point out that the existing examination scheme is not conductive to the proper development of children. The following are some of its shortcomings, that have been time and again pointed out by various educationists and commissions appointed for the purpose:

Student does not Study the whole Year. For the present examination system, the student is not compelled to exert himself through the entire session, but achieves competency for it by labouring only through the last few weeks before the examination. In this manner, the student does not attain any real ability or capability even through he passes the examination. He forgets a lesson just as soon or as rapidly as he learns it. During the first two or three months of the session, it is a rare student who is seen at his desk. In this manner from the educational viewpoint, a major portion of a student's time is completely wasted.

Studying from Question-answer Books and Key Books. In the present context, a student's ability is guaged from the scores he obtains in the examinations. And for obtaining good marks in the examinations, there is no need to wander into a maze of extensive reading and comprehensive knowledge. In every examination paper, the student is required to do four to five questions out of nine or ten that are set. The consequence is that even without having gone through more than one-third of the course prescribed for study, the average student finds three or four questions that he is in a position to answer. And four to ten pages of writing are considered adequate in answer to each question.

Fear of Examination. In the modern examination system, the examination is taken at the end of the session with the result that the student is fearfully conscious of the examination right through the session.

Success in Examinations a Matter of Luck. In the way examinations are conducted at present, success is more a matter of luck than anything else. His entire future is to be decided in two or three hours. No matter what skill a student has gained in his subject through constant labour during the entire session, his effort is completely wasted if for some reason or the other he fails to exhibit his skill in these three hours. Some students fail to attend the examination through some contingency such as illness during the examination period, or an accident or any other human involvement. On the other hand, even through they are in a position to attend the examination, they fail to give their best performance. The only consequence in such a case is that their whole year's effort is wasted.

Mechanical Method. In this way, the existing system of education is a machine in which conclusions are reached, no importance being attached to the human elements involved. Hence, people have devised new methods of succeeding in the mechanical set-up. Some students do not bother to put in more than a few week's effort for the examinations, during which they do nothing more than make a cursory study of guess papers and question answer books. As a result, they are in a position to come to grips with the paper, even though there is no element of mastery involved. And in subjects in which the question paper out does expectation, and unexpected questions crop, the contingency is overcome by fraternizing with the examiners and having their marks surreptitiously increased. And in the case of such a success in any examination, it is only natural for the individual to be devoid of any skill whatsoever in the subject in which he has passed the examination.

Defects Concerning Evaluation of Answer Books. Under the present system of examination, a student's achievement in any subject is measured by the marks that he obtains during the examination. Hence, his fortune depends upon the evaluation of his effort in the answer book. Such a method is susceptible to numerous faults.

(i) If the teacher's mental condition is disturbed, he does not evaluate the answer books correctly. What most often occurs is that the few copies in the bundle sent to him are examined with due care, but as he gradually tires and reaches the stage of growing exhaustion, the subsequent copies are gone through as a matter of necessity and duty.

(ii) It is only too apparent that all copies are not examined from the same standpoint or standard. Of course, different examiners would award differing marks to the same copy, but even if the same examiner is asked to examine the same copy, it is quite likely that he will award it different marks on different occasions.

(iii) The maximum number of marks that any student may be awarded depends upon the examiner's mental tendency.

(iv) It often happens, that due to a very great variety of causes, the examiner has very little time at his disposal to examine the copies.

(v) Many of the examiners are completely prejudiced or biased in their thinking, having only the most incomplete knowledge of their respective subjects. Secondly, some teachers even fail to understand the actual implications of the question asked in the question paper. It is only to be expected in such circumstances that there is no justice done to the student.

Long Examination Period. The present examination system allows the period of examination to spread over a very considerable period of at least a month. It is often seen that students get some weeks between two individual examination dates. Such a long period of inactivity has the worst effort upon the student's attitude towards the examination as it tends to lull him towards the seriousness of the matter. Secondly, the provision of time. periods between various papers is not at all proportionate. He gets no more that a few hours between two papers while between another two he has a few days at his disposal. Evidently, the opportunity available for the preparation of each subject is unequal.

Wrong Objective. The present aim of examination is to obtain marks in order to get a degree, not the desire to gain skill in any subject. Hence, the main attention in any examination is concentrated upon getting good marks so that one can have proof of one's ability or skill. There are innumerable methods of obtaining an adequate number of marks in the examination though all of them are not proper.

Defects of the Essay System. Under the existing scheme of examination, the student is required to answer each question in the form of an essay, with the result that the educational system has acquired all the defects inherent in the essay type examination. In this method the students pay much greater attention to learning answers to questions than to understanding the subject and delving deep into it. In the examination hall, they do no more than reproduce these learned and remembered answers on the answer books. Once the examination is over, the facts learned for it are as expeditiously forgotten, since once they have been put in the answer book, they no longer possess any importance for the student. One natural outcome of this method is that even though the student may have done exceptionally well in the examination, he is more or less blank on all the subjects that he has made a pretense of studying.

Suggestions for Improvement

Many thinkers, educationists and education commissions have pointed out the above defects in the existing scheme of examinations in this country, but there are many difficulties that hinder the complete replacement of it. The main difficulty is financial besides which the extremely large number of candidates makes it difficult to evolve a different examination system for them. Hence, the practicable solution is to maintain the existing scheme of things and make efforts to effect definite improvements. Main suggestions in this respect are the following:

Certificates should not be Required for Services. If the tradition of requiring certificates for various jobs and services is given up, and individuals are separately tested for qualities that the job requires, then, people will give up the race for obtaining certificates and degrees, and turn their attention to development of qualities required in the professions of their choice. It must, of course, be kept in mind that this method is not practicable in all professions nevertheless, it should be used in as many as admit of its use.

Improvement in the Evaluation of Answer Books. The method and system of examining and evaluating answer books should be improved. The remuneration of evaluating copies should be enough to induce the examiner to attend to them himself, and to do his work efficiently and well. The time allowed to the examiner of revaluating the answer books should be sufficient to allow him to work in peace, so that no haphazard work results from hurry or strain. There should be a definite standard of reference concerning the answers of different questions. Every examiner should be required to send copies that the he is to examine as samples so that his standard of judgement can be measured, and he should be requested to evaluate the remaining copies similarly.

Terminal or Monthly Examinations. Nevertheless, the student's knowledge of his subject cannot be properly gauged once in a year in a sitting of only three hours. For this it is essential that the teacher should examine the students in the class every fifteen days or a month in the subject matter that he has taught till then. The results should be announced on the basis of these monthly tests as well as the annual examination. This method will compel the students to spread their labour over the whole year.

Examination in Other Aspects of Development. The aim of education is not only to impart information but to achieve the complete development of the individual. It is only information that is examined in the present examinations. Hence, it is essential that the child's physical, emotional and social development also be examined, even though the marks obtained therein may not be made the reason for detaining him if he fails. Yet, these marks will help in advising and improving him. If the children understand that it is essential for them to pass in these respects also, they themselves will try harder to improve themselves.

Re-examination. Examinees, who, for one or the other legitimate reason such as disease, accident, etc., fail to take their examination at the regular time, should be given a chance to be examined once the reason for their abstaining from the regular examination has been confirmed. Their efforts during the entire year should not be allowed to waste.

Discouragement to Rote Learning. Questions in the examination papers should be such as discourage the practice of rote learning but encourage the expression of the student's skill in the subject.

Change in Questions. Questions should vary radically from year to year so that the practice of basing preparation and guess papers on questions asked in previous years and then rote learning answers to them is discouraged and ultimately discarded.

Covering Entire Course. Questions in the paper should cover every aspect of the curriculum even if more than one questions are given, and the solution of one is required. Such methods will induce the students to study all that is prescribed rather than making a selection from it.

Paper Scheme. During the period of examinations the distribution of papers should be equitable and proportionate, the normal period of inactivity not streching over more than one or two days. Only one paper should be set for one day.

Sufficient Number of Examiners. The number of examiners should be considerably increased so that all of them can conveniently judge a smaller number of copies in the period of one or two weeks provided them for the purpose.

Punishment for Wrong Practices. Strict measures should be adopted for punishing all examinations or obtaining certificates.

Responsibility of Teaching. Finally, the fundamental fact that must be pointed out is that the improvements in the existing scheme of examinations depend upon the teachers themselves. It is for them to encourage the students in their classes to attain high degree of skill and efficiency in the subject rather than to prepare them for the examinations. In educational institutions, the principal and teachers can specially attend to this aspect of the matter. Cooperation between teachers and the various examining bodies can help to improve the system of examinations.

23

Teacher Education

Training Educators

In olden times, there was no systematic provision for the education of teachers but it was assumed that, he alone had a right to teach who had acquired complete mastery over knowledge and could also translate it into practical life. In general, an individual won the right to teach when he had arrived at the stage of Vaanprastha ashram. By the time an individual had reached this age, he had acquired complete experience of life, and this was, in essence, the real training. In India, the imparting of education has always been regarded as a noble task, and the teachers of this country had so much renown and prestige that students from Tibet, China and Japan came here to study under them. In foreign countries, too, Indian teachers imparted education with a unique devotion. Society gave these teachers the highest respect because they were committed to bringing about the comprehensive and harmonious development of the student's personality. This sentiment is succinctly expressed in the statement *'aacharya devobhava'* which occurs in the 'paitriya Upanishad.

Even during the Buddhist and Jain periods, a teacher occupied a very respected place in society. It was presumed that he gave the student real self-knowledge. Respect was shown to him by saying *"Na devah shri guroh"*.

During the Middle Ages, *maktabs* and madrassas came into

existence when the Arabic and Persian language won state patronage. A person well versed in religious rituals and performances was regarded as a good teacher. Some evidence of the monitorial system is found in each one of these three ages. The brilliant students guided their juniors in their studies and thus assisted their teachers.

The need for systematic education of teachers was felt during the British period. Its growth can be divided conveniently into three parts.

Monitorial System. Teachers used to give informal training in the art of teaching to their favourite students. The method was referred to as the class monitor method, in which each class or the whole school was divided into groups, and each group was placed under the charge of a brilliant student. This student taught his own group, and in this way he learnt the art of teaching by actual practice.

Teachers' Training. It was in 1881-82 that the Indian Education Commission, for the first time, put forward a suggestion for the training of teachers. First of all, the missionaries from Denmark set up the normal School at Serampur. Later on, similar schools came to be set up at Bombay, Calcutta and Madras also. The Commission offered the following suggestions for the training of teachers at the primary and secondary levels :

1. Training schools should be established at place from which they can conveniently fulfil the demand for teachers in all primary schools. At least one training school should be set up within the area administered by one inspector of schools.
2. Proper arrangements should be made for the setting up of normal schools and training of school inspectors from the funds made available by the regional governments for primary education.
3. Training schools should be spread over the entire country.
4. There should be separate curricula for graduate and pre-graduate teachers, and the programmes for their training should also be different.
5. Training should be an essential pre-requisite for teaching.

A training school was set up at Madras in 1826, and between 1849 and 1859, the government established four Model Schools. Similar training institutions were set up in Uttar Pradesh (the erstwhile United Provinces) also. In 1904, the Indian Education Policy laid special stress upon the appointment of able and highly trained individuals to the Indian Education Service. A training period of one year was fixed for graduate teachers, and, in this training, importance was given to theory as well as practice. As a result of this recommendation, teacher training institutions began to grow in number. Different curricula were prepared for pre-graduate and graduate teachers and, in addition, model schools were attached to each teacher training centre. In 1913, the government took the definite step of declaring the policy that no individual should be allowed to teach, in the modern educational system as long as he did not possess a certificate providing his ability as a teacher. In 1910, the Calcutta University Commission introduced education as a subject at the intermediate and graduate levels. In 1929, the Hertog Committee suggested the introduction of refresher courses, and the idea was again stressed later by the Mudaliar and Radhakrishnan Committee. The Kothari Commission gave great importance to the establishment of intensive education colleges for the training of teachers. Many suggestions were also given to eradicate the alienation which had crept into teacher education.

Various Types

Today, the educational process is divided into a number of levels or stages and for each stage, different kinds of teachers are required. Consequently, we have five distinct levels of teacher training.

Normal School. In these institutions, teachers are trained for imparting education to primary classes, and their training comprehends both basic training and general training.

Secondary Training School. In these schools, teachers are trained for giving education to students of middle schools.

Training Colleges. Teachers in these institutions are trained to teach high school students.

M.Ed. In these institutions, the emphasis is upon imparting training for research in the curricula of education after the candidate has obtained his B.Ed. degree.

Specialised Training. In these institutions, teachers are trained for imparting education in home science, art, industry, physical education and the pre-primary level, or in other specialised subjects.

Basic Issues

Absence of Synchronisation between Training Establishments. According to K.G. Saiyidain, the candidate's knowledge of theory and actual conduct in the class-room remain two discrete elements, instead of blending with and strengthening or reinforcing each other. Hence, it is necessary that there should be a balance between theory and practice, so that the gulf between the schools and the training establishments is effectively bridged.

Imbalance between Theory and Practice. Training schools normally lay too much stress upon the principles or theory of teaching, whereas equal importance should be given to practice teaching and theory.

Lack of Suitable Curriculum. The curriculum of training is defective. The student is compelled to study subjects which bear no relationship whatsoever to actual teaching.

Neglect of Human Values. During training, the entire focus is upon objectives , goals, etc., while human values are completely neglected. In the opinion of K.G. Sayidain, the candidates are unable to visualise the fact that education is a specific social and cultural process. Because of lack of foresight and undue emphasis upon minor details or technical necessities, the close relationship of the school with society, the living problems of schools, and other important issues are lost sight of.

Absence of a Free, Untramelled Atmosphere. In training schools, the atmosphere of freedom is noticeably lacking, and because of the oppressive atmosphere, students are often seen indulging in flattery so that they may obtain good divisions.

Problem of Selection for Training. At present, training colleges are facing the problem of granting admissions, and undoubtedly, the choice of able and suitable individuals for training as teachers is a major problem.

In-service Training. In-service training takes within its ambit such activities as refresher courses, short term intensive curricula, practical knowledge of workshops, seminars, professional conferences, etc. However, even those suffer from numerous problems.

Traditional Influence. Even today, the curriculum is an ancient and traditional one, the ideal lessons are patently unpsychological, teaching aids are not used effectively and intelligently, considerable indifference and neglect are often displayed. In addition, the opportunities for frutiful discussion are few and far between, hostel facilities are often lacking, and opportunities for mutual contact and co-operation are negligible. S.N. Mukerjee has pointed out that in order to raise the standard of teacher training, attention should be paid to a proper management and organisation of the teachers' education programme, administration,' finance educational institutions, election for admission, pre-service education, practical training, in-service training, research into and publication of teacher training research work, preparation of college teachers and lack of concourse.

The Guidelines

Prof. K.G. Sayidain has put forward the following suggestions for overcoming the shortcomings and problems of teacher's education:-

1. Each state should, with the assistance of its training colleges and department of education, carry out a survey at least once in every five years to ascertain the need for male and female teachers in all the schools of the state. Admissions to teacher training establishments should be based exclusively upon this estimate.
2. Short-term curricula should be prepared for the old and experienced teachers, who, for one reason or the other, could not take admission to training colleges. On receiving systematic training, these teachers will add to their efficiency, win promotions to higher ranks and feel more secure in their jobs.

3. Having made arrangements for the training of old and experienced teachers in the manner outlined above, the question now remains of those individuals who, having completed their college or university admission, wish to secure admission to a teacher's training institution. From among these candidates, only those individuals, who really possess the potential for becoming able and successful teachers, should be chosen.

4. The rough and ready, stereotyped methods in use for the selection of new candidates should be replaced by more effective, adequate and scientific techniques of selection. These techniques should be capable of accurate evaluation of the aspiring candidate's moral and mental qualities.

5. Individuals interested in adopting the teaching profession should keep in mind the needs of their future profession so that they do not acquire piecemeal knowledge and then seek admission to a training establishment. Such individuals should shun all knowledge which bears no relationship to teaching, which is to be their future profession.

6. As is the case in some universities, the science of education should be made one of the alternative or optional subjects.

The view of the Kothari Commission and the Secondary Education Commission is that in order to make professional education more effective, it is necessary to link it, on the one hand with universities, and on the other, with schools. Only then can the development of both aspects take place conveniently.

The following are the views of the Commission:-

1. Education should be introduced as an elective subject for the first as well as the second degree.

2. Universities should set up education colleges which may provide assistance in training teachers and research.

3. In order to bridge the gulf between training institutions and schools, there should be extension service departments at the pre-primary, primary and secondary levels in each training establishment. There should also be an organisation of old students, and it should offer its

suggestions regarding the curriculum of training. Candidates receiving training should be sent to recognised schools. The supervisory staff should be transferred from one school to another at regular intervals.

4. The distance and barriers between particular subjects such as arts, physical education, etc., should be done away with.
5. Training colleges should be raised to the same status and level as that of the colleges of universities.
6. State boards of education should be established at the state level.
7. The period of training for those who have received secondary education should be two years, while graduates should receive training for one year.
8. Proper arrangements should be made for part-time education.

Dr. Sampurnananda has stated that the nation should be conscious of the sentiments and needs of its teachers. On the other hand, it is expected of the teachers that they will provide able and devoted leaders in every sphere of life, despite the fact that the teachers themselves are compelled to live in circumstances which are not conducive to efficiency, skill or even self-respect.

In the context of teacher's education, Dr. Radhakrishnan has observed truthfully that the teacher occupies a very important place in society because he brings about the transfer of the intellectual tradition from one generation to the next. At the same time, he maintains the level of technological skill and keeps the light of civilisation burning bright. He not only guides the individual, he shows the whole nation the right direction. The Kothari Commission, too, has been constrained to observe that the most important thing is to create satisfactory conditions of work for the teachers of our country.

The Terms

At the present time, the conditions of service and working conditions of teachers are truly pitiable. Today, we have two kinds of schools- (1) government administered, and (2) privately administered. Both kinds influence the conditions of service and work in their own respective ways.

Service and Working Conditions in Government-managed Schools. In schools managed by the government or local administrative bodies, the conditions of service are generally acceptable and tolerable. The teacher has no fear of losing his job, but when an educational plan is set into motion by administrators ignorant of the process of education, disorganisation is created. Teachers are often transferred to unsuitable places, and often, the transfers are the result of political influence, vested interests or individual influence. Only those teachers are able to derive any advantage who have contacts with officials in the administration. As a consequence, teachers feel constrained to seek the protection of some political pressure group or the other.

Privately Managed Schools. Private management of educational institutions has proved a curse at every level of education, in the context of service and working conditions of teachers. In fact, some schools and colleges have been turned into proftable business organisations. In these institutions, teachers are treated as no better than menials and slaves, and thus, the teachers are compelled to lick the boots of the managers. In other schools, the in-fighting between teachers themselves poses a danger to their very existence. The situation is so grave that even universities have fallen prey to such influences. And, there is no dearth of schools in which the teachers who work devotedly and seek to raise the standard of teaching and education through writing and authorship are served notices and subjected to pressures which render them intellectually impotent.

The Mudaliar Commission noted the sad state of teachers. It said that during its survey, it was sadly compelled to take note of the fact that the social level, salaries and other working conditions of teachers were very far from satisfactory. It was the committee's general view that the teacher's conditions had gradually deteriorated instead of improving.

The suggestions of the Mudaliar Commission with regard to service and working conditions of teachers are as follows:-

1. There should be a uniform policy throughout the country for the selection and appointment of teachers.
2. There should be a committee for the selection of teachers in all privately managed schools as well as those managed

by local bodies, and the principal should be a member of this committee.

3. The period of probation should be one year.
4. The Triple Benefit Scheme should be implemented.
5. The principle of equal pay for equal work and equal ability should be applied.
6. Difficulties should be sorted out through the panchayat system, which should include the education director or his representative also.
7. At every stage of education, the children of teachers should be provided free education.
8. In order to improve the social position of teachers, their profession should get respect from all other classes of society.

The foregoing suggestions were put forward for improving the service conditions of teachers, but all that they did was to add to the grandeur of the report of the commission. No noticeable improvement, in the working and service conditions of teachers materialised.

Commission's Report

The Kothari Commission felt that in such creative activities as research and teaching, stimulating opportunities are absolutely essential for professional development and improvement. They are no less important for attracting talented individuals to this profession, and for ensuring that they remain in the profession. The working conditions in schools should be such that they aid the teacher in achieving the highest levels of efficiency and skill. For this, they should receive certain facilities, such as : (1) facilities in the classroom, (2) necessary teaching materials, (3) facilities of libraries and laboratories, and (4) a proper ratio between students and teachers.

In addition, teachers should also possess adequate freedom to make experiments' in creative activities. They should be free to structure the curriculum according to the conditions existing in the classroom and to make modifications in the method of teaching.

Hours of work should be similar to those of administrative officials, and these should include the time consumed in actual classroom teaching in preparing lessons, correction work, evaluation, organisation of teaching materials and extra-curricular activities, tutorials, seminars, guidance of students, student welfare activities, etc.

If the professional abilities and skills of teachers are to be improved, other facilities such as providing liberal leave facilities for attending seminars, for self-study and other intellectual activities, and giving opportunities for promotions to higher levels, are also essential. Reflecting on the rational of such facilities, the Kothari Commission opined that teachers should be given a concessional railway ticket for travel throughout India at least once in five years.

Equal Status

Teachers can be expected to provide satisfactory results only when the working conditions created for them are suitable and satisfactory. In governmental institutions, service conditions are relatively satisfactory, but the real problem exists in privately managed institutions. In the latter, the administration does not hesitate to neglect or violate the rules laid down by the government. Managers and secretaries work according to their own sweet will. Rules pertaining to educational services should be different from those prevailing in administrative activities because the teachers cannot be tied down by such rules and procedures. For this reason, the Kothari Commission has forcefully suggested the framing of separate rules for the educational service. These rules should be conducive to the professional and individual growth of the teacher. The problems existing in privately managed institutions are : (1) private management boards have not laid down suitable conditions of service for the teachers, (2) the managements can, and do, terminate the services of teachers without due cause.

In order to overcome this difficulty, it is essential that the working and service conditions of teachers should be uniform. As far as termination of service is concerned, there should be a necessary condition that the teacher should be given a fair opportunity to present his case before a group of arbitrators (panchayat). This group should also contain at least one representative of the department of education.

The problem of housing is a very serious one for teachers. In rural areas, this problem is even more grievous. Because of it, the teacher's efficiency is undermined, and he has difficulty in establishing fruitful relations with the community. The following suggestions have been offered for overcoming these difficulties : (1) Every possible effort should be made to increase the housing facilities for teachers in rural areas. (2) The problem should be recognised and accepted as the responsibility of the local community. (3) Wherever possible, the state government should extend all possible aid. (4) Even in urban areas, the problem becomes very acute at certain times, though at others it may be less grave. Hence, programmes for housing construction should be taken up, and teachers should also be given a house rent allowance. (5) Teachers should be given a place in official housing schemes and also loans for constructing their own houses.

Facilities should also be provided to teachers in universities and affiliated colleges. Experience has shown that the universities which do offer housing facilities take advantage of renowned scholars by offering housing accommodation as a major inducement.

Source of Earning

One major source of additional income for the teacher is tuition. Private tuitions have increased to such horrifying extent that only students from well-to-do families are able to take advantage of them, and hence, other students do not get equal opportunities of education. The education department of Rajasthan has issued an order to put an end to this malpractice. Other states should take similar steps.

Private coaching or tuition is an evil of the educational system. Efforts should be made to ensure that the need for private coaching does not arise at all. It has often been observed that this practice flourishes either because the number of students is too large or because teachers do not perceive their responsibility correctly. The department (Education Department, Rajasthan) believes that the practice cannot be completely eradicated, but if all persons concerned with the problem become aware of it, its evil effects can certainly be mitigated. For this purpose both creative and administrative action is necessary.

At the school level, additional income is generated through guidance and the work of evaluating examination papers. Till the present, it was an established practice that the teacher was required to deposit a part of this income in the school. The Kothari Commission is of the view that a teacher should not be required to part with a percentage of his additional income as long as such additional income is less than 50 per cent of his salary.

The Growth

It is essential that the profession of teaching possesses avenues and prospects of promotion, because this is an important factor for attracting capable individuals to the profession. For this purpose, the following steps can be taken.

At the School Level. Trained teachers should get opportunities for progress in the future. These opportunities can take the following forms :

1. In primary schools, able and trained teachers should be promoted to the ranks of headmasters or inspectors.
2. The trained graduate teacher, who is doing praiseworthy work in his field, should be given the grades of post-graduate teachers.
3. Teachers of secondary schools possessing the requisite qualifications and ability should be given an opportunity to become teachers in colleges or universities. They should also be given research fellowships for further studies.
4. Teachers doing commendable work in the sphere of teaching can be given advance increments. In general, the teacher's pay scale stretches over 20 years. For 5% teachers at least, opportunities can be provided for reaching the maximum of the scale within ten years.

At the University Level. Though there is no provision for formal training of teachers at the university level, and neither has the need for this been felt, the following suggestions have been given to ensure their progress :

1. In universities, general temporary posts can be created for those honoured and devoted teachers of a scholarly nature who could not get promotion because of the lack of general permanent posts.

2. In post-graduate departments, posts of teachers should be created according to the actual needs of the department.
3. In consultation with the UGC, the pay scale of 1600-1800 can be given to teachers of proved ability.
4. The pay-scales and dearness allowances should be re-assessed every five years, and the dearness allowance should be equal to the allowance paid by the government to its other employees.

Welfare-promoting Activities. Now, some thought is being given to the question of welfare of teachers, but much remains to be done in this direction. The following steps can be considered:

1. A welfare fund for teachers should be established in the states as well as union territories. Teachers should contribute 1.5% of their salaries to this fund. It should be administered by a committee consisting of representatives of teachers and government officials. At a suitable time, the government should establish its own fund for this purpose and.amalgamate the teacher's fund with it.
2. New pay-scales should immediately be given to teachers, and the central government should help the state governments in doing so.

Post-retirement Facilities. The facilities available to teachers after their retirement are almost non-existent. Consequently, no ambitious and able person feels attracted towards this profession. Some suggestions in this regard are :

1. Facilities of this nature should first be made available to teachers retiring from government schools, though later on they should be extended to teachers in private schools also.
2. For internal management, the Triple Benefit Scheme (pension, provident fund, insurance) should also be implemented.
3. The age of retirement should, in general, be 60 years, in schools as well as in colleges. Under special circumstances, this age limit may be raised to 65.
4. Teachers should get adequate interest on their provident

fund. Their money should be invested responsibly and profitably.

Other General Facilities. Teachers are deprived even of the common facilities that are available as a matter of course to other ordinary citizens. These facilities, outlined below, should be made available to teachers also:-

1. Teachers should have the right to make the best use of their civic rights, such as contesting local, district, state or national level elections or work on any social position, though while engaged in such activities, they must take leave from their institutions.
2. There should be an increase in women teachers at every level. Besides, provisions must also be made for part-time employment.
3. In rural areas, housing facilities must be made available for women teachers.
4. The central social welfare department should introduce and propagate a condensed course for adult ladies.
5. Facilities for postal or correspondence education should be extended.
6. In rural areas, additional allowances may also be given to lady teachers, wherever such allowances are needed.
7. Teachers working in tribal areas should be given special allowances. Arrangements should be made for their housing as well as the education of their children.
8. Teachers working in tribal areas should be given special training also.

Teacher Organisations. Teachers will have to build up their own professional organisations to safeguard their own interests, as other professions have done. Events of the past have proved that teachers have been able to get their rights only through the medium of such organisations. The Kothari Commission has offered the following suggestions on the subject-

1. State and Central governments should recognise those unions of teachers which aim at the growth and development of education and the profession of teaching.

2. At the state level, joint teacher councils should be organised, and it should be entrusted with the task of reflecting on the problems of teachers.

National Awards. The Education Ministry should consider the following suggestion's relating to national awards for teachers : (1) the number of national awards should be increased, (2) the selection for the awards should be objective, (3) the person selected for the award be given a travelling allowance equivalent to that of a Class I officer.

The development and growth of skill and efficiency in teaching means national development, but this becomes possible only when teachers possess a high social and moral status. And, respect for the teachers in the other classes of society will be generated only when their economic and social standards are improved. By making provision for the full use of civic rights by teachers, the Commission has taken a definite step towards winning for them a more respected place in society. It has suggested that teachers can contest local, district, state or national elections and also hold social positions.

The powerful vision of the Kothari Commission has fallen not only upon the other problems of education but also upon the real status and conditions of teachers. As a result, the Commission has sought to win for the teachers same social, economic and cultural position which was responsible for teachers being called gods, teachers and fathers in every preceding age. The truth is that, in the process of social struggle, the teacher had lost his position. Now, the Commission has made the government aware of this fact, and sought to restore to the teacher his pristine glory and importance.

Further Development

The standards and criteria of teacher's education have changed. Today, it has become a powerful and inalienable aspect of national development. Its progress has taken place in the manner outlined below :

Training Facilities. In the last few years, facilities for training of teachers have grown manifold, and, as a consequence, the number of trained teachers has risen from 5% in 1951 to 38% in

1971. The following table reflects this growth for each level of education.

Progress in Teachers' Training

Schools	% of Trained Teachers	
	1951	1971
Primary	58.8	82.9
Middle	53.3	84.9
Secondary	53.8	81.2

This percentage had gone up even further by the end of the Fourth Plan period. The number of trained teachers has risen because of an expansion in facilities and the fact that training has become a compulsory prerequisite for teaching profession.

In spite of this, the facilities available for such training vary from state to state. When it has been accepted that training is essential for teaching, each state should make arrangements for training every teacher at the primary, middle and secondary levels. Thus, in Himachal Pradesh, Haryana, Punjab, Rajasthan (with the Exception of the Middle level), Andhra Pradesh, Kerala, Tamil Nadu, Gujarat, and the Union Territories (Chandigarh and Delhi) almost every teacher is a trained one. In the five year plans, further arrangements are being made for training of teachers. It has been envisaged in the sixth plan that for the trained teachers who are unemployed special schemes have been prepared.

In-Service Training. Because of the expansion in training facilities, it has become possible to bring about an increase in the number of trained teachers. Despite this, there are teachers who are untrained or those who have to develop their abilities, and for this in-service training facilities have been provided. Surveys have revealed that at the primary and secondary levels, two-thirds of the untrained teachers are below 30 years of age while 80% of such teachers are less than 35 years. Obviously, these teachers are going to teach for many long years, arid hence it is essential that special arrangements should be made for their education. The following table throws light on the statistical findings of the second educational survey:-

Experienced Untrained Teachers

Experience (Years)	Primary	Percentage Middle	Secondary
4 years	58.24	59.21	62.55
5-8	19.03	19.61	17.87
9-12	9.36	9.44	8.36
13-16	5.36	5.59	4.87
17-20	4.05	3.22	2.94
20 & above	3.67	2.85	3.38

It has been noticed that the untrained teachers are not only young, they also possess a few years of teaching experience. Most of them need formal training. State governments must give fiscal as well as other incentives so that they may willingly obtain formal training. Special training programmes will also have to be introduced. Such teachers must be given knowledge of educational psychology, educational sociology, educational principles and school organisations, etc. Correspondence courses introduced by extension service centres can fulfil this need, while teachers already possessing formal training may supervise the practical aspect of this training.

Educational Qualifications. In order to make school education effective, it is essential to keep in view the educational qualifications of teachers. With the recent expansion in primary, secondary and graduate education, schools have now begun to employ only qualified teachers, but, in spite of this, there is no dearth of teachers in our schools even now who do not have the requisite academic qualifications. The following table provides the statistical details:-

Qualification of Teachers

Edn. Qualification	Primary	Middle	Secondary
Below Middle	1.92	13.09	0.31
Middle Pass	49.65		

Matric	41.27	49.65	8.75
Inter	4.64	11.83	5.25
Graduate	1.39	14.91	54.72
Post-Graduate	0.11	2.55	20.70
Others	0.98	7.92	10.70

The above statistical details have been taken from the second educational survey. From 1965 onwards, the situation has improved further, and yet, there are not a few teachers whose qualifications must be improved. Training establishments provide condensed courses for such teachers to fill the gap in their education.

It has also been observed that the dearth of educational facilities still exists, and that it has a negative impact. Hence, expansion of training facilities is essential. Besides, it is also noteworthy that many training establishments that do exist suffer from lack of laboratories, buildings, resources and other essentials.

Affiliation of Institutions. Many states do not have adequate training institutions and hence they fail to fulfil their demands for trained teachers. Secondly, the standard of training must also be improved. Efforts should be made to ensure that institutions lacking the requisite standards should not come into existence at all. And therefore, affiliation should be offered to them only when they fulfil all the necessary conditions and requirements. Consequently, the responsibility of the State Teacher Training Councils becomes even more onerous. Universities should offer affiliation to training schools only on the recommendation of this council, and in addition, these institutions should be subject to periodical and regular inspections and surveys.

Curriculum Reforms. There are many areas of the training curriculum which are crying out for suitable reforms, for which there are many programmes which do not involve substantial financial outlays. Reform of the curriculum is an important step in this direction. A critical evaluation of the curricula of training schools and colleges is essential, and its objective should be to eliminate unnecessary elements and to utilise the time thus saved for more important elements. The objectives of education should be clearly defined and programmes should be designed for achieving them. The teachers should have knowledge of teaching methods, not only content knowledge. The curriculum should be so designed that the teacher has context knowledge, he is trained through corrective teaching, he should have the cooperation and assistance of institutions and schools, and his vacations should be utilised creatively. Practice Teaching should be initiated at two distinct levels- (1) training should initially be given for one or two weeks to acquaint him with actual classroom conditions, (2) the Internship should be of a long duration, during which the trainee should remain in the school for his entire time and seek solutions to the problems he has faced.

Since the requirements of primary schools are different, the curriculum for this stage is in urgent need of reform. And, since the curriculum differs in nature in the tribal areas, this fact should also be kept in view. Special training will have to be given for teachers of single teacher schools as well as tribal schools. The teacher must remain in contact with the latest methods of imparting knowledge in reading, writing, arithmetic and other subjects. The teacher, teaching class first should develop his knowledge of health education, citizenship, community relations as well as aid to his work experience.

Criteria for Admission. Clearly specified criteria for admission to training institutions should be designed and laid down, the basis for which should be general mental ability as well as educational achievement. What is most important is a natural inclination towards teaching. The most able and interested individuals should be attracted towards teaching. In addition, training programme should also keep in view the needs of the teachers. There is almost invariably a shortage of teachers for certain subjects, such as science and mathematics. In many states, teaching of these subjects is being done by unqualified teachers. The imbalance between demand and supply, in this sphere. is due to the fact that sufficient caution is not exercised at the time of giving admissions to training schools. State governments, in order to make plans for long-term educational development, should keep in view the demand and the supply, as well as the available manpower.

In-Service Training. Pre-service training is not the end of a teacher's professional preparation because it is essential for the teacher to remain in constant touch with the latest methods of teaching as well as the changes in content knowledge. Provisions should be made in service rules so that the teacher is compelled to receive in-service training. Similarly, the education code should also lay down rules compelling private schools to send their teachers for in-service training and refresher courses at regular intervals. The education departments should also be aware that such regulations are in fact being followed or not.

In-service training should be compulsory for every school and college, and wherever necessary, additional staff should be made available to these institutions. In addition, adequate financial aid should also be available to them. The purpose of refresher courses is two-fold : to increase the teacher's knowledge, and also to increase his content knowledge. For this purpose, summer courses (or courses during vacations) must be organised. for this, the teachers of colleges can be asked to extend their cooperation. In addition, it is equally necessary that extension service centres be set up in each training establishment, with adequate funds. Initially; the financial aid can be provided by the Union Government, while the NCERT can provide the necessary technical aid.

Training of Untrained Teachers. Even today, almost one-fourth of the teachers in primary and secondary schools are untrained, and in the eastern regions, the situation is even more deplorable because their percentage is even higher. During the fifth Five year plan, the following courses were introduced- (1) a training, course of one to two years for teachers with less than 8 years' experience and below 35 years of age, and (2) correspondence courses along with the necessary practical training for the teachers with more than 8 years of experience and above 35 years of age.

Pace Setting Institutions. The qualitative objective or aim of teaching cannot be fulfilled. Training schools are prevented from carrying out experiment because of lack of material as well as faculty-related necessities. Hence, the activities of these institutions are stereotyped. Because of this, revolutionary changes are required in their role, mode of working and facilities. There is a need to increase the number of trained teachers, but for this an unmanageable load cannot be thrust upon education. However, some selected institutions can be used for this purpose. Hence, it becomes necessary to establish a certain minimum standard for each training school and college, to establish a few institutions of this kind in each state, and to develop them accordingly. These institutions should be able to experiment with new ideas and methods and also help to guide other institutions.

Organisation of Teachers Education. In each state, the teachers' training programme should be organised in the best possible way. for this, an autonomous state teachers training council should be brought into existence, and the following functions entrusted to it:-

1. Making a long-term (five year) plan for the welfare of teachers.
2. Establishing teacher's training schools in accordance with the demand for teachers.
3. Providing advice regarding affiliation to universities and the state government.
4. Maintaining the standards of the state's training institutions.
5. Distributing aid to these training establishments.
6. Preparing the curriculum for training schools and colleges.
7. Making arrangements for in-service training.
8. Creating the necessary teaching materials and literature.

Teachers' Welfare. For the welfare of teachers (1) there should be a teacher training centre in each district (tehsil) where arrangements should exist both for entertainment as well as professional development, (2) on a co-operative basis, there should be provision for house construction as well as medical facilities and services. For this, the fifth plan has made a provision of Rs. 6.36 crores. In addition, a sum of Rs. one crore has been provided by the NCERT for research. Rs. 4.24 crores have been set aside for teacher training.

The teaching community, today, is divided into a number of classes or sub-classes, among which there is little or no inter-change or intercourse. The primary teacher regards himself as inferior to the secondary, college or university teacher, just as the university teacher regards himself as far superior to all these other teachers and remains proudly alienated from them.

This alienation can be seen at three levels-

Isolation from University Life. The professional education of the primary teacher is not seen from the view-point which applies to university education. The professional education of the teacher at the secondary level is related to universities, but even that is little relationship with the other subjects taught in the university.

Distant from School Life. Teacher's education at the primary and secondary levels is distinct and distant from the modern development of colleges and college education.

Alienation from Each Other. In various ways, the various teacher training institutions are also alienated from each other, with the result that they have failed to create a cohesive community even among themselves.

Now, we will reflect upon the factors which may help alleviate the alienation pervading the sphere of teacher's education.

The Kothari Commission has felt that the nature of 'education' is different from that of other academic subjects, but despite this, it should be available to the common masses. In its view, education should be included in the main flow of the academic life of the university. In India, education is mainly associated with pedagogy, i.e., it is taught almost exclusively in training institutions, and only to those who have decided to enter the teaching profession. From the educational view-point, in the advanced countries, education is regarded as a separate, specific subject, comparable to any other social science. After assuming that education is a process of social, political and economic change, it is regarded as far removed from implementability or practicality like other philosophies or subjects. It is also worth mentioning that philosophers as well as social scientists, of recent years, have begun to pay special attention to education in their respective fields of specialised reflection. Having considered these factors, the Education Commission has. put forth the following suggestions for putting an end to this distance from the universities.

In order to make education significant and to increase its scope, it is essential that education be recognised as a social science, as an independent subject of academic study. In addition, education as a subject for study at the graduate and post-graduate levels, i.e., as an optional subject, should be offered on the basis of the following arguments:-

1. At the graduate level, the curriculum laid down should be oriented into three spheres - the sociological, philosophical, and psychological bases of education. The contributions of the great educationists, comparative education and some modern educational problems should form parts of the curriculum.

2. At the post-graduate level, there should be provisions for an M.Ed. degree. After the conclusion of the first degree, the time period of this latter degree should be two years. Besides, at this level, it should also be possible to combine the various subjects of the sciences and the humanities with education. Initially, it should be kept as an additional option also, and in order to encourage its study, scholarships can be offered to those who study it in order to become teachers.

3. In each of these curricula-the graduate and the post-graduate - there must be a certain minimum of teaching practice as compulsory, just as laboratory work is a compulsory part of science. The student may be required to go through a period of internship or compulsory in-service summer course teaching so that he may become a fully qualified teacher.

The Kothari Commission has also recommended that, to bring about the desired result, the foregoing programme should be implemented by the University Grants Commission. In addition, it has also recommended the setting up of 'schools of education' in certain selected universities. In these, in addition to the normal teaching of various subjects, there should be provisions and facilities for training and research in education. Their functions should be as follows :

1. Laying down the curriculum for the graduate and post-graduate levels.

2. Making arrangements for the vocational training and education of teachers of various grades at the pre-primary, primary and secondary levels.
3. Arranging for the setting up of Extension Services in some training institutions at every level.
4. Organising summer courses and in-service courses in professional and other courses of study.
5. Conducting research into the curricula as well as methods of teaching with the help of students of all kinds.
6. Encouraging and developing research in education and considering the potential for interdisciplinary approach and research into it.
7. It has also been the considered view of the Commission that reputed scholars in various subjects should be attached to these institutions for short periods of time. These scholars should create acquaintance with the progress that has taken place in their various disciplines. Such programme will have two advantages-(1) The study of education will take place without teacher training or combined subjects ; (2) Many talented students, after studying these subject, will be attracted towards teaching.

The distance from schools emanates from various causes, the main ones being the notion of standard and the idea of being superior or inferior. Training colleges can offer their cooperation for putting an end to this alienation, by offering their advice, at least to neighbouring schools, on such matters as planning of work, modes of teaching, etc. This extension work will benefit the training institutions as well as the schools. The Education Commission has recommended that at every level of training-pre-primary as well as secondary-there should be extension service centres, and their creation should be an integral part of the programme of training establishments. Members of the staff should participate in it regularly.

In this context, it is also worth mentioning that the NCERT has done commendable work in this direction. It has spread extension services to 50% institutions. Similarly, the National Institute of Basic Education, the State Institute of Education, etc., have also done some satisfactory work in this field.

In addition to the steps outlined above, there is another way in which training establishments can eradicate this distance, and that is through maintaining contact with their old students. These institutions should have old students associations through which, from time to time, there should be contact between old and new students, during which immediate educational problems can be discussed, along with new experiments, the implementation of new curricula and new methods and the possible problems that may arise in doing so.

In addition, the Education Commission has also suggested that this alienation may be ended by introducing internship programmes in training institutions. Under these, the teacher-students should spend their entire time in schools and participate in every activity of the school. But for the success of any such internship programme, close co-operation between schools as well as training institutions is of the essence. Obviously, teaching experience through actual practice can only be the consequence of a partnership between the producers (the training colleges) and the consumers (the schools). The educational department should give special recognition to schools selected for practice teaching, and as assisting schools, these should be given a special maintenance grant. In these spheres, the regional colleges have done pioneering work.

Apart from the internship programme, other schemes can be devised for eradicating this harmful alienation. These are, for instance-(1) Progressive teachers working in schools may be appointed on deputation to training colleges ; (2) teachers working in schools may be invited, from time to time, to participate in programmes organised in the training colleges ; (3) teachers from. the training colleges should go to the assisting schools for teaching work at regular intervals.

Programmes of this kind will produce the following advantages:-

1. Teachers of the training colleges will teach at least one unit of a subject to the students of a school for at least one month ; the effect of this can then be accurately evaluated.
2. Teachers will implement new methods of teaching and the principles of training and thus benefit the student teachers directly.

3. Schools will also come gradually to offer their cooperation in professional studies and educational research, and thus become active partners in a process intended, ultimately, for their own benefit.

At various levels, there is complete absence of harmony of exchange between the teachers themselves. Teachers working at the pre-primary and primary level have secondary level qualifications. Besides, there is a difference in their pay scales also. the distance between them is evinced thus :

1. Training institutions at the primary and pre-primary levels differ from those meant for the secondary level.
2. The pay-scales in these Institutions differ from each other.

Having reflected on both these factors, the Kothari Commission declared that an important reform in this direction is to develop the training establishments for the pre-primary and primary levels to the level of training colleges. Thus, the distance in teacher's training will come to an end.

The actual objective of this programme is- every kind of teacher's training should come within the jurisdiction of a university. It should be so organised that the co-operation of the educational unions and teachers' unions in the states may be advantageously exploited. Some universities have made considerable efforts for the education of teachers at the secondary level, but so far their attention has not turned to the pre-primary and primary levels. Hence, it is essential that this, too, should come within the jurisdiction of the university so as to ensure both the necessary freedom and autonomy as well as intellectual and educational efficiency at every level.

Considering this problem, the Education Commission has recommended that this programme should take three forms -

(i) Establishment of Comprehensive Colleges.
(ii) A programme for raising all training establishments to the college level.
(iii) Establishment of a State Board of Education which may become a link in the organisation of every such programme.

We will now reflect on each of these three situations.

The concept of a Comprehensive Education College implies an institution which provides education at every level of teaching : primary, secondary, post-graduate, research, domestic science, arts and crafts. Such institutions will improve the standard of teaching. In Chandigarh, Allahabad, Kurukshetra, Trivandrum, and other universities, there are provisions only for M.Ed. and research. But, in fact, no obstacle really exists for dedicated and determined individuals.

Comprehensive Colleges. With reference to the Comprehensive Colleges, the Kothari Commission has opined that such colleges should be located at places where teachers for every level can be trained and prepared. Already, there are a few such institutions and they have produced good results. Now, the thing that is needed is that other institutions must be organised in a planned manner so that they may provide curricula and courses of study intended to produce pre primary, primary and secondary teachers through suitable education. So far, such schools produce teachers for the secondary level alone.

Improvement of Pre-primary and Primary Training Institutions. These institutions comprehend those establishments which train successful secondary or high school students for appointment as teachers at the primary level. For the improvement of these institutions, there is a dire need for a dynamic programme. The responsibility for devising a suitable curriculum and laying down the standards for admission should be taken by universities, and for this purpose, the Education Commission has suggested a period of 15 to 20 years.

State Board of Teacher Education. Today, teacher training is going on through the education departments and universities. A state board of teacher education can function as a bridge or link between the two. It should be constituted from among teachers of universities, representatives of the education departments, principals of teacher training colleges and representatives of teachers' unions, and it should be completely responsible for every conceivable kind of teacher's education at the state level. Its functions should be -

(i) Determining the standards in the teachers' training establishments.

(ii) Developing the curriculum, framing programmes, improving the examination system, arranging for and producing books as well as instructional materials for teachers' education.
(iii) Determining the essential conditions for training establishments and subjecting them to periodical inspections.
(iv) Giving advice to the institutions.
(v) Obtaining a commitment that the student in such institutions will be working in the state's schools after receiving training.
(vi) Making short as well as long-term programmes for the qualitative as well as quantitative improvement of teacher's education.

In this context, the Kothari Commission has suggested that, in each state, such a council should be set up by the state itself. It should also have a full-time secretary. The State's Institute of Education should be affiliated to it. Such a council should take upon itself all the functions of the institutions of pre-primary training, and also advise the training establishments producing teachers for the secondary levels, though such institutions may actually be affiliated to the universities.

The Betterment

The responsibility for the growth and development of the nation is thrust upon the shoulders of teachers, and, to a certain, extent, this is an undeniable fact. The training of the future generation is undoubtedly in the teacher's hands. It is, therefore, obvious that if the education of teachers does not improve qualitatively, the results for the future generations may well prove to be disastrous. When we speak of a qualitative improvement in this context, we mean an increase in the teacher's ability, skill and a broadening of his mental horizon.

What is urgently needed for a qualitative improvement in teacher's education at every level is Reorganisation, a reorganisation which must take place in the following spheres:-

Reorientation of Subject Knowledge. The purpose of such a scheme is that, during training at the primary and secondary level, the trainees should be imparted knowledge of the subject apart from information upon the modalities of teaching. The Kothari Commission's caution is that such a programme should be carefully planned. In it, the use of the given information in the light of basic facts and school subjects should be made sharply explicit. In addition, text books and other teaching materials should be presented at the level of the school as a measure of aid and help. At least 20% of the entire training time should be given over to a study of the subject itself.

In the context of any training there is the eternal question regarding the period of training essential for a specific level. In this context, the Kothari Commission has given two kinds of suggestions-

(i) At the primary level, the training period should be of two years. Where the period is at present of one year, it can conveniently be extended to two years:

(ii) At the secondary level, where the existing curriculum extends over one year, it should be extended to two years, as justice is never done to the curriculum in the short period prescribed at present.

However, the biggest obstacle in this context is that this task is not desirable from either the economic viewpoint or the practical. Consequently, the Education Commission has most wisely suggested that the working days in a year should be increased, from the present 180 or 190 days to at least 230 days. Since such an experiment has proved eminently successful in some training institutions, the Commission suggests that the change should immediately be implemented elsewhere also.

At the secondary level, the cooperation of teachers of the other departments of universities should also be sought for improving content knowledge. The Commission suggests that any such reorientation programme should be composed of the teaching method relevant to the subject as well as special techniques. The traditional ways of preparing lessons should be abandoned.

In this connection, another. suggestion of the Commission is the introduction of integrated curricula. A curriculum combining general as well as vocational elements should be evolved. Some experiments have been conducted in the USA in this direction. In

India, too, the Education College of the Kurukshetra University prepared a four-year curriculum for post-high school studies, and five-year course was initiated in the regional college of education. But the departments of education and universities have, as yet not given recognition to these integrated curricula. Doubt has been expressed regarding the validity and success of such courses on the following grounds:-

1. After passing matriculation, the student is unable to decide whether he should become a teacher or not.

2. Students studying under the integrated curricula have not shown better than, or even comparable results, as those studying under the one-year curriculum.

With reference to the success of such. integrated curricula, the Commission has opined that if these integrated curricula are completely integrated, then, in its opinion, they will have a definite place in a new, varied and flexible system.

Vitalising Professional Studies. Many of the topics forming a part of professional or vocational studies at present lack real utility, and hence they should be eliminated. Professional studies should consist exclusively of topics which are useful for student teachers. It has been suggested that the real need is for the synthesizing and harmonising various curricula according to Indian conditions. The Commission's view is that these curricula suffer from the following two defects -

(i) In Indian conditions, because of the total absence or a minimum of research, the teacher educators generally take only theory, and their elaboration is replete with examples taken from foreign countries.

(ii) Teacher education is unfortunately replete with platitudes. The reason for this lies in the absence of a tendency to read the best books on the science of education. At the primary level, there is a distinct tendency to read cheap 'guides' or 'notes'. Another major obstacle is the lack of knowledge of a foreign language.

Improving Methods of Teaching and Evaluation. In training institutions, the methods for evaluating the performance of students, teachers are the traditional ones. Students adopt the following methods for getting the highest possible grades in the practical examinations - (1) pleading with the principals, doing domestic chores to please them, or indulging in back-biting against other teachers, (b) offering unnecessary gifts to the principals.

In the same manner, the principals either neglect or actually hinder the student teachers so that the latter may feel pressed to offer them gifts, work for them without charge, offer them refreshments, etc. At the time of examination, this neglect reaches its peak, and thus leads to a marked increase in gifts to the principals in the form of cash. It has also been noticed that such principals accept very expensive and numerous gifts from the aspiring candidates, with the result that first divisions are scattered broadly , while students too indigent to indulge in such gifts have to suffer loss of career. Obviously, there is urgent and dire need for a change in the modes of evaluating and testing-teacher's education. For this purpose, the Commission has offered the following suggestions:-

(i) Student-teachers should be brought to the required level of maturity through contact, experience, study and debates, for which independent 'study and the cooperation of students is essential. Unfortunately, they do not come with the pre-formed habits of self-study and independent thinking. Training institutions must try to overcome this handicap and accustom students to thinking, Belt-study and discussion. Individual work in the library, preparation of reports and analyses, case studies, project work, seminars, debates, conferences, etc., should be an integral part of the curriculum of training schools.

(ii) The attitudes of the students should be developed and made mature on the basis of human relations, and stress should be laid upon the importance of social values in the development of education.

(iii) In the developed countries, methods of teaching are constantly changing and developing. Such tools as radio, television, film-strips, programme instruction, language laboratories etc., have come into common use there. In India, too, radio and television have begun to broadcast lessons for schools.

Besides, an equally necessary improvement is the change in the system of examination. As in schools, so too in training schools, arrangements are made for external examinations. As long as examinations are not modified and improved, teachers will not adopt the modern methods of evaluation, and hence, there will be no improvement in evaluation through examinations at the school level. Hence, internal assessment must necessarily be recognised as an essential part of evaluation. Training schools should maintain cumulative records of the performance of their students, and the trainees must also be trained in the proper analysis of such records.

Improvement of Student-teaching. The lessons imparted to student-teachers for training are not suitably planned, examined or evaluated. Most of the lessons are not examined at all, and, in addition, the period of practical teaching work is almost never more than 2 to 6 weeks.

In view of this, the Commission has suggested that student-training should be split into two stages:-

(i) The student-teacher should be made fully aware of the conditions in the schools as well as the actual conditions prevailing in the classroom during teaching.

(ii) The student-teacher should, at the second stage, be made to teach for a continuous period of at least eight weeks. Such teachers must be made to work as integral parts of the teaching staff, not as appendages.

Development of Special Programmes and Courses. As already pointed out above, it is essential for the development of education that new curricula and courses be developed. The Education Commission has spoken in terms of introducing 'education' as a subject at the graduate and post-graduate levels. There should be special courses for principals, and short-term courses for those about to assume the charge of a principal. Short courses should also be devised for educational trainers at the primary and secondary levels. There should be other programmes after the completion of which they can teach higher classes. At the primary and secondary levels, there should be composite courses. The Commission stresses that the devising of such programmes should be the combined responsibility of the NCERT, the department of education, and the National Association of Teacher Education.

Revision and Improvement of Curriculum. The Commission has expressed the hope that the curriculum be revaluated in the light of the suggestions of the Teacher Education Commission. This revaluation should be oriented primarily towards utility. Its suggestions in this regard are:-

(i) The curriculum of teacher training is divided into two parts. In the theoretical part are the principles of education, child development and the psychology, modalities of teaching, organisation of schools and health education. In the practical aspect are such activities as practice teaching, craft, community life, etc. These subjects should be so reoriented as to create insight in the teacher regarding the school.

(ii) At the primary level, general education should be coextensive with training. They need a curriculum which can evolve a suitable social and cultural attitude to life.

(iii) For the purpose of practical teaching, conditions which are in consonance with the needs of modern society should be created. Fundamental facts should be kept in view while seeking solutions to problems.

What is noteworthy in this connection is that the general and vocational curriculum outlined above should prepare students to recognise and understand the role and importance of education in social, religious, political, economic change and development. As far as the question of initiating the study of 'education' at the M.A. level is concerned, the Commission has laid special stress on it. In its view, the prevailing curriculum fails to develop the requisite insight in the students.

The Commission has suggested some of the following points as the. basis for the curriculum of education at the M.A. level:-

(a) A core curriculum which affords the students opportunities to study the problems of education on a scientific basis.

(b) There should be specialised courses such as educational planning and administration, guidance and counselling, evaluation of teaching, or the psychological foundations of teaching, etc.

(c) Methods of research.

(d) Preparation of Dissertation.

Experience indicates that the standard of M.Ed. students is unsatisfactory because the qualification for admission is B.Ed. If M.A. (Education) is introduced, students will have developed a suitable attitude towards education by the time they arrive at this level, and the time period for this course of study may if necessary be increased from two to three, or even more, years.

The Institutions

The standard of teacher's education depends, to a large extent, upon the qualities, work and prestige of the training institutions. In general, such institutions are of two levels- (1) secondary, (2) primary.

The qualitative improvement of these institutions requires thinking in terms of teachers, students and facilities.

Teachers. According to a survey, 40% of the teachers at the secondary level institutions are only graduates, 55% teachers possess post-graduate degrees while 20% of them have Doctorate degrees. Their pay scales are almost equivalent to those of principals of other colleges. Hence, the teaching community of training colleges should be constituted thus- (i) In order to teach the secondary training course, post-graduate qualifications in two subjects should be necessary. Some of them should also have Doctorate degrees. They should also have experience of teaching and training teachers. (ii) They should not have specialised professional training.in special subjects such as science, sociology, psychology and mathematics. In order to develop such a programme, the summer institutions should be well planned and organised.

Students. Students coming for teachers training do not possess sufficient content knowledge. In many states, teachers are required to teach even those subjects which they have not studied even at the graduate level. There are some subjects which the student studies only at the graduate level. At the secondary level, it is often difficult to get teachers with post-graduate qualifications in certain subjects. There is a serious dearth of good and qualified teachers for mathematics, science and english. For this, the Commission has suggested that - (i) No student should be allowed to specialise in any subject which he has not studied at the B.A. Level. (ii) Teachers should be required to teach at school only those subjects which they have actually studied at the graduate level. If they are given other subjects, it must be necessary for them to obtain the requisite qualifications in those subjects. (iii) Only first and second class students should be selected for teachers training, and they should also be given necessary scholarships.

Facilities. Many of the training establishments are lacking in hostel facilities. The Commission has laid stress on the creation, use and improvement of libraries, reading rooms, laboratories, teaching aids, etc.

Training establishments responsible for preparing primary teachers are in an even worse plight. Their development should encompass the improvement of teachers, students and facilities.

Teachers. The teachers in such institutions come from secondary schools, though completely lacking the ability to train their wards. Their pay scales are also low. Good teachers do not prefer to go to training institutions. The following are the suggestions of the Commission for bringing about the desired improvements- (a) Teachers imparting training to primary teachers should have post-graduate qualifications, apart from possessing B.Ed. degrees. Primary teachers should possess special training. (b) Only those individuals should be employed as teachers in primary schools who have themselves completed a minimum of 10 years in school, though a little flexibility in this rule may be observed with respect to women and tribal areas.

Students. Another problem in these establishments is the advent of students, because most of the applicants have not received even general education. The following suggestions have been preferred- (a) Liberality must be exercised for education through posts as well as granting leave for studies. (b) Students who have passed their B.A. and wish to teach in primary schools should be required to pass special courses. (c) The period of training should be two years.

Facilities. The following facilities should be made available for a qualitative improvement of training establishments for primary teachers- (i) Tuition fees should be eliminated, and instead, loans and scholarships should be made available. (ii) Every training establishment should have an experimental or demonstration school. (iii) There should be adequate housing facilities for the staff as well as the students. (iv) Libraries, laboratories, workshops, etc, should be available. (v) Similar improvements on the same basis should be made for the other teachers also.

State of Affairs

The Education Commission has suggested that the following general conditions for the qualitative improvement of training institutions should also be considered:-

Provision of Facilities

Opportunities for training should be made available on a priority basis. The purpose of this is, that, at the time of appointment, the applicant should be trained. If he is not trained, he should be sent for training. In view of this, the Commission has opined that:-

(i) Each State should expand and enlarge its training colleges according to its needs, and make arrangements for in-service training also.

(ii) Part-time as well as correspondence education should be expanded, but, in doing so, care must be taken to ensure that the standard of full-time institutions does not deteriorate.

(iii) Untrained teachers should be trained at the earliest.

(iv) The size of training colleges should be large, and they should also be properly planned.

On the Job Training

Knowledge is expanding and growing at such a rapid pace that if teachers do not keep in touch with it, their existing knowledge will soon lose its utility. Hence -

(i) At every level, every teacher should be compulsorily

required to undergo a three-month in-service training course once in five years.

(ii) Summer Institutes should be expanded for the purpose of in-service training.

Further Training

It is generally observed that teachers engaged in higher education apparently do not need training but when they are faced with the actual classroom situation, they get into serious difficulties. Hence -

(i) There should be arrangements for the proper training of junior lecturers.

(ii) Newly appointed teachers should be given an opportunity to assimilate themselves with the institution. They should be given chances to listen to old and experienced teachers with a reputation for scholarship.

(iii) Provisions should be made for orientation courses for new teachers in every college.

(iv) Such orientation courses should be run permanently by the universities.

The Scales

At present, the standard of teacher's education is determined by traditional knowledge and methodology, but, as time changes, the standard of teacher's education is changing. In view of this -

(i) At the national level, the UGC should take upon itself the responsibility for fixing the standards for teachers. At the state level, the responsibility for improving the standards of teachers should lie with the State Board of Teacher Education.

(ii) The UGC should possess requisite funds under the various plans for, improving teacher education.

It is evident that any improvement in the quality of teacher's education can really be expected only when the above suggestions are seriously considered, and equally seriously implemented.

Noble Profession

One question that has perennially been asked is whether teaching is a profession? Is it, like other professions, to be considered exclusively as a means to a livelihood? A glance at the pages of history dispels this notion. It tells us that it has never been an ideal vocation. Speaking about Brahmanic education, Lord William said that these places of teaching were constructed out of ordinary mud. Generally it was the teacher who made these huts at his own expense, and the teacher begged, not merely. to create the hut, but even to feed his students. This shows that teaching has always been a profession which makes human beings, a profession with its own unique traditions. In this connection, the regional service/extension department of the National Educational Organisation has put forward the following eight points:-

1. A profession should be necessarily equipped with intellectual tendencies.
2. A profession should have opportunities for various kinds of specialised skills and abilities.
3. A profession should also possess opportunities for regular and systematic promotion during the period of service.
4. A profession should possess opportunities for the necessary special training and preparation of those engaged in it.
5. A profession provides an occupation and a permanent membership for the entire life of the participant.
6. A profession generates its own standards.
7. A profession generates the desire for service even more than for personal gain.
8. A profession possesses strong professional organisations associated with it.

On the basis of these eight points or elements, T.M. Stinnet and Albert J. Huggett have established that education is not merely one of the professions, but the creative source or mother of all professions. Having accepted that education is a profession, it is essential to realise the programmes that are essential for making it a success. The Education Commission has offered numerous suggestions for making this profession attractive and interesting, the important ones being the following:-

1. Each State should formulate plans for creating facilities for training teachers on the basis of demand and supply.
2. Correspondence course and part-time curricula should be introduced on a large and extensive scale.
3. The size of training institutions should be enlarged and more facilities should be provided.
4. Teachers should be given opportunities for improving their professional skill during their period of service.
5. If a teacher lacks training at the time of appointment, he should be required to obtain training within three years.
6. At the level of higher education, junior lecturers should be given suitable opportunities for professional training and education.
7. New lecturers should be given a chance to listen to the lectures of old, experienced and scholarly teachers.
8. There should be orientation courses for new teachers.

The following are the suggestions of the Commission for improving the standards of teacher's education:-

1. The UGC should assume the responsibility for improving standards of teacher's education throughout the country, at the national level.
2. At the state level, this responsibility should be borne by the Teacher Education Council. It should also specify the acceptable standards.
3. Funds should be allocated for this purpose in the five year plans.
4. A permanent committee or council should be set up with the help of the UGC and the NCERT.

Education is a profession which, keeping itself completely away from black-marketing, corruption and other evil practices, gives rise to healthy traditions and thus helps to make concrete the dream of national development. When we accept that education is a profession, we must also accept its responsibilities and its burden. Dr. Carr's view is that an analysis of the existing circumstances and the potential for the future makes it evident that there is a universal tendency towards changing the new power and energy of the teacher- (1) people think that education and school are synonymous with each other, (b) seeking education means becoming a victim of the fad prevailing in education, (c) the greatest fear is that the public loses faith in the teacher.

Charles Lamb's view of the teacher is that he is aware, but he has no place of his own in the society of his own level. Amongst his young pupils, he comes as a Gulliver, but he cannot communicate his awareness to you. He cannot meet you at the crossing. He is so busily engaged in his teaching that he would like to teach even you. Lamb's statement reflects the devotion, the majesty but also the neglect of teaching. Prof. Vernan points out that the low level at which the teacher is compelled to work is the gift of those adults who, during their own student days, suffered from an inferiority complex.

Today, conditions have changed. The teacher will have to win to his own cause all those who believe him to be the maker of the nation. How can the teacher be the architect of his country? In the absence of a national educational policy, who will make the nation? The low salaries of the teacher are dispensed by the administration, the exploitation is done by the administration, the conditions of work are made insufferable by the administration, and yet it is claimed that it is the teacher who will build the nation. For this, the reason is that the teacher's objections make no dent upon the mind of the legislators. In view of this, it is necessary that the administration and the community must change its attitude towards the teacher who is being grounded to dust between the two grinding stones of the administration and the management.

The first duty of the administration is to nationalize education. The greatest advantage of such a move would be to put an end to the innumerable problems created by the community, and also generate a sense of equality. It should also modify the declared national educational policy to bring it into consonance with national requirements. It must also make every effort to isolate education from parochial politics so that education may devote itself to the building of a future society instead of seeking immediate and personal gains.

The following suggestions are taken from the 21st Conference of the Universal Teachers Council, for the improvement of teaching profession:-

1. Teachers should be given professional training and the latest knowledge.
2. Teachers at all levels should be treated as equals.
3. Teacher trainees should be kept in contact with actual conditions.
4. All teachers should be given equal opportunities for developing and improving themselves.
5. Unions of teachers should be established to safeguard the interests of the teachers.
6. The Administration should seek the cooperation of teachers in its work.
7. Educational programmes should be planned properly.

The profession of teaching should be developed as a technical profession. Teachers should get equality in such matters as scales of pay and facilities. They should also be remembered when posts with social status and awards are being distributed. If these steps are not taken, the poor teacher, who is living in an atmosphere of distrust and neglect, will once again have to take to revolutionary means to win for himself what society owes him.

The profession of teaching should be developed as [illegible] profession. Teachers should [illegible] [illegible] [illegible] [illegible] [illegible] and [illegible]

24

Free Education

To universalize higher education open university system is a unique experiment in India. Since 1958 to 1985, an individual had to go-through the formal stream of education to get the entry into the gateway of university. If any person deviated from the stream, he had to face a lot of difficulties to regain the same. The first step was to give permission to the individual to appear as private candidate for university examination. Second step was - correspondence courses for the various subjects and standards. Finding increasing craze for getting higher education, India felt the need to establish open university on the lines of England.

Open Universities

Open university is an experiment recently introduced to universalize higher education in the world. Through this system an individual wants to keep himself upto-date in the process of emerging new knowledge. An Open University is meant for those who want to gain higher knowledge and develop higher learning skill. Following are the main characteristics of an Open university:

(i) There is no need of any qualifying examination to get admission in the university.

(ii) There is no age limit for selecting admission.

(iii) Individual belonging to any State or region may seek admission.

(iv) There is no time limit for examination.

(v) There is no formal campus for study.

It is to be noted that Open university has curriculum, study and examination just like traditional universities.

The Cultivation

The pressure is regularly increasing on the universities. To solve this problem, in 1979 the first opened university was open in Britain. There 25,000 candidates were registered in the first year. By 1985, there 1,00,000 candidates had been registered. This number is increasing day by day. This university uses 300 study centres, Radio, Television and other means of communication for conducing studies. Now a days, there are Open universities in China, Japan, Thailand; Korea, Spain, Netherland, Pakistan, Sri Lanka and India.

Since 1970, the efforts were made to open Universities. In 1982, the first Open university was started in Andhra Pradesh ; the name of this university is Annamalai University. This university imparted instruction for B.A., B.Sc., B.Com and Post-graduate degrees in various subjects as well as B. Ed., M. Ed., and LL.B.

The first open university in India was S.N.D.T University, Bombay. Formerly it was a university for women. Later on the structure of this university had been changed. Many useful curricula are being run for women by this university through distance education. Seeing the achievements of Open universities Homeberg has rightly said that real study is basically an individual effort. This effort comes out through inner urges. Open universities were called Air Universities. Later on, these universities were renamed as Open Universities.

Open Universities are becoming popular and this experiment is quite successful. The achievements of this experiment are as follows:-

1. This is a successful experiment to universalize higher education.
2. There is no need of any qualifying certificate to seek admission in it.

3. Radio and Television are frequently used to impart education.
4. Every individual who wants to seek admission, may get opportunities for the same.
5. Individual is free to select the lifestyle and way of progress of this media of higher education.
6. Through correspondence the teaching material along with complete instruction is sent to the candidates. They send it back to the office for evaluation.
7. This university has complete structure - Academic and Administrative. There is a central body to control over the functions of the university.
8. There are university study centres in States.
9. In each district, there is an arrangement for study centre.

The Organisation

In an Open university, there is a three tier system of evaluation (i) self-education, (ii) education by the tutor, (iii) education by the university. After completing three stages a certificate is awarded to the candidate.

New Policies

New Policy of Education, stressed over the need of Open university. There is 4.9% higher education in our country. Therefore a policy is adopted to universalize higher education and keep the individual upto-date with knowledge. In the policy following points have been stressed:-

(i) Open university system has been introduced to democratise education and increasing educational opportunities for the common man.

(ii) Indira Gandhi Open University established in 1985 will cater the needs of learners.

(iii) The development of this powerful educational media will be done with great care:

The strategy of an open university is as follows:-

Evaluation Structure. Evaluation will be done by the candidate himself, by the tutor and by the university.

Execution. This programme has been started since 1987 and new curriculum, have also been started since 1988. A separate channel on TV is introduced for educational programmes. Orientation Courses are being introduced for men and women. This programme is framed on the pattern of Modulus are credit system. University Grant Commission will give sufficient grant for the promotion of this programme. Courses for Agriculture, Industry and many other fields, National norms for curriculum and evaluation will be developed. State open universities will seek guidance from the National Open University.

Ideal University

In 1985, Indira Gandhi National Open University had been established through an Act passed by the Parliament. President of India is a visitor of this university and head of the university is vice-chancellor. For his assistance there is an Executive Council, Academic Council, Planning Board, Finance Committee and Board of Recognition. There is Pro-vice chancellor and Directors for assisting Vice-chancellor. There is a Registrar who is Administrative head and a Finance Officer. Its headquarters is at New Delhi.

Structure. There is a different structure for Open University. There is no boundary for learners. Audio-visual aids, audio equipments, Television, edited teaching material and contact programme are used in place of teacher. Guidance programme is introduced in contact place. Co-ordinates of study centres are responsible for conducting the contact programmes.

Teaching Programmes. Diploma in Management, Diploma in Distance Education, Nutrition, Creative writing and B.A., B. Com., B. Sc., etc., have been started in 1987. Besides these Diploma in Management, Studies, Local Self Government, Energy Resources, Horticulture, etc., have been planned. Qualifying examination for the admission is Intermediate or its equivalent. There is an admission test for those who are not Intermediate.

Regional Centres. There are Regional Sectors to run the programmes of university smoothly. Head of the Sector is called Director. State Governments provide this sector building and other facilities. These sectors are co-ordinating units. There are libraries and other teaching material in every sector.

Curriculum. B.A., B.Sc., B. Com. courses under Three years degree scheme have been started by Indira Gandhi N.O.U. The student is expected to complete this degree within eight years.

Homeberg has rightly said that this system influenced the outlook and perspective of the learner. This system has made them a critic and has removed their doubts. The feeling of co-operation is developed. There is a solution to remove unemployment by providing them up-to-date knowledge and skill, fine behaviour and impressionistic discipline.

Open university is a vital organisation to meet the demand of the growing higher levels of learners. Those, who have not enjoyed any opportunity for colleges and universities, may get the chance to fulfil their ambitions. The persons, who are working on the basis of old knowledge and skill may also keep themselves up-to-date.

Open universities are trying their best to minimise pressures of the regular system of higher education by using the means of communication. In new education policy, it is said that modern technology of communication has controlled over the time and space. This technology has opened new dimensions in the field of teaching, learning and national development. To improve the quality of teachers' training, in service programmes, consciousness towards art and culture, developing permanent human values, this system will be a boon.

It is hoped that open universities, to be opened under New Education Policy will cater to the need and aspirations of the masses. The objective of New Education Policy is to prepare the manpower for national development ; such type of manpower is not merely a degree earner but in real sense curious and keen thinkers. We need such type of education which caters to the real knowledge and skill among the learners instead of spoon feeding by the teachers. There must be development of thoughtful-process which is responsible for the exposition of the inner self. India is committed for the exchange of knowledge and national development; therefore it is necessary to provide the maximum opportunities of fast growing and emerging knowledge to the citizens of India.

25

Student Unrest

The phenomenon of student unrest started in India with the agitation of 1905 led by Calcutta and Dacca students to oppose the partition of Bengal. This marked student involvement in agitations. As a part of National struggle it was encouraged by all political parties and welcomed by the public. Therefore, since then the student's participation in national political movement in India increased at every stage particularly in Quit India Movement in 1942. Most of the national leaders were students during the period of national struggle. They left the colleges and the universities to participate in National Movement at the call of their beloved leaders M. K. Gandhi, J. L. Nehru and B. G. Tilak, etc.

Student Unrest in the World

Students' involvement in politics is nothing new. In Germany, Russia and France a large number of students participated in political activities in the 19th century. In 20th century the student activities in South Korea were effective in changing the iron regime of Syghman Rhee. In Japan the students demonstrated against Prime Minister Kishi. In Indonesia and Vietnam the students protested against U. S. interference. In England and America one occasionally witnesses student demonstration against expansion of nuclear weapons. Peace marches are a usually scene. A large number of students in Afghanistan were fighting as gorillas against Russians. In Dacca students have several times strongly demonstrated on national issues. In U. S. S. R., however, the phenomenon of disturbed campus is not traceable. On the other hand, in almost all the other countries of the world one finds students' participation in demonstrations, strikes, processions and mass meetings.

Role of Political Parties in India

In India by the participation in national struggle the students learned agitational methods of protest and realized the power of student unity. After the country achieved independence this experience was utilized to highlight student's sentiments on local, regional, national and even international issues. Since the political parties were in the habit of using students as the youth power in political agitations, most of the political parties encouraged students as the youth power in political agitations, most of the political parties encouraged students organizations on political basis. Thus, while B. H. U. has been dominated by rightist students, J. N. U. is the centre of leftist activities. Congress-I, B.J.P., Janata and D.M.K. all the political parties have been maintaining their student wings since independence in India. Therefore, it is quite understandable that the disturbed campus is not a temporary phenomenon. Disturbance is only.a symptom, a fruit whose roots are being nourished by all the political parties.

Growth of Youth Power

This, however, does not mean that the students have themselves no political consciousness and that whatever they do is at the instigation of the political parties. Leadership is a phenomenon which is nourished and grown in institutions of higher learning everywhere. This is necessary for the growth of youth leadership in the country. This is most welcome though when it takes wrong turns it becomes a headache to the government and the people alike. In recent years several universities have witnessed growth of student power. In most of the universities the student unions have their own buildings, budget extending to thousands of rupees and all the paraphernalia of a political party. During the period of elections the whole campus and even the city is on siege. All types of methods of propaganda are utilized. Vote catching devises are practised even more shrewdly as compared to the techniques of general elections. Propaganda material worth lakhs of rupees is utilized. Posters come up on all the walls of the city. Hundreds of vehicles of all types are utilized. Money flows from the capitalists and the political parties. And when the winners celebrate they are blessed by the benign presence of the national leaders belonging to the political parties to which they owe allegiance.

The Modus Operandi

After the leaders are elected, they take stock of the situation local, regional and national. If the issues are not pointed enough, even the flimsiest issue is taken up for starting agitation. It is not because there is something to do that the political activities go on but because the leaders have to justify their election and to show their presence that issues are created. This, however, does not mean that all the activities are baseless. Some student activities have undoubtedly cleaned the campus, made the teachers more responsible and kept the administration awake. From time to time the student leaders do the cathartic function of unveiling the mask from the face of the administrators and powerful teacher politicians to show them in their true colours. This service is of signal importance.

Phenomenon of Indiscipline

Indiscipline is the initial symptom as well as result of a disturbed campus. While discipline is the adherence to rules and regulations, indiscipline is their contravention. According to the report on the problem of student indiscipline in India in 1960 presented by the committee appointed by the U.G.C. to investigate student indiscipline, "Indiscipline is a mass moral turpitude and collective defiance of authority and the use of techniques in seeking redress of real or imagined grievances which are not appropriate for students to use." This definition was formulated after a close study of the disturbed campus. The acts of indiscipline noted by the committee involved discourtesy to teachers, misbehaviour towards women students, student riots, damaging college building, disruption of the normal life of society, squatting on tram lines and rail tracks, stopping and burning the buses, physical violence against this or that individual and group and a host of other activities resulting into disruption of the educational process, growth of violence and general elimination of peace and order.

These acts of indiscipline start on any issue and led by the student leaders followed by thousands of enthusiastic students. The committee called these techniques in appropriate. This is far from convincing since it suffers from the dual standard, allowing the use of these techniques to political leaders and disallowing them to students. This double standard is far from convincing to the student leaders.

Multisided Phenomenon

Thus the phenomenon of the disturbed campus is multisided. Physically, it maybe seen in acts of violence, damages to property, impediments in the normal working of the educational institutions, mass meetings, hunger strikes, agitations, processions, etc. The psychological aspect, however, is more important. This is made of power mongering on the part of the leaders and frustration among the students. So many lapses on the part of the government administrators result in a sense of frustration on the part of the students. One of the most glaring factor creating frustration is the phenomenon of educated unemployment. The student leaders on the other hand are constantly on the look out to lake an issue to show their power to the student community on the one hand and to the administrator, the government and the public on the other. It is notable that it is from the ranks of these student leaders that some of the most famous national leaders in India have grown. Their example serves to encourage the ambitions of every student leader. By taking up an issue he makes promises to the student community and exercises pressure by threats and coercion upon the administrative authorities.

Psychological Factors

In brief the following psychological factors work at the root of the phenomenon of disturbed campus :

Loss of Faith in Aim of Education. As more and more students become disillusioned about the goals of education in the colleges and universities, they withdraw from studies and involve themselves in union activities.

Loss of Faith in the Means. Even if the goals sought by educational institutions maybe sound, loss of faith in the means of education may result into frustration. This may be concerning any part of the educational machinery such as admissions, appointment of teachers, discipline among teaches, time-table, curricula, methods of teaching, rules of discipline, rules concerning hostels, efficiency of the general administration and finally the mode and validity of examination and evaluation methods. It is a truism that in India at present all these aspects of education are full of problems which do not appear to be solved in near future.

Lack of Internalisation of Values and Attitudes. It is well known that without teacher's involvement in the process of education, no betterment in educational institutions is possible. This involvement, however, requires several conditions. If so many teachers are known to be having side jobs, running tuition shops, doing insurance business or things like that, they can hardly have any involvement with teaching in the educational institutions.

This involvement requires more conscientiousness among teachers. The teachers themselves should be free from politics before asking the students to do so. If the teacher unions are functioning like labour unions how can they suggest anything different to the student unions. The repressive techniques of the research guides can only help to increase frustration rather than any real creative work among the research students. But while the teachers know that there is no necessary correlation between teaching methods and evaluation techniques their enthusiasm in teaching cannot be maintained, unless the teacher-management relationship, the teacher-principal and the teacher-student relationship is improved. The involvement of the teachers is not possible if the teacher-taught ratio is beyond a certain proportion. No educational institution can remain undisturbed without solving this problem. Therefore, the values and attitudes demanded from the students should be first created among the teachers. And before asking for involvement on the part of teachers, suitable conditions for its natural growth must be created.

Sociological Factors

In The Sociology of Education in India. NCERT (1967) Mr. S. H. Asthana and Suma Chitnis have analysed the phenomenon of the Disturbed Campus under two heads as follows :

Goals of Education. The minimum goal of education is training for earning a livelihood. The maximum goal of education is socialization, diffusion of knowledge, values, attitudes and norms of realtionships, required for playing adult roles in society. In a healthy system of education both these goals must be realized.

Failures of Educational System. The above mentioned goals have not been realized. The growing number of educated unemployment clearly shows failure of our educational system to provide livelihood. During British regime even a matric fail could find a job. Now persons with postgraduate degree are unemployed in a great number. And this number is constantly growing. This failure may be attributed to the following causes:

No Accurate Assessment of Manpower Needs. As there is no accurate assessment of manpower needs there is no correlation between the number of educated persons growing every year and the number of employment opportunities. Expansion in education has been more rapid than generation of job opportunities.

Prejudices. Caste, region, language, religion and nationality have been the basis of appointment in non-government and even government agencies. Therefore, the organization failed to provide livelihood on the basis of merit.

Irrelevance of Education to Occupations. A general criticism of the present educational system is about irrelevance to occupations other than white-colar jobs. The values created by academic education do not create initiative and necessary, qualities of character such as national integration, equality, patriotism, democratic attitude to life, etc.

Lack of National Integration. Casteism, communalism, linguism, and parochial tendencies are fast disintegrating Indian society. Far from eliminating these tendencies, the education sometimes, encourages them. For example, in most of the colleges and universities linguism, regionalism and casteism are rather the rule than exception. Communalism, though not much rampant, may also be seen particularly in the educational institutions organized and run by a particular community. Unless national integration is maintained the conflict among various groups of students and teachers is inevitable.

Absence of Democratic Values. It is an irony that the student unions which were primarily established to fulfil the demands of democratization of education have themselves become source of the disturbed campus. Equality may be declared in policy but it is not properly practiced. Liberty takes the form of indiscipline and rowdy behaviour. Fraternity is conspicuous by its absence. In the words of H. S. Asthana and Suma Chitnis, "Democracy, to many, is voicing an opinion insisting on one's right, student unions give an excellent exercise in these qualities. But the more important concept of democracy as a partnership of free men, united in the common purpose of national development, does not emerge."

Examples of Teaching. Unfortunately the examples of academic fraternity set by the teaching community is far from encouraging this value among the students. Most of the university departments in every residential university exhibit cut throat factionism among teachers. This factionism sometimes goes to the extent of teacher's activities against the research students and disciples of rival colleagues. Every university department has become a den of favouritism, in-fighting, casteism, communalism, regionalism, hatred and jealousies. In this atmosphere no youth can learn democratic values. Team work is a phenomenon unknown to Indian scholars. While in the West most of the valuable academic advancement has been achieved through team work, in India hardly a group of scholars can see eye to eye on any problem. Seminars exhibit leg pulling and personal aggrandisement, vain show and manerism rather than any solid contribution to knowledge. Lectures are organized to oblige friends. Examinerships are exchanged. Ph. Ds. are distributed on clique basis. Appointments are made on the basis of personal favour. In the face of such a low level of character and behaviour *among gurus,* it is small wonder that the new generation learns that opportunism, nepotism-politicking, wire pulling, back-biting, cut-throat competitions and ruthlessness are the values and traits required for progress in life. It has been rightly lamented by Asthana and Chitnis, "The academic community in India is not a partnership in quest of knowledge. Mutual response between teachers and administrators swings between the two extremes of callous flouting of authority and a subservience that smothers self-respect. A mood of lethargy and pessimism prevails."

Norms, Sanctions, Values and Attitudes

Change in Norms. Formerly, it was's the norm in education that the teachers were respected. According to Indian philosophy of education academic achievements are correlative to respect toward teachers. This norm has been now reversed since education is linked with payment of fees. The modern students have hardly any respect towards their teachers, the idea of serving the teacher is beyond their comprehension. This discourages the teachers to give their best to the student. The modern teacher is stimulated by the challenge he faces in the class. The old teacher was encouraged to give his best because of his love and sentiment of service, dedication and sacrifice for the academic cause. Thus, the norms both on the part of teacher and the taught have been reversed.

Change in Sanctions. Formerly, the teacher's attempts to maintain discipline was sanctioned by the administration, the community and even by the students themselves. Even corporal punishment was appreciated. Today attempts to discipline the students do not receive sanction from the community and the students. The administration is helpless against the strength of the student unions. It is a common feature in the universities that rustication of rowdy student leaders is opposed by student unions tooth and nail. It sparks off protests, strikes and even violence. The students turn a deaf ear to the teachers, the principal and the vice-chancellor. The parents do not approve punishment any more. Corporal punishment is opposed by the parents.

The most important sanction to discipline in education comes from social ethos. Formerly, the social ethos emphasized reverence for elders. The children were asked to obey their parents and teachers. Today the emphasis is on freedom-freedom to think, freedom to act, freedom to react and even freedom to all kinds of indiscipline. In almost every sphere of life today the only value is self regard or selfishness. In the absence of the sanction of the social ethos discipline cannot be created in educational institutions.

Change in Values and Attitudes. Indian society was formerly authoritarian. In the wake of democratic values authoritarianism has been substituted by liberty. Not only in the field of education but in marriage and family modern boys and girls do as they like. The age of marriage is growing, making norm for twenty to twenty-five for girls and twenty-five to thirty for boys. Till then boys and girls stay in universities and colleges. Therefore, they learn all types of individual ways of behaviour and conduct. They are not governed either by parents or by teachers. The media, the film, literature, radio, television and every thing else are laying emphasis upon personal choice irrespective of what it means to others. Therefore, the values of equality and fraternity have been often set back by liberty. In fact, of the three democratic values, fraternity is the proper basis for equality and liberty. Liberty, on the other hand, cannot be the basis of equality and fraternity. Unfortunately, the modern youth lays emphasis upon liberty as the highest value. Therefore, there is no wonder that he is only concerned with himself.

Onesided Value System. In Indian axiology *Dharma* was the highest value while *Artha and Kama* were subordinate to it. *Moksha* was the ideal of life. This was an integral value system. It has now been substituted by a onesided value system of *Artha* or *Kama* as the only values to be cherished. According to Indian wisdom while Artha *and Kama* are provided by destiny, *and Artha and Kama* are actively pursued. The history of culture in different human societies has shown that mammon worship leads to cultural degeneration and final deface. This is the inevitable result of the present day culture. In such circumstances the youths learn to fulfil their aim by hook or crook. The emphasis is rather on smartness than culture, mannerism than character, general knowledge than scholarship. Therefore, mediocrity is the rule and excellence is exception. Scholarship, simplicity and hard work are no more necessary values. Not excellence but success is the goal. Not *Dharma but Artha* and *Kama* are the aims to be achieved. The Modern student aims at enjoyment. The emphasis is on fashion, excitement, novelty, speed and enjoyment. Heterosexual relationships are gradually breaking all norms of decency and restraint. Student politics knows no level. All means are adopted for self-aggrandisement. The techniques taught by M. K. Gandhi are being used in educational campus all over India for achievemnt of goals which are far from decency, discipline and even student welfare.

Youth Unrest in India

The analysis of disturbed campus in India shows several features. While some of it is revolt against oppression most of it may be termed indiscipline. While some of it may be attributed to exuberance of young, most of it is delinquency, vandalism and even crime. While some of it aims at general welfare of student community, most of it is for the calculated benefit of a clique of student leaders. While some of it may genuinely represent uprising of Indian youth, most of it is due to the inroad of political parties into campus. Most of the union activities are guided not even by the union leaders but by their political mentors outside the campus. While some of the budget of the student unions is covered by contributions from the student, most of it is met by secret donations from political parties and vested interests. Therefore, it goes without saying that the disturbed campus requires corrective measures.

Basically the disturbed campus in India is the result of youth unrest. Youth unrest in India is a phenomenon exhibiting moral perplexity, lack of ideal educators, defective system of education, political gansterism, groupism among educators, repressive policies of the state, social disorganization, absence of teacher-parent relationships and finally, the psychological defects of character. An analysis of these causes of youth unrest in India will pave the path to the means of curing them.

Causes of Youth Unrest in India

The following are the causes of widespread indiscipline among the youth in the country:

Moral Perplexity. The youth of today is in a dilemma because he does not know what is right and what is wrong. Most of the teachers express such completely contradictory opinions on moral problems that the educand is confused. On the one hand, he finds very strong arguments being advanced for a materialistic philosophy by some teachers, while other educators are found supporting the cause of idealism with equally valid arguments. The confusion is made worse by the differing opinions on the subject of religion also. Some educators are devout religionists while other are complete atheists. On the one side are the educators who believe in the ancient ideal or abstinence as the sole means of developing character. On the other, one finds more liberal educators who believe that the casual mixing of sexes and social intercourse, etc., are the most important formative .influences in character development. They argue that sex is natural and there is no need for any restraint. It is only something natural that the educand should be stupefied and left completely adrift when he is faced with such contradictory alternatives. Consequently, he finds it difficult if not impossible, to act according to any rational principle. He has no choice but to do as he likes, and one finds that his more animal tendencies are being manifested in the form of indiscipline.

Lack of Ideal Educators. Most of the youth forming part of the existing educational structure arc completely lacking in ideals. Some of the causes of this materialism are the bad economic conditions of the educators, uneven and often insufferable working conditions, nepotism and favouritism in appointments, absence of any social prestige, etc. But, whatever the causes, it cannot be doubted that the majority of teachers at the primary and secondary level of education are individuals without ideals and principles. In fact, many of them are morally degenerate and there is little cause for surprise if indiscipline among educated persons increases when they are guided by such individuals. But, it must also be remembered that the government is also very much to be blamed for this situation. Fairly recently, ' the staff at the primary level in U. P. went on strike to support its demands for increase in pay. It was argued by the educators that the government could not expect good teaching at the salary it offered to the educator. The government countered this with the suggestion that it wanted the educands taught 3R's not ideals. If the government itself exhibits such lack of concern towards the fundamental principles which guide civilized life, it can blame only itself for the difficult situation created in the country by increasing indiscipline.

Defective System of Education. After India had won her independence, a series of committees and commissions have criticised the existing system of education and pointed out its defects. In spite of this the system continues till today. It was introduced by the East India Company with a view to producing qualified clerical staff. There has been no change for the better, in fact, there has only been a steady erosion of standards. Corruption at all levels is not rampant but accepted as another fact of life. Accepting bribes to give better marks, co-operating with another educator to give better marks to his candidate, favouritism in the evaluation of doctoral research theses, are some of the common practices. In fact, one can sum up the entire situation by saying that now, there appears to be no correlation between hard work and study, writing the correct answers in the examination answer books and getting good marks. There is, therefore, no occasion for surprise if one finds that the educand's only aim is to secure degree by fair means or foul. Apart from the system of examination, the education system is further eroded by such defects as an impractical teacher taught ratio in the class-room, absence of extra-curricular programmes, the prescription of sob-standard text-books, etc. It is only manifesting one's ignorance if one imagines that indiscipline can be removed when the education system is so beset with defects.

Political Gangsterism. Most of the colleges and universities in the country have become nothing more than hotbeds of political gangsterism and polemic. Most of the students unions are dominated by stooges of some political parties, and they are concerned only with achieving their own ends by using the students unions. Such influences not only lead to gangsterism in the institution, they also create the possibility of misusing the students for political ends. One finds that during elections, political parties become even more active in their efforts to woo the educands to their side. There is no denying that political parties have played a sufficiently destructive role in bringing about indiscipline and the consequent problems although it would be unfair to imply that political interference is the sole cause.

Grouping Among Educators. If an individual takes it upon himself to attend the functions and gatherings of teacher's unions of some institution on three or four occasions, he will soon arrive at the conclusion that the groupism found among teachers perhaps exceeds that which is found among the members of any other professional group. Students are not only aware of this groupism, but they are deliberately made aware of this, because in many cases they are directed by one group to observe the activities of the other group of educators and to report it to the First. Thus, the educand becomes conscious of existing rivalry between the various groups among his educators. All this has a very detrimental effect on the educand's mind, because he feels that such activity must be justified.

Repressive Policies of the State. Clashes between the students and police have become a regular feature in almost every state. One hears of many incidents in which the police thrashed the students, carried out a baton charge, entered the college campuses, destroyed property, attacked students inside the colleges, even resorted to firing and killing students. Lack of discipline among the students cannot be compared to revolution and rioting, and it should not be treated as such. At the root of it there are some causes which have to be understood and then eradicated. Adoption of a repressive policy only adds fuel to the fire, and ultimately this fire spreads from one part of the country to another, until it engulfs most of the country.

Social Disorganization. Social disorganization is a condition in which the organization, control and mutual co-operation that normally exists between various social institutions and committees deteriorates and practically ceases to exist. This kind of disorganization leads to the disorganization of such fundamental institutions as marriage and finally, ultimately leading to personal disorganization. Indiscipline is just "-instance of this kind of disorganization. Hence, one cause of the indiscipline found among students today is the general disorganization of society.

Absence of Teacher-parent Relationship. In a more normal situation, the absence of relationship and contact between teachers and parents is another cause of indiscipline. Both the teacher and the parent are unaware of the difficulties of each other, and thus they blame each other for the defects of the students without making any effort to improve the student. In fact, the responsibility for the student's indiscipline must be equally divided between the student, the parent and the teacher, but mutual cooperation and contact between the latter two can solve this problem to a great extreme.

Psychological Causes. At its root, indiscipline is a psychological defect of character. Among its more prominent causes are abnormalities concerning sex, inferiority and superiority complexes, feelings of insecurity, absence of any aim, etc. All these factors contribute to the frustration of the educand, which is converted into violence. This violence is manifested in the facts of indiscipline which are universally condemned. The responsibility for giving rise to such psychological symptoms rests upon bad and morally degenerate films and literature, lack of character among the educators, social class distinctions, absence of any normal relations between girls and boys in the college, neglect of moral education, etc.

The most important factor among those outlined above is the

defective nature of the system of education, because all other causes have their origin in the basic sortcoming. The existing system of education cannot do with some small changes. It needs to be completely overhauled, in fact, scrapped and replaced by a different system altogether. It should be made to conform to the cultural characteristics of the nation, education should be imparted through the medium of the national language, and it must incorporate better working conditions for the educator, and a more efficacious and reliable system of examination.

Suggestions for Dealing with Youth Unrest

The means of curing youth tension can be inferred form the foregoing account of its causes. The following suggestion have been made in this regard:

Improvement in the Teacher's Conditions. This comprehends increase in salary, better conditions of work, more just and impartial selections and appointments, reasonable prospects of advancement, etc. If these conditions are met, the educators will be able to live satisfactory lives, and thus they will be encouraged to impart some idealism to their educands.

Improvement in the Teacher's Conditions. This comprehends increase in salary, better conditions of work» more just and impartial selections and appointments, reasonable prospects of advancement, etc. If these conditions arc met, the educators will be able to live satisfactory lives, and thus they will be encouraged to impart some idealism to their educands.

Presentation of Right Ideals by the Educators. Since almost all educands imitate their educator both consciously and unconsciously, it is necessary that the educator must present the correct ideal in every sphere of conduct.

Youth Unrest in India

Improvements in the System of Education. As far as possible the defects in the system of education pointed out by various committees and commissions should be removed immediately.

Preventing Political Influence in Schools. No political party should be given the chance to penetrate schools and college life.

Control of Unwarranted State Interference. More often than not, the vice-chancellors appointed to the universities are appointed on any consideration except that of merit. These appointments are made by the government, and hence are illustrations of undue state interference in education. It is undesirable for the state to interfere in the working of education in this manner.

Protection of the Independence of Educational Institutions. Of the many incidents of violence and destruction by the students in the recent past, many were inspired by the entry of the police into college compounds, either without the permission or in violation of the express command of the college authorities. All educationists agree that no government employee has the right to enter the premises of the educational institution without the permission of the principal. If this rule is not violated it would be easier to prevent manifestations of youth unrest, from becoming violent and destructive.

Contact between Educators and Parents. Another method of curbing youth unrest is to encourage contact between educators and parents so that they can meet and discuss the problems of educands and thus remove the causes leading to indiscipline.

Moral Education. Most thinkers agree that absence of moral education is responsible for youth unrest and character defects of the educands. In any case moral education will definitely curb indiscipline.

Creation of Proper Atmosphere to Colleges. The psychological factors at the root of youth unrest can be eliminated by creating the proper atmosphere in schools. As far as possible, the atmosphere should resemble that of a large family in which the relations between boys, girls, educators, students, etc., would be morally and psychologically healthy.

Youth unrest is a complex problem having its social, political and psychological aspects. In order to remove it, these aspects must be understood and the cooperation of educators, parents and state must be used to solve this problem.

Improvement of Student Unions

The role of student leaders in campus is not negative. Student unions cannot run on the pattern of labour unions. Instead of aiming at student's unity and demand of students rights, they should rather aim at furthering the cause of education and strengthening teacher-taught relationship. This, however, requires a periodical survey of the needs and demands of the students by the government and the administration and prompt remedy to them. Restriction on admission of black listed students is a necessary condition for checking indiscipline on the campus, the following suggestions may be advanced for the better organization of student unions.

Student's Participation in Management. In the college government by managing committees the student leaders may be given representation in the managing committees so that they may get their demands directly fulfilled without any confrontation with the principal.

Limitation on Expenses. There should be restriction and proper auditing of budget of student unions. If evidence for spending much beyond it becomes clear, enquiry should be made into the extra source of income.

Restriction on Activities in Public. The activities of student unions should be-confined within the campus. They should be restrained to do anything in city.

No Permission for Litigation. All the controversies concerning students should be decided by the principal, the Vice-Chancellor or the district administration. At no time the student union may be permitted to go to court for pressing its demand.

Proper Permission for Activities. The student union is governed by campus rules. They should give prior information and seek sanction for every activity from the principal in the college and the Vice-Chancellor in the university. Activities should be organized not only by prior information but prior sanction.

Correlation of Manpower Needs and Educational Planning. This point lias been repeatedly emphasized by every education commission Education planning includes educational guidance. Manpower planning depends on vocational guidance. Vocationalisation of higher education is necessary for practical use of educational facilities. Job efficiency should be the criteria for organization of courses, method of evaluation and modes of instruction.

Better Teacher-taught Relationships. Peace on the campus depends on proper teacher-taught relationships. This requires satisfaction and involvement of the teachers as well as the taught. This depends upon proper policies concerning admission, curriculum, methods of teaching, administration, evaluation, appointments and general facilities.

Better Socialization. This requires elimination of paro-chialism, casteism, communalism, linguism, regionalism and faction from the campus. On the other hand, national integration should be propagated by all means.

In the end it should be remembered that some sort of disturbance is a part of the normal life in the campus. It is only when indiscipline crosses limits that action should be taken. Prevention is always better than cure. This is particularly true in the case of educational campus.

26

Universal Education

Internationalism is a synonym for humanism, with the emphasis on what is universal in man-his strivings for self-expression within the larger community and for its ultimate benefit. National contributions must not be glossed over by internationalism in education. On the contrary they will be stressed, just as individual contributions are stressed in democratic society. But those contributions will be stressed as part of man's larger heritage and not as a nation's jealously guarded monopoly.'

Need for an International Attitude in Education

Internationalism implies the awareness of all human beings as members of a single human society, irrespective of national boundaries and other differences. The modern period has seen a remarkable transformation of the means of transport and communications, the tremendous spreading of education, the notable increase in the mutual contact between citizens of the world. As a consequence the world has shrunk in size, -which in itself has led to local problems influencing areas and peoples far removed. For example, it is now being recognised that the excessive increase in poverty in any one part of the world is almost certain to affect the economic conditions of other-countries as well. If peace and prosperity are to be created in one country, it becomes necessary to create good living conditions all over the world. Now that man has set foot on the moon, there is an increasing demand for international understanding. Besides, the two world wars of the century have enforced the useful lesson that, in this age of nuclear weapons, the people of the world have to live and die together. Communist and non-communist countries both feel that they cannot hope to maintain their status in the world, unless they make efforts to spread their ideology in other countries. The failure of the League of Nations depressed the desire for internationalism. For this reason its successor, the United Nations, is aiming at cooperation not merely in the field of politics but also in the economic, educational and cultural spheres. UNESCO, one specialized body of the U.N.O., is dedicated to the spread of international understanding through the medium of education in every part of the world.

Internationalism in Modern Indian Education

Modern educational philosophers in India have supported the notion of internationalism for a specific and unique reason. This attitude is based on the philosophy of the ancient Upanishads which taught that God lives as soul in the bodies of all human beings, irrespective of differences of race, nation, area, sex, etc. Vedanta philosophy provides the strong foundation for it Sri Aurobindo was a staunch internationalist, inspite of his very emphatic expression of nationalism. He expressed the opinion that, just as the ideal nation is one in which the individual's freedom and perfection is harmonized with the development and organisation of society, the freedom and development of an international society should be harmonized with the development and perfection of humanity in its entirety.

Of the many modern thinkers, Rabindranath Tagore expressed such vehement support for internationalism that people misunderstood him and took him to be opposed to nationalism. His creation, Shanti Niketan, is the concrete manifestation of the international attitude in education. Dr. Radhakrishnan, the chairman of the Indian Universities Commission drew attention to the need for an international attitude in education. He expressed regret at the failure of the current educational system to propagate feelings of internationalism and universal brotherhood. An educational system should be such that it may create a new generation of individuals who believe that all human beings are brothers and that differences of caste, region, community or nation have no significance. True education leads to internationalism. Dr. Radhakrishnan commented that we must make efforts for the unity of the world. We should try to a create a new generation which has faith in the nobility of intellectual life, in purity, in a feeling of brotherhood towards humanity, in love and peace. There should be no national educational plan which proves an obstacle in the growth and spread of this feeling. In fact, there is no opposition between nationalism and internationalism, but if it becomes necessary to make comparisons, both Rabindranath Tagore and Dr. Radhakrishnan incline towards internationalism. Education must aim at making every man and woman a citizen of the world, by developing within each one such thinking, concentration, insight and intellectuality or spirituality that they can perform useful roles in life. Peace in the world can be expected only when this ideal is pursued by education in every country. These ideas of Dr. Radhakrishnan have found echoes in every part of the world, and there is consensus of opinion among educationists everywhere that training men and women in internationalism through education is the only way of avoiding a third world war.

Propagation of Internationalism By UNESCO

The role of UNESCO in spreading internationalism is notable. This body is a special organ of the U.N.O. dedicated to the spread of international understanding. It has been said in its constitution that "since wars begin in the minds of men, it is in the minds of men that the defence of peace must be constructed." The breadth of its scope can be judged from its name, the United Nations Education, Scientific, and Cultural Organization. In order to achieve its goal of spreading international understanding, it performs the following functions:

1. This organization transmits knowledge of the literature, art, science, etc., of one nation to all other nations.
2. It also provides many opportunities to thinkers, scientists, teachers and artists to meet each other and exchange ideas and put forward creative plans for promoting world peace and justice. Efforts are made to prevent the people from beings influenced too much by narrow parochial thinking.
3. UNESCO also seeks to improve the mutual relations

between various nations and remove fear, suspicion and lack of confidence between them.

4. Considerable financial aid is given by UNESCO to improve the teaching facilities in backward and exploited countries.
5. UNESCO also provides guidance in modifying texts prescribed in various syllabi in order to make the books more internationally oriented. The organisation does its best to root out illiteracy and lack of education from the poor countries.
6. In order to promote international understanding, UNESCO provides facilities to students and teachers to visit abroad and to exchange views and also gain experience in international living.
7. It also organises art and literature exhibitions at the international level to promote feelings of love and friendship.
8. Research is also encouraged by UNESCO, for it provides financial help and other facilities to researchers.

It is evident from the varied functions of UNESCO that the organisation is particularly aiming at creating an international feeling in education but this objective cannot be achieved by UNESCO alone. For this it will be necessary to make proper arrangements for education in many countries.

Synthesis of the National and International Points of View

Here it is essential to understand how the national and international standpoints can be synthesized and reconciled with each other. Nationalistic feeling attaches the greatest importance to the nation's interests. Inspired by such feelings individuals are even willing to lay down their lives in order to protect the honour of their nations. It is only by awakening such feelings that manynations have gathered so much military power and have attempted to extend their own frontiers. But, if carefully examined, it will be seen that this is a distorted form of nationalism. In its best form nationalism does not oppose internationalism. It has helped various nations to collect power in their hands in orders to throw off the yoke of a foreign nation. Nationalism has played a vital role in throwing out colonialism. But despite these great advantages and positive qualities, nationalism underwent a change and became colonialism itself. As a result of the nationalistic feelings, people focussed their eyes on their own country and lost interest in anything other than their own sectarian interests. Just as any interest turns into an ism by becoming narrow and thus harms the more liberal interests, in the same way, this narrow minded nationalism has become an obstacle in the development of internationalism. It is this nationalism which inspired many nations of Europe to establish big colonies in Africa and Asia. Later, Germany and Italy became jealous of the English and French colonies, a feeling which manifested itself in the first and second world wars. After the first world war, an international organisation known as the League of Nations was established, but it came to a premature end due to the narrow minded nationalism of its members. It was the precursor of the United Nations Organisation which came into being after the second experience of a global conflict. Despite the lessons learnt earlier, many nations continue to constitute a very grave threat to international peace because of their own interests. One concrete example of this is South Africa which continues to exercise its policy of apartheid, despite the many warnings given by the U.N.0. It is now universally felt that it is only the distorted form of nationalism which hinders the growth of internationalism.

On the other hand, healthy nationalism is a boon to internationalism. As has already been pointed out, it is only nationalism which has inspired many nations to throw off foreign rule. It is nationalism which has helped even the smallest nations of the world to raise their heads and stand proudly by the side of their mightier brothers. In fact, nationalism can be used or misused by human beings. The two international wars of the present century should be sufficient to teach human beings that there is need for balance and synthesis between nationalism and internationalism. There is a parallel to be drawn here. Individuals sacrifice the interests of family, race, town, etc., for the benefit of the nation, because they realise that these also gain when the nation gains. In the same way, national interests can be allied with international goals. National interests can be restricted for this, and it cannot be questioned that progress of isolated groups also depends very much upon the progress of the world as a whole. This fact must be realized first of all by the rich, powerful and the prosperous nations, because on them lies the onus of the world's development In fact, it is the realization of their responsibility which is persuading the rich nations to extend a helping hand to their poor neighbours, but when some political strings are attached to the aid given, it defeats the purpose of encouraging internationalism. It must be remembered that there would be no international feeling in the absence of a national one, for it is the latter which inspires the former. No nation should become an obstacle to the progress of another nation in trying to achieve greater prosperity for itself. Secondly, progressive nations must help the underdeveloped ones. The principle of Panchsheel is a fine example of a synthesis between the nationalism and internationalism, but for this peaceful co-existence itself is not enough. Active cooperation is more important.

Means of International Education

In order to encourage the growth of internationalism, it is necessary to make satiable amendments and modifications in the objectives of education, in the syllabus, and the methods of teaching. The following suggestions have been put forward:

Aims of Education. With the intention of spreading international feeling, the following aims of education should be paid special attention :

Development of Independent Thinking. Education must help every student to think for himself so that he should not blindly accept every statement favourable to his own country, and blindly reject everything in favour of another. He must be able to arrive at an independent judgement of the worth of some fact relating to his own country or another.

Developing a Feeling of World Citizenship. Education must also seek to teach children that they are citizens of a world state. When this feeling is developed in them, they will have no difficulty in rising above national interests and understanding international interests, which they will try to achieve.

Creating Faith in Humanity. Rabindra Nath Tagore, the strongest supporter of internationalism among the contemporary Indian educational philosophers, based his concept of internationalism upon the philosophical background of humanitarianism. Humanity is the true religion of human beings, while all the great religions are only different forms of it. All great religions have placed great stress upon the equality of human beings. Human perfection has been accepted as the goal of human life. Once this concept is understood, it becomes easy to have faith in humanity and to love all human beings irrespective of their country.

The following changes in syllabi are suggested, if an international feeling is to be created :

1. All syllabi should include paintings, literature, music, etc., which are typical of different countries.
2. The children should be acquainted with all attempts at humanitarian work carried out in every part of the world.
3. Efforts should be made to overcome narrowmindedness and blind faith in children through a scientific education.
4. The teaching of geography should be supplemented with knowledge of the singleness of the world.
5. The teaching of history should concentrate primarily on the efforts of great figures who have contributed to the history of the world.
6. In teaching civics, the educator should explain to the students not only the rights of a citizen but also the rights and duties of a person to the international community as a whole.
7. Teaching should not be restricted to bookish teaching alone, but must also extend to visits to different parts of the country and also to other countries.
8. Pen friendship should also be encouraged.

Methods of Teaching. Certain suggestions about the changes and improvements in syllabi also imply some changes b teaching methods, if education is to have an international impact. The points to be noted in this connection are :

Stress on World Citizenship. During the process of teaching, it is desirable to stress points which may help in evolving an all encompassing love and world citizenship.

Stress on Similarities. The teaching of history, geography and civics, should concentrate not upon the differences between and tensions among nations but on the similarities so that sympathy for other nations and nationals is awakened in the mind of the educand.

International Viewpoint of Educator. But an international viewpoint cannot be generated in the educand if the educator himself lacks it. When the educator is possessed of it, he will inspire the educand through his conversations, his ideas, training, and by setting an example. Hence, the first step in the process is to educate the educator.

International Contact. The various committees for the various sciences and arts that are constituted at the university level should be encouraged to develop contact with national and international institutions of the same kind. What is really required is international contact at all levels of life and among people of every walk of life, scientists, scholars, literary figures, teachers, doctors, in fact every profession. Such contacts can be evolved by international meetings of local committees concerned with different professions, and also through mutual exchange of scholars and learned people.

Finally, it has also been suggested that every national plan of education, in every country, must make a specific provision for developing international feeling through education. Educators and educational institutions should be given specific instructions concerning this. Only this will awaken sufficient enthusiasm in local institutions, and only thus can the aim of international education be fulfilled.

Means of Spreading International Education

Apart from the formal education of colleges and schools, certain other media can also be useful in spreading international feeling, the major ones being:

Pen Friendship. Quite a few of the contemporary magazines, in all parts of the world, more particularly, the magazines meant for children and adolescents carry this kind of information. Such magazines publish the reader's interests, age, bobbies other relevant information, and sometimes even a photograph of the person interested in penfriendship. Thus many children and aaolescents form penfriends in all parts of the world, and later on exchange pictures, postal stamps, books and other things. Penfriendship is thus the most important means of increasing feeling for people of different parts of the world.

Exchange of Gifts. Another modern practice is the sending of gifts by the children of one Country to the children of other countries, India, for example, has gifted elephants to the children of other nations. Such actions strengthen international feeling by attracting children of one country to another. Sometimes, some gift packets are also distributed in schools. These packets contain things that the children can use. It is only natural that when the children get these gifts packets, they harbour kind and friendly feelings for the donor. The American Redcross distributes such gifts parcels among Indian children from time to time.

International Competitions. Now-a-days cultural com-petitions over the display of dance, drama, art, music, etc., take on an international colour because people from many countries participate in them. This brings people into contact with the result that the world seems like a vast home.

International Exhibitions. Such exhibitions also play an important part in promoting international understanding, because they help to acquaint people with the art and culture of different countries.

Cine Films. People derive a lot of information by seeing foreign films, because they see their mode of living. Besides, it also encourages the feeling that human beings are the same everywhere, in their happiness, pain, pleasure, problems, joys and sorrows. This helps international understanding.

Radio and Television. Radio and television play practically the same role as films because foreign programmes help the audience to understand life in other parts of the world.

Literature. Now-a-days, the literature of almost every country is available in every other country of the world. This can help in increasing acquaintance with life as it is lived in different parts. In addition to such literature certain books specialize in compiling the stories of lives, characters, interesting incidents and surprising objects in various parts of the world. This is a kind of international literature.

Contribution of Universities. Finally, it can be said that universities are the most important medium of propagating international education because they provide opportunities for the meeting of artists, scientist, literary figures and scholars. This creates international understanding at a very high level.

Various Institutions of U.N.O. Many institutions of U.N.0., more particularly, UNESCO, are engaged in directly and consciously promoting international understanding and the growth of international feeling. It is desirable that their sphere should be further expanded, and that more nations should participate in their programmes so that their objectives can be achieved more easily.

Developing Intercultural Understanding

India is a big country in which one finds groups distinguished from each other on the basis of language, religion, race, mode of dress, etc. There are numerous racial groups living in different parts of the country who not only posses different cultures, but possess cultures which do not resemble civilized groups. One finds differences of living standards, languages, style of dress, etc. among the people living in different parts of the country., but even more remarkable is the difference in values of life and ideas. In fact, that which is called Indian culture is not a single culture, but a composite culture made up of the synthesis of numerous cultures. This was born even before Aryan civilization, and other cultures have added to it from time to time. In view of the numerous instances of conflict which have been seen recently due to linguism, regionalism, communalism, casteism, etc., it can be said that schools have failed to create unity and mutual sympathy among the different groups. These influences are also seen constantly working in the country in the garb of partiality for a person of one's own region. This had led man educationists to reflect upon this issue and to give valuable suggestions.

Suggestions for Inter-cultural Understanding

Inter-cultural understanding implies particular attitude, the attitude of understanding members of another culture, of recognising their merits, of sympathising and being liberal towards them. And since India contains many different cultures, inter-cultural understanding is essential, for, in its absence, conflict can never be curtailed. This inter-cultural understanding can be created through education. An emotional unity is the first essential thing for this. Besides, in the absence of inter-cultural understanding, it is impossible to generate a genuine internationalism which is necessary in view of the substantial differences between the numerous cultures found in different parts of the world. And as long as human beings do not rise above their petty differences and understand all human beings to be members of the same group, and learn to appreciate other cultures, international understanding cannot be created. The following suggestions are put forward for creating inter-cultural understanding:

Study of Cultural Anthropology. Cultural anthropology, one branch of anthropology, provides knowledge of the origin of various cultures, their development and their inner content. By studying the fundamental elements of this discipline, educands can comprehend the different cultural patterns and characteristics which are found. By studying the origins of various cultures, they will be able to understand that differences in culture arise out of the different circumstances in which the cultures are born. This will lead to a more charitable and liberal attitude to culture differences.

Encouragement to Tourism. Travelling to different parts of the country is a valuable experience in that it helps one to realise that despite the obvious differences in various groups, all of them are Indians. This promotes inter-cultural understanding.

Encouraging Mutual Meetings. Indian universities regularly organise cultural programmes in which students from different universities present cultural shows. Such meetings give the young people to meet young people of other cultural groups, with the result that they get a chance to understand the other culture. This helps to free their minds of narrow thinking.

Propagating the Theory of Unity in Diversity. People who believe either in the destruction of diversity in order to create uniformity or in the destruction of unity to maintain diversity forget that unity in diversity is a natural characteristic of human society as well as of the entire creation. Happiness lies in following this principle. If this principle is accepted, internationalism will be encouraged, but not at the cost of nationalism. Today, all the different cultures that are growing in the country must be allowed to flourish. None of them should be destroyed, because each represents a specific pattern of adjustment with the environment existing at a particular place, and hence it has its own value. Each culture is the product of the local conditions, climate and natural environment, and represent an adjustment to that environment. Therefore, each culture must be given the opportunity to grow further. But this does not necessarily imply that the country will inevitably be divided into numerous different cultural groups or that this should be allowed to happen. Cultural unity can be promoted even after maintaining cultural variety and identity. This cultural unity can be created by using education to promote inter-cultural understanding. If people can be made to realize that both unity or conformity and diversity or individuality are part of the theory of unity in diversity, it will be possible to take care of and eradicate much of the prejudices, partiality, differences, etc., that arise out of cultural differences.

In addition to the above measures, it is possible to utilize many other things for the purpose of creating inter-cultural understanding. Young men and women can, for example, be encouraged to establish contact with members of other cultures through the medium of pen-friendship. Even inter-cultural marriages can be of immense value in this respect. It is possible to create situations in which members of different cultures come into contact with each other. Tourism, in particular, should be encouraged. Young students can tour the country in groups and thus acquaint themselves with the different cultures existing in remote parts of the country. It is possible to generate a liberal, sympathetic and kind hearted attitude towards other cultures among the younger generations through the medium of magazines, literary publications intended for the young, and other similar channels. Exhibitions of literature and art can achieve the same thing. Films can also make valuable contributions in this respect. Besides, once the teachers themselves have understood the importance of this aim of education, they will provide many illustrations to their students to create inter-cultural understanding.

Bibliography

Addaval, S.B. (ed.): *The Third India Year Book of Education Educational Research,* NCERT, New Delhi, 1968.

Aggarwal, J.C. : *Development and Planning of Modern Education with Special Reference to India,* Vikas Publishing House, New Delhi, 1982.

Anastasi, Anne. *Psychological Testing.* London: Collier Macmillan Publishers, 1982.

Andrew W. Halping (ed.) : *Administrative Theory in Education,* The MacMillan Company, New York, 1967,

Aparna Basu : *The Growth of Education and Political Development in India 1898-1920,* Oxford University Press, Delhi, 1970.

Beck, Carlton, e. *Philosophical Foundations of Guidance.* Englewood Cliffs, New Jersey: Prentice Hall, 1964.

Biswas, Dutt Sunnittee and R.P. Singhal: *The New Educational Pattern in India,* Vikas Publishing House. Delhi. 1916.

Bhatia, S.C.: *Education and Socio-Cultural Disadvantage,* Xerxes Publications, Delhi, 1982.

Brij Raj Chauhan, G. Narayan and T.R. Singh : *Scheduled Castes and Education,* Anu Publications, Meerat, 1975.

Buch, M.B., *Second Survey of Research in Education 1972-1978,* Society for Educational Research and Development, Baroda, 1979.

Charles Jeffries : *Illiteracy : A World Problem,* Pall Mall Press London, 1967.

Chotia, F.S. and Mehta, H.P. "*A Brief Account of Vocational Guidance Movement in India.*" Journal of vocational and Educational guidance, 1955.

Crow, Lester D., and Crow, A. *An Introduction to Guidance Principles and Practices.* New Delhi: Eurasia Publishing House, 1962.

Cottle, W.C. and Downie, N.M. *Preparation for Counselling.* Second ed. Englewood Cliffs. N.J.: Prentice Hall, 1970.

Cronbach, L.I. *Essentials of Psychological Testing.* New York: Horper, 1970.

Denis, Lawton : *Education and Social Justice, Sage Publications,* London, 1977.

Desai, A.R. "Social Change and Educational Policy", in M.S. Gore and Others (ed.,), *Papers in the Sociology of Education in India,* NCERT, New Delhi.

Dharni, P. Sinha: *Descriptive-cum-Critical Study of Education System in Andhra Pradesh,* Administrative Staff College of India, Hyderabad, 1976.

Don Adams : *Education and Modernisation in Asia,* Addison Wesley Publishing Company, London, 1970.

Erickson, Clifford E. *A Basic Text for Guidance Workers.* Englewood Cliffs: Prentice Hall, 1955.

Frank, H. Krouse. *Counselling Technique with Youth.* Ohio: Charles and Mervil, 1960.

Froehlich, C.P. and Hoyt, K. *Guidance Testing.* Science Research Associates Inc. 1959.

Fletcher, F.M. and Riddle, W. *"The Guidance Movement in India."* Personnel and Guidance Jouranl, 1962.

Garret, A. *Interviewing: Its Principles and Methods.* New York: Family Service Association of America, 1942.

Gaur, J.S. and Saraswat, R.K. *Occupational Literature: An Annotated Biblography.* New Delhi: NCERT, 1978.

Ginzberg, E. *"Towards a Theory of Occupational Choice."* Personnel and Guidance Journal, 1952.

Goel, S.C., *Education and Economic Growth in India,* The MacMillan Company of India Ltd., Delhi, 1975.

Gore, M.S., and others (ed.) : *Papers in the Sociology of Education in India,* NCERT, New Delhi, 1967.

Gunnar, Myrdal : *Asian Drama - An Inquiry into the Poverty of Nations,* Abridged by Seth S. King, Allen Lane, London, 1972.

Hamrin, S.A. *Initiating and Administering Guidance Services.*

Bloomington: McKnight and McKnight Publishing Company, 1959.

Haragopal, G. : *Administrative Leadership and Rural Development in India,* Light & Life Publishers, New Delhi, 1980.

Hoose, William N. Van (ed.). *Counselling and Guidance in the 20th Century*. Boston: Houghton Mifflin Co., 1979.

Humphrey, J. Anthony and Traxler, Arthur *E. Guidance Services*. Chicago: Science Research Associates, Inc., 1954.

Iqbal Narain, K.C. Pande and Mohan Lal Sarma: *Panchayati Raj and Educational Administration,* Aalakli Publishers, Jaipur, 1976.

John W., Hanson and Cole S. Brem Beck: *Education and the Development of Nations,* Holt, Rinehart and Winston, New York, 1966.

Joshi, R.N.: *Education—Elsewhere and Here,* Bharatiya Vidya Bhavan, Bombay, 1979.

Knapp, Robert H. *Practical Guidance Methods for Counsellors, Teachers and Administrators. New York:* McGraw Hill Book Co., Inc. 1953.

Kishore Gandhi : *Issues and Choices in Higher Education: A Sociological Analysis,* B.R. Publishing Corporation, Delhi, 1977.

Kochhar, S.K. : *Pivotal Issues in Indian Education,* Sterling, New Delhi, 1981.

Kroth, J.A. *Counselling, Psychology and Guidance.* Springfield, Illinois: Charles C. Thomas, 1973

Lakshmana Swamy Mudaliar A.: *Education in India,* Asia Publishing House, Bombay, 1960.

Louis Malassis : *The Rural World : Education and Development,* Croom Helm, London, 1976.

Majid Rahnema, "Iran," in Suresh Gosh (ed.) : *Educational Strategies in Developing Countries,* Sterling Publishers, New Delhi, 1976.

Matarazzo, J.D. *Wechsler's Measurement and Appraisal of Adult Intelligence,* Baltimore: Williams and Wilkins, 1972.

Miller, Carroll H. *Foundations of Guidance.* New York: Harper and Brothers, 1961.

Miller, Frank W. *Guidance—Principles and Services.* Ohio: Charles E. Merrill Books, 1961.

Mukherji, S.N. (ed.) : *Administration of Education in India.* Acharya Book Depot, Baroda, 1962.

Munson, Harold L. *Foundations of Developmental Guidance.* Boston: Allyan and Bacon, 1971.

Naik, J.P. : "Education", in Dube S.C. (ed.), *India Since Independence,* Vikas Publishing House, New Delhi, 1977.

Nirmalya Bagchi : *Cheep Poison,* Chalti Duniya, Calcutta, 1974.

Niblett, W.R. : *Essential Education,* University of London, London,1955.

Oldhan, J.N. : *Village Education in India : The Report of Commission of Enquiry,* Oxford University Press, London,. 1922.

Panchamukhi, P.R.: "Financing of Primary Education in India". in *Primary and Work-Oriented Education,* NCERT, 1970.

Pasricha, Prem. *Guidance and Counselling in Indian Education.* New Delhi: NCERT, 1976.

Patterson, C.H. *Therories of Counselling and Psycho-therapy.* New York: Harper and Row, 1973.

Pepinsky, Harold B. and Pepinsky, Pauline Nichols. *Counselling Theory and Practice.* New York: The Ronald Press Company, 1954.

Peters, H.J. and Hanson, J.C. (ed.) *Vocational Guidance and Career Development.* New York: Macmillan, 1968.

Prem Kripal : *A Decade of Education in India,* Indian Book Company, Delhi, 1968.

Raghunath Safaya : *Innovations and Latest Trends in Education,* The Associated Publishers, Ambala Cantt., 1976.

Raju, V.B.: *Commentaries on the Constitution of India,* Eastern Book Company, Lucknow, 1973.

Rao, Narayan. *Counselling Psychology.* New Delhi: McGraw Hill Publishing Company Limited, 1981.

Rao, V.K.R.V. : *Education and Human Resource Development,* Allied Publishers, Bombay, 1966.

Roeber, E. C., Smith, G. E. and Erickson, E.E. *Organisation and Administration of Guidance Services* New York: McGraw Hill, 1955.

Rudolph & Rudolph (ed.) : *Education and Politics in India Studies in Organisation, Society and Policy,* Harvard University Press, Cambridge, 1972.

Saini, S.K.: *Development of Education in India : Socio-Economic and Political Perspective*, Cosmo Publications, New Delhi, 1980

Sateswari Saxena : *Education Planning in India : A Study in Approach and Methodology*, Sterling Publishers, New Delhi, 1974

Sharma, G.S. : *Educational and Cultural Development of the Minorities—A Study in Social Effects of the Judicial Trends in India*, ICSSR, New Delhi, 1973.

Shertzer, Bruce Stone, Shelly, C. *Fundamentals of Guidance*. Boston: Houghton Miffin Co. 1976.

Shrimali, K.L.: *A Search for Values in Indian Education:* Vikas Publishers, Delhi, 1974

Shukla, P.D. : *Towards the New Pattern of Education in India*, Sterling Publishers, New Delhi-1976.

Singla M.M. : *The Constitution of India-Studies in Perspective* The World Press, Calcutta, 1975,

Slocum, Walter L. *Occupational Careers: Sociological Perspective.* Aldine Publishing Co., 1968.

Smith, H M. and Eckerson, L.O. *Guidance Services in Elementary Schools.* Washington: Government Printing Press, 1966.

Spearman, C.E. *The Nature of Intelligence and Principles of Congnition.* London: Macmillan, 1923.

Stewart, N.R. and others. *Systematic Counselling*. Englewood Cliffs, N.J.. Prentice Hall, 1978.

Sundaram, P.S. and A.B. Shah : *Education or Catastrophe?* Vikas Publishing House, New Delhi, 1976.

Tiwari, D.D. : *Education at the Cross Roads*, Chugh Publications, Allahabad, 1975.

Thomas, F. Station. *Dynamics of Adjustment*. New York: MacMillan Co., 1953.

Tolber, E.L. *Counselling for Career Development*. Boston: Houghton Miffin, 1974.

Tyler, L.E. *The Work of the Counsellor*. New York: Appleton Century Crafts, 1969.

Vernon, P.E. *Intelligence and Cultural Environment*. London: Methuen, 1969

Warters, Jane. *Techniques of Counselling*, New York: McGraw Hill 1964

Singh, S.K., [illegible] Publications, New Delhi, 1980.

[illegible] Study in [illegible] and [illegible] Publications, New Delhi, 197[illegible].

[illegible] of the [illegible] India Book, New Delhi, 19[illegible].

[illegible] Houghton Mifflin Co., 19[illegible].

[illegible] Publishers, Delhi, 19[illegible].

[illegible] Publishers, New Delhi, 197[illegible].

[illegible] Press, Calcutta, 19[illegible].

[illegible] Co., 19[illegible].

Smith, H.M. and [illegible] Washington: Government Printing Press, 19[illegible].

[illegible] 197[illegible].

[illegible] 197[illegible].

[illegible] House, New Delhi, 197[illegible].

[illegible] 19[illegible].

[illegible] 19[illegible].

[illegible] Boston: Houghton Mifflin, 197[illegible].

[illegible] 19[illegible].

[illegible] London: [illegible] 19[illegible].

[illegible] New York: [illegible] 19[illegible].